Other Prima Books by Currid & Company

Computing Strategies for Reengineering Your Organization
Software: What's Hot! What's Not! 1994 Edition

Other Prima Business Books Available

Wave Three: The New Era in Network Marketing
Managerial Moxie
Going Public
Smart People Sometimes Wear Plaid
Breakthrough Thinking, Revised 2nd Edition
Doing Business in Mexico
Doing Business with the U.S. Government
Importing into the United States, Revised 2nd Edition
Exporting from the United States, Revised 2nd Edition
Leadership and the Computer
The Making of Microsoft
Almost Perfect
Julian Block's Year-Round Tax Strategies for the $40,000-Plus
  Household, 1995 Edition (Avail. Sept.)

How to Order:

For information on quantity discounts, contact the publisher: Prima
Publishing, P.O. Box 1260BK, Rocklin, CA 95677-1260; (916) 632-
4400. On your letterhead, include information concerning the
intended use of the books and the number of books you wish to purchase. For individual orders, please turn to the back of the book for
more information.

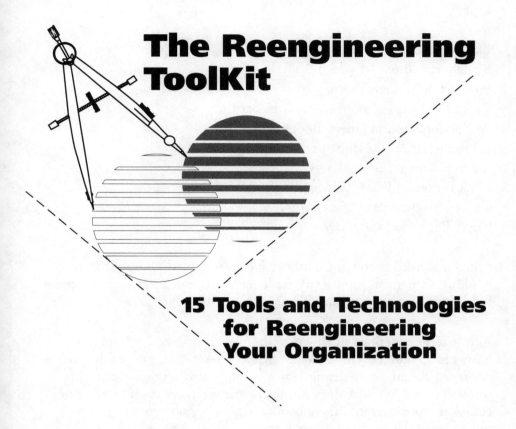

The Reengineering ToolKit

15 Tools and Technologies for Reengineering Your Organization

Cheryl Currid & Company

Prima Publishing
P.O. Box 1260BK
Rocklin, CA 95677-1260

Executive Editor: Roger Stewart
Managing Editor: Neweleen A. Trebnik
Project Editor: Stefan Grünwedel
Cover Production Coordinator: Kim Bartusch
Production: Susan Glinert, BookMakers
Copyeditor: Dan Rosenbaum
Indexer: Brown Editorial Service
Book Designer: Susan Glinert, BookMakers
Cover Designer: Page Design, Inc.
Cover Illustrator: Judy Sava

Prima Publishing and the authors have attempted throughout this book to distinguish proprietary trademarks from descriptive terms by following the capitalization style used by the manufacturer.

Information contained in this book has been obtained by Prima Publishing from sources believed to be reliable. However, because of the possibility of human or mechanical error by our sources, Prima Publishing, or others, the Publisher does not guarantee the accuracy, adequacy, or completeness of any information and is not responsible for any errors or omissions or the results obtained from use of such information.

ISBN: 1-55958-504-8
Library of Congress Card Number: 93-48147

Printed in the United States of America
94 95 96 97 RRD 10 9 8 7 6 5 4 3 2 1

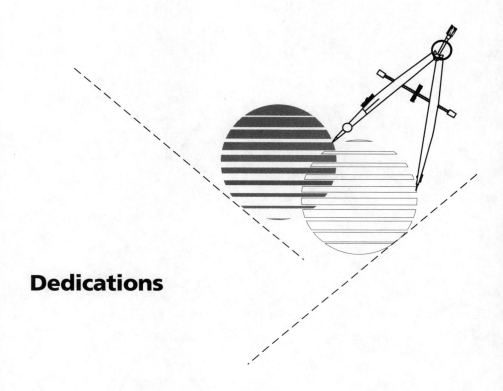

Dedications

To Ray, Tray, Justin, and Katherine. Thanks for your wonderful support.—Cheryl Currid

To Brian, my understanding and supportive husband. Thanks for playing Mr. Mom while I spent long hours researching and writing my chapters.—Linda Musthaler

To Me—whoever you are. You feel good about your contribution to this effort. Allow yourself some time to enjoy that feeling and what it might mean.—Bill Pearson

To Tom, for the gentle challenge; Linda, for your encouraging wit; Diane, for your editing efforts; Cheryl, for the opportunity; and most of all to my lovely wife, Vita, for the nights and weekends when I was "so quiet" mentally composing.—Sam Rose

To my wife, Linda, for her support and understanding and for her incisive editor's eye.—Thomas J. Howard

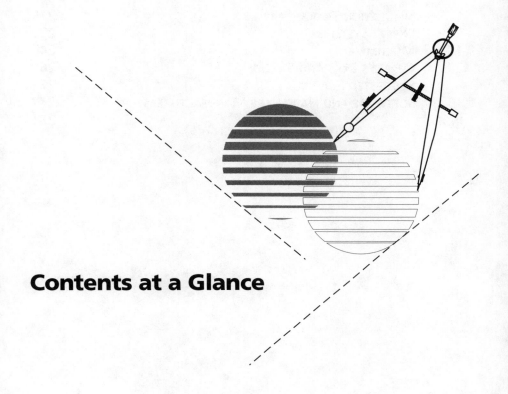

Contents at a Glance

1	WHAT IS REENGINEERING?	5
2	REENGINEERING TECHNIQUES	21
3	TEAMS FOR REENGINEERING	37
4	FUNDAMENTAL TECHNOLOGIES FOR REENGINEERING	53
5	RAPID APPLICATION DEVELOPMENT TOOLS	63
6	VOICE SYSTEMS	77
7	AUTOMATED INPUT	87
8	GIS AND GPS	99
9	WORKFLOW	113
10	DOCUMENT MANAGEMENT AND IMAGING	121
11	ELECTRONIC MAIL	133
12	GROUPWARE	155
13	ELECTRONIC COMMERCE	167
14	MOBILE AND REMOTE COMPUTING	183
15	WIRELESS COMMUNICATION	193
16	KNOWLEDGE BASES & AGENTS	205

17	Simulation Tools	219
18	Expert Systems	229
19	Multimedia	245
20	Currid's Do's and Taboos	265
A	Suggested Reading	271
B	Software and Hardware Manufacturers	277
Index		281

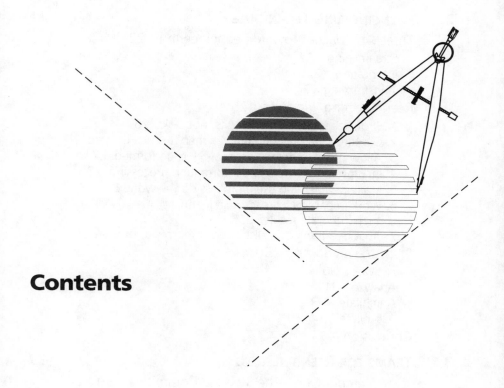

Contents

PART I   THE QUICK AND THE DEAD   1

1   WHAT IS REENGINEERING?   5

Entering the Age of Reinvention   6
Why Companies Are Doing It   8
Defining Reengineering   9
   Functions versus Processes   10
History: How Did We Get This Way?   15
   We're Stuck with Straight Pins   15
   More Ways to Divide   16
Reengineering versus Other Theories   17
   How Is Reengineering Different?   17
   Who Is Reengineering?   18
Conclusion   19

2   REENGINEERING TECHNIQUES   **21**

Three Approaches toward Reengineering   22
    Streamlining   22
    Integrating   23
    Transforming   24
Reengineering Principles   25
    1. Organize work around results, not tasks. 26
    2. Capture data only one time—when it is first created. 26
    3. Allow decision points where work is performed. 27
    4. Incorporate controls into information processing. 28
    5. Make people who use a process do the work. 28
    6. Work in parallel instead of sequentially,
        then integrate results. 29
    7. Treat geographically dispersed resources as one. 29
Steps to Get Started   30
    Activate   30
    Analyze   31
    Annihilate   33
    Assimilate   34
Conclusion   35

3   TEAMS FOR REENGINEERING   **37**

Team Number One—The Steering Committee   39
    Roles for the Steering Committee   39
Team Number Two—The Reengineering Team   41
    Roles within the Reengineering Team   44
Conclusion   47

PART II   THE 15 ENABLING TECHNOLOGIES   49

4   FUNDAMENTAL TECHNOLOGIES FOR REENGINEERING   53

Networking—First Stop to the Information
Superhighway   54
    Begin at the Beginning   55
    Planning for the Information Superhighway   55
    A Technology Checklist for Networks   56
Databases   57
    Database Technology   57
    A Technology Checklist for Databases   58
Desktop Tools   59

Consistent Tools 59
Multitasking Tools 60
Data Sharing of Tools 60
A Word about Hardware and Quality Components 60
Conclusion 61

5 RAPID APPLICATION DEVELOPMENT TOOLS **63**
Four Points to RAD Success 64
How You Can Benefit from RAD 65
The Deadline Pressure 66
RAD Tips for Success 67
Computer-Aided Software Engineering (CASE) 67
The Old versus the New 68
Using What You Already Have 69
Why You'll Have Trouble with RAD 71
Who's Confused? 72
Choosing the Right Tool 73
Supporting the Seven Principles 74
Conclusion 74

6 VOICE SYSTEMS **77**
Justifying a Voice System 78
Voice Mail 79
Interactive Voice Response Systems 80
Fax-Back 82
Business Audio 83
Voice Recognition 84
Supporting the Seven Principles 85
Conclusion 85

7 AUTOMATED INPUT **87**
How Automated Input Fits In 88
Not Just a Cash Register 90
Touch-Activated Screens 92
Magnetic-Strip Readers 92
Scanners 93
Optical-Character Recognition 94
Magnetic-Ink Character Recognition 94
Voice-Activated Systems 95

A Case Study   95

Supporting the Seven Principles   97

Conclusion   97

8   **GIS AND GPS**   **99**

Geographic Information Systems   100

Problems with GISs   101

The Cost of a GIS   103

Uses for GIS Technology   105

The Global Positioning System   107

How Does the GPS Work?   108

Receivers Are Becoming Abundantly Available   108

Taking Mapping and GIS Mobile   109

GIS and GPS Success Stories   109

Continental Insurance of New York   109

Federal Emergency Management Agency   110

Sylvania   110

Crime Prevention   110

Conclusion   111

9   **WORKFLOW**   **113**

Managing Your Workflow   115

Loans in an Hour: A Case Study   118

Supporting the Seven Principles   120

Conclusion   120

10   **DOCUMENT MANAGEMENT AND IMAGING**   **121**

Defining Document Management   122

Managing All That Paper   123

How Can Technology Help?   125

How Will Standards Help?   128

Document Management in Banking   128

Supporting the Seven Principles   130

Conclusion   131

11   **ELECTRONIC MAIL**   **133**

Just What Is E-mail?   134

E-mail's Role and Promise   136

E-Mail versus "The Old-Fashioned Way"   137

Changing Corporate Culture 139
   E-mail Is the Great Equalizer 139
   E-mail Changes Expectations for Communication 140
   E-mail Extends Our List of Correspondents 141
   E-mail Extends Our Reach 141
E-mail's Role in Reengineering 143
E-mail Features and Capabilities 144
   Electronic Calendars and Scheduling 145
   Task Tracking 146
   Message Routing 147
   Remote Access 147
   E-mail Gateways 148
   Filtering Agents 148
   And Coming Soon... 149
The Issues of Implementing and Using E-mail 149
   Achieving Critical Mass 150
   Electronic Etiquette 150
   Interoperability 151
   Distributed Directories 151
   Network Traffic 152
Conclusion 152

12 GROUPWARE 155
Groupware? What's That? 156
How Groupware Gets Used 158
   Vennet: A Comprehensive Communications Network 158
   Compaq's Worldwide Data Repository 159
Types of Groupware 160
   Shared Information Bases 161
   Meetingware 162
   Videoconferencing 163
   Group Scheduling 164
The Effects of Using Groupware 164
Currid's Do's and Don'ts for Groupware 165
Conclusion 166

13 ELECTRONIC COMMERCE 167
What Is Electronic Commerce? 168
The Benefits of Electronic Commerce 172
   Reduced Paperwork and Administrative Costs 172

More Accurate Data   173
Better Customer Service   174
Additional Services and Incremental Business   174
Electronic Data Interchange   175
EDI's Role in Reengineering   176
The Information Superhighway   178
The Issues of Electronic Commerce   179
Standards   180
Privacy and Security   180
Government Regulations   180
Coordination of Services   181
Conclusion   181

14   MOBILE AND REMOTE COMPUTING   183
Telecommuting's Promise   184
What Drives Telecommuting?   186
The Downside of Telecommuting   187
Key Factors for Telecommuting Success   187
Technologies for Telecommuting   188
Mobile Computing in Action   188
How Does Mobile Computing Support Reengineering?   190
Mobile Computing Technologies   190
Key Points of Mobile Computing   191
Conclusion   191

15   WIRELESS COMMUNICATION   193
New, But Already Productive   194
Wireless Emerges   195
Today's Wireless Technology   196
Local Wireless   196
Short-Distance Wireless   197
Remote Wireless   197
Emerging Wireless Technologies   198
Who Uses Wireless?   198
Key Players in the Wireless Infrastructure   199
Ardis   199
RAM Mobile Data   200
CDPD   200
Nextel Communications   201
Nationwide Wireless Network   201

Metricom 201
Orbcomm 202
Supporting the Seven Principles 202
Conclusion 203

16 KNOWLEDGE BASES & AGENTS **205**

The Value of Knowledge Bases 207
The Major Services 208
What You Use Them For 209
Knowledge Bases for the Professional User 211
Knowledge Bases for the Personal User 213
Agent Technology 213
Agents at Your Command 214
How Telescript Agents Work 215
Creating Your Own Knowledge Base 216
Supporting the Seven Principles 217
Conclusion 218

17 SIMULATION TOOLS **219**

Why Use Simulation? 220
Image Processing 221
Imaging 222
Print Processing 222
Drawing 223
CAD/CAM 223
Virtual Reality 225
Modeling 226
Supporting the Seven Principles 227
Conclusion 228

18 EXPERT SYSTEMS **229**

What Is an Expert System? 230
The Requirement for an Enterprise Model 232
The ES: Where to Begin 233
The Company IQ 235
Decision Making: Where Is the Information? 237
Who's Using Expert Systems? 239
Learning from an ES 240
Neural Networks: An ES Variation 241

Supporting the Seven Principles   243
Conclusion   243

19   MULTIMEDIA **245**
Multimedia: Our Definition   248
Why Use Multimedia?   249
The Elements of Multimedia   250
  Text and Graphics   250
  Audio   250
  Video   251
  Animation   251
Isn't This Pretty Expensive?   252
What About Standards?   253
Gotchas, Do's, and Don'ts   254
Reengineering with Multimedia Magic   255
Hospital Use of Multimedia   256
Conclusion   259

PART III   GETTING IT TOGETHER **261**

20   CURRID'S DO'S AND TABOOS **265**
Do's   266
Taboos   268
Conclusion   269

A   SUGGESTED READING **271**

B   SOFTWARE AND
HARDWARE MANUFACTURERS **277**

INDEX **281**

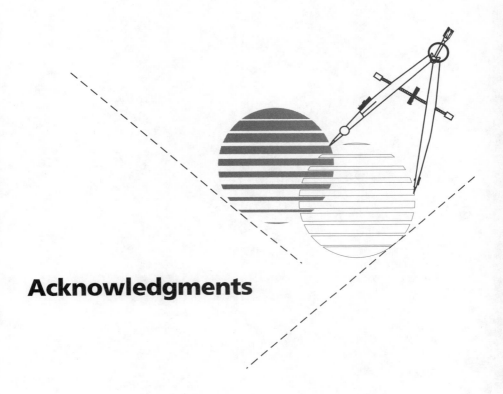

Acknowledgments

This book, like many others, is the result of a remarkable team effort. It involved collaboration, dedication, hard work, and long hours. We want to thank the effort of the entire team at Currid & Company. We especially want to acknowledge the work and effort of Diane Bolin, our project coordinator. Thanks, Diane, for all the late nights, the reading and re-reading all the words, and—most especially—for helping the rookies learn the ropes.

We also thank the people at Prima Publishing who were involved in this effort, especially Stefan Grünwedel, for his extra work and support.

All the research we did on this book involved several very helpful people who were kind enough to share their experiences with us. Rather than list them all here, let us simply say, "thanks for the effort!"

A special acknowledgment is due to the people at Compaq Computer Corporation who helped us with this project, without whose efforts it would never have happened.

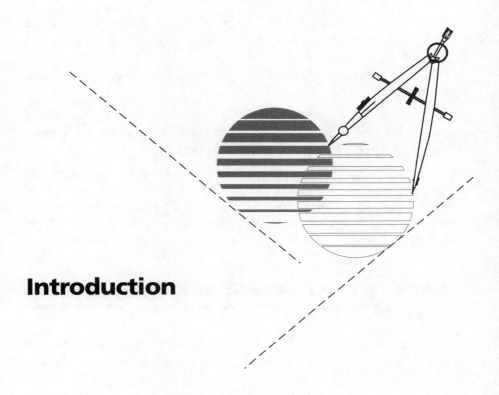

Introduction

Picture the consummate company of the 21st Century: active, agile, and aware. It produces perfect-quality products, delights its customers with superior service, and empowers an info-savvy workforce to create and make decisions.

It can't be beat. The organization busted its bureaucracy long ago and broke with time-honored (but time-wasting) traditions that didn't make sense. It can turn on a dime to seize an opportunity, respond to market changes, or create a new business. It knows how to harness the best of both people and technology. This company can reach around the globe to pull together the best teams of talent. And through the miracle of communications and computer technology it can do so in an instant. This company knows no bounds, it has vision, and it can execute.

Sound good? Now picture competing with this organization.

Would you have a chance? Answer honestly. You wouldn't if you are like many organizations. Especially if you still have processes designed by workers of the 1950s—and despite the fact that these people are long gone, their policies and procedures linger on, and on, and on.

How can you change? Follow the lead of smart companies. Look over, under, around, and through your organization for the symptoms. Chances are you'll find bad business practices marbled in.

That's where reengineering comes to the rescue. Business process reengineering—the fundamental rethinking and radical redesign of business processes—lets you reinvent your company. A recent bestseller explained why companies should reengineer, but just how do you do it? We believe you do it by pulling out the Reengineering ToolKit.

What Is the Reengineering ToolKit?

You'll need three sets of tools to reengineer your organization. You need to pack your ToolKit with the right techniques, teams, and tools. An artisan wouldn't think about starting a job without a plan, nor would he consider doing the job with broken or worn-out tools. Similarly, you should refrain from changing your business until you know what you can do—and how to do it.

In your ToolKit, you will want to carry a set of techniques for reengineering—the basics of how to rearrange organizations and work. You'll also want to select carefully the human resources—creating a well-rounded reengineering team. And finally, you'll want to know about technology tools for your ToolKit.

Admittedly, our focus for this book is technology. We have seen, studied, and used paradigm-busting technologies that virtually let people change all the rules about work. Why pass a multi-part form to 17 people to sign when an electronic note simultaneously sent to three decision makers will do? Why spend 100 hours a week matching up purchase orders, receiving tickets, and invoices when an on-line database will match up information automatically?

Information technology can help you defy time, space, and location. Used creatively, technology can help you improve the speed and quality of work—or help you eliminate some work all together.

How We've Built the ToolKit

In **Chapter 1** we introduce the concept of reengineering. Reengineering is changing all the rules for the way business arranges itself. We define it, we talk about where it came from, what it is, and what it is not.

In **Chapter 2** we talk about the techniques for reengineering. We introduce seven guiding principles or overriding techniques for reengineering. These principles describe how to take work apart and put it back together again. We discuss each of these.

In **Chapter 3** we turn our attention to forming teams for reengineering projects. We describe what it takes to make a team system work in your organization—how to arrange a reengineering team, whom to put on it. Then we describe the personality types, the skills and disciplines you need in order to create a successful team structure.

In **Chapter 4** we begin to focus our attention on technologies and stay there for the balance of the book. We open Chapter 4 with the fundamental technologies you need to have in place to make the Reengineering ToolKit work. We will talk about three key technologies: networks, databases, and desktop tools. These are the foundation technologies—necessary for effective use of other technologies.

In **Chapter 5** we explore the world of rapid application development tools. These are software tools that are designed to help developers build applications software faster.

In **Chapter 6** we look at voice systems. In this context, we define voice systems as computer applications linked to telephone applications. We also touch on voice applications not associated with the telephone—voice recognition, voice activation, and business audio.

In **Chapter 7** we investigate automated input devices such as barcode readers, scanners, magnetic-card readers, and point-of-sale terminals. These devices allow data to be automatically input into a computer system, capturing data as they are created and avoiding multiple processing.

In **Chapter 8** we discuss geographic information systems (GISs) and the global positioning system (GPS). GISs arrange data, such as sales or delivery route data, in a geographic context. The GPS allows us to pinpoint the physical location of something, regardless of where it is in the world.

In **Chapter 9** we look at workflow management. Workflow software automates sequential processing of work, such as the approval of an expense report or purchase order. It is sometimes oriented towards the movement of paperless forms through an organization.

In **Chapter 10** we investigate document management and imaging systems. These systems automate the process of storing and retrieving documents. In this context, "document" has a vary broad meaning which includes letters, e-mail, faxes, spreadsheets, and images.

In **Chapter 11** we explore the world of e-mail, which allows people to transmit messages across the office and the world.

In **Chapter 12** we turn our attention to groupware and workgroup computing—a combination of hardware and software that enables collaborative work within and among groups.

In **Chapter 13** we discuss electronic commerce, a broad category of systems that automate business transactions. Examples of electronic commerce are electronic data interchange, automated teller machine systems, and computer-to-computer systems that manage ordering, invoicing, and bill-paying.

In **Chapter 14** we investigate mobile and remote computing—that is, hardware and software that lets people work away from their traditional offices. This is particularly important to the remote office worker, the traveling worker, or the homebound worker. This technology also opens up options for new work styles, such as telecommuting.

In **Chapter 15** we examine wireless computing. Wireless computing consists of communications technology that transmits data without wires. It extends the options of mobile computing. The technology can support communications between computers in the same building, across a campus, or very remote—around the country.

In **Chapter 16** we turn our attention to knowledge bases and agents. A knowledge base is a software system that collects and indexes large amounts of information. An example is the Dow Jones News Service. An agent is software that performs a process, acting on behalf of a user, to get information or perhaps even make decisions.

In **Chapter 17** we look at simulation tools, such as CAD, CAM, modeling, and virtual reality. These are specialized tools that perform or simulate an activity such as design or modeling.

In **Chapter 18** we discuss expert systems. These apply a set of rules and conditions that vary, depending on the data being processed. Examples of this technology can be seen in automated stock trading systems or sophisticated loan approval systems which make decisions or recommendations.

In **Chapter 19** we look at the world of multimedia, which is the incorporation of sound, video, and computing technology into an application. Multimedia is usually associated with education, training, or presentations.

Through many years of observing and helping many companies go through the process of change, we have gathered a tremendous amount of experience. In **Chapter 20** we provide you with a few helpful hints about what to do, and what not to do, as you reengineer your business processes.

In **Appendix A** we provide you with a list of references and company names that assist you in putting your ToolKit together.

This book is the product of many years of experience and research into the various ways that techniques, teams, and technologies can be used. At Currid & Company, we study the effects of new technologies and how they affect work results and personal ability to perform. We believe that technology extends people and, when used correctly, makes us smarter and more effective in our jobs.

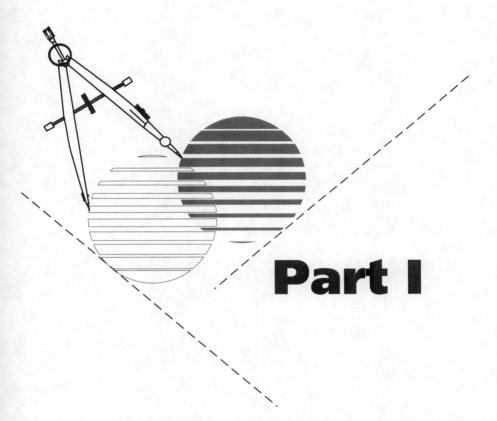

Part I

The Quick and the Dead

Welcome to business, 21st Century style. Chances are, we will know only two types of companies: the quick and the dead.

Breakneck advances in technology, rapid changes in the rules for global competition, and the quest to meet the demands of an ever-fickle customer continue to change the fundamentals of business. These changes send out the call: swim or sink; adapt or evaporate; move or get crushed. The picture below gives you the general idea. If you're smart, you'll pick the one on the left.

Businesses that plan on being around in the 21st Century need to learn how to operate at warp speed or suffer the consequences. They need to rethink, reinvent, and reengineer anything that slows them down.

The Quick and the Dead

CHAPTER 1

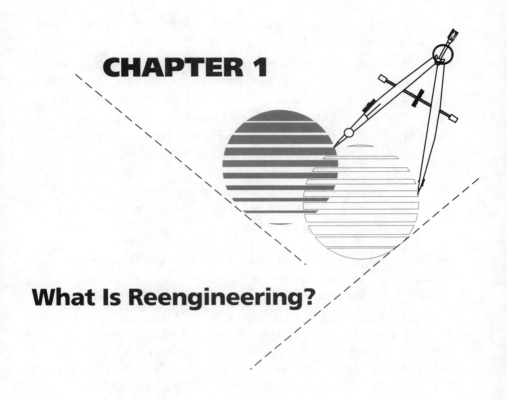

What Is Reengineering?

Oh no, Toto. This doesn't look like Kansas anymore.
—*Dorothy,* The Wizard of Oz

It's simply not business as usual in many industries today. New challenges from global competition, changes in customer preferences, and constant innovations in technology alter the business scenery almost daily.

Sometimes the results can be disastrous. Even the smartest managers at the biggest and richest companies find themselves in strange surroundings. Consider:

≜ IBM saw its high-margin market for large computers begin to evaporate in the late 1980s. Failing to turn around and refocus its business fast enough, the company posted staggering losses of $12 billion and shed nearly 200,000 jobs.

≣ Ford Motor Company wallowed in $3 billion worth of red ink from 1980 to 1982 as Japanese competitors out-gunned and out-designed U.S. car makers. The automaker's problems continued well into the 1990s.

≣ GTE's front-line customer service was so fragmented that only 1 in 200 support calls was resolved while the customer was still on the phone.

≣ And, speaking of poor customer service, patrons of British Airways rated its service so bad that they nicknamed the flagship carrier "bloody awful."

The managers of these organizations saw the bad news travel fast —straight from the boardroom to the bottom line. What's worse, the path back up is not well marked. Some companies never make it.

Companies attempting to recover must learn both a new landscape and a new mindscape. It takes strong action. It requires people willing to question and possibly change everything from organizational goals to the methods of achieving those goals. The organization must challenge itself to ask and answer very basic questions, such as:

≣ What is the company's purpose? (What do we do?)

≣ Where do we want to be in three to five years? (How do we face and influence the future?)

≣ What processes should the company use to achieve its goals? (How do we do it best?)

Entering the Age of Reinvention

Call it reengineering, rethinking, redesigning, rebuilding, redirecting or any other of the "re" words, but the pressures of the business world have sparked an era of reinvention. Companies, in both public and private sectors, are pulling out the stops and beginning to challenge everything from the way they answer the phone to the way they manufacture goods or provide services.

A 1994 CSC/Index report surveyed over 400 U.S. and European businesses and discovered that 75 percent had major formal process improvement efforts under way. Nearly 70 percent of the respondents expected major changes in corporate culture, and most predicted big changes in jobs and organizational structures. Moreover, 77 percent felt that information technology was very important to the success of the efforts.

No process is sacred. Every activity is (or can be) scrutinized. And, the results of challenging the status quo are remarkable.

Many organizations are shocked when they realize the effects of time-honored (but time-wasting) processes. Consider a few examples:

- IBM Credit, the organization that finances computers, software, and services sold by IBM, learned that the actual work required to process a new customer could be completed in only 90 minutes, instead of the six days to two weeks it used to take.

- Ford Motor Company learned that it employed 100 times more people in its accounts payable department than Mazda. Even after adjusting for Mazda's smaller size, no one could justify the head count or the processes that required people to manually match up 14 data items between the purchase order, receipt record, and invoice.

- Vice President Gore's National Productivity Review unearthed an inconceivable (and unmanageable) 100,000-page human resource policy that was administered by 40,000 people. In his report to the President, he wrote, "The personnel code alone weighs in at over 1,000 pounds. That code and the regulations no longer help government work; they hurt it. They hurt it badly, and we recommend getting rid of it." Gore's review also found that the U.S. government still maintains 10 pages of regulations on how to make an ash tray even though smoking has been abolished in most government office buildings.

- A study in the health care industry showed that 84 percent of hospital employees' time is spent on non-patient-care activities such as keeping records, scheduling, and attending meetings. Another study revealed that paper-intensive practices of U.S. health organizations cost an average patient $500 a year. That's 3.3 times higher than in Canada.

≋ A life insurance company studied its process of handling new customer applications. It discovered dozens of discrete steps and many hand-offs to people who performed only small parts of the process. The work passed between doers and checkers more than 30 times. The actual work took less than 20 minutes to complete, but insurance applications disappeared for over three weeks—moving from desk to desk, department to department—while processing took place.

In each case, people found that processes, policies, and politics prevented them from working efficiently. Small, sometimes innocent, procedures added up over the years to create bloated bureaucracies and slow response to customers. Such are the ingredients that stir up the environment right for change.

Why Companies Are Doing It

Organizations look at reengineering for one of three reasons. They either:

≋ Are on the brink
≋ See storm clouds on the horizon
≋ Seek a quick competitive advantage

Organizations on the brink must change or face extinction. In some cases, they experience competitive threats; in other cases (like IBM) the market simply changes and core products and or services are no longer in demand.

In other situations, a company can see problems appearing on the horizon. GTE predicted the effects of having too many people filling jobs that could be handled by technology. Instead of waiting for the red ink to roll over their financial reports, they struck back. In early 1994, GTE announced a huge restructuring that will affect 17,000 jobs over three years. GTE's chairman and chief executive officer, Charles Lee, was quoted as saying, "Technology is driving our industry. No matter what the legislature, the administration or the regulators do, we're going to have a competitive marketplace in the not-too-distant future. And we have to have competitive costs." The company staved off problems by restructuring before it had to.

Finally, some organizations see reengineering as a means to gain a competitive advantage or improve customer service. This is a popular quest of service industries such as stock brokerages. For example, Fidelity Investments changed the way its customers could buy and sell securities when it implemented its "TouchTone Trader" system. Customers, with no more than a push button telephone, can dial a toll-free number, check the status of their accounts or initiate a transaction. The customer can do work for himself or herself—taking the broker out of the picture. The system is fast, accurate, and easy to use.

Defining Reengineering

From banana farming to banking, business people are reexamining business processes. They are changing the way business does business. They look for ways to do things better, faster, or not at all.

That's where business process reengineering (BPR) comes in. With little argument, business process reengineering has become the preeminent business tool for redesigning business. Proponent Michael Hammer defines Business Reengineering as:

> The fundamental rethinking and radical redesign of an entire business system.

It takes into consideration everything from the business processes themselves, people's jobs, organizational structures, management systems, values and beliefs.

In their book *Reengineering the Corporation,* Hammer and co-author James Champy define reengineering's goal as "achieve[ing] dramatic improvements in critical contemporary measures of performance such as cost, quality, service and speed."

Business process reengineering's chief tool is a blank sheet of paper and an open mind. Hammer and Champy call it "...a creative process with an uncertain outcome."

The basic steps of reengineering are:

≋ Define objectives
≋ Analyze existing processes
≋ Invent new ways to work
≋ Implement the new process

Hammer and Champy say that the ability to use insight, imagination, and a willingness to challenge all assumptions are key to BPR. In practice, reengineering lets people change the rules. Often, they must change the rules of the entire business, not just those of a small department or work group.

For example, Ford started to challenge only its accounts payable activities. Instead, it ended up changing its entire materials acquisition process. When it first studied the process, Ford found that a lot of unnecessary time was being spent matching up purchase orders, receiving tickets, and invoices. Now, when an order is initiated by Purchasing, an entry is made into an on-line database. When goods arrive at the factory, a clerk at the receiving dock checks the database to be sure the shipment is correct and to register its receipt. Ford's suppliers no longer need to send invoices either, since Ford pays from its own records. The result? A 75 percent reduction in staff, a simplification of material control and improved accuracy in financial reporting.

Functions versus Processes

Without a doubt, there is still plenty of confusion about the key elements of business process reengineering. Some of it stems from the difficulty of understanding the differences between business functions and processes.

Most organizational structures designed before 1990 are function-based. They arrange people into stovepipe departments like those shown in Figure 1.

Typical business functions include accounting, purchasing, or marketing. Most companies have structured business organizations by

Function-based Organizations

Finance   Sales   Logistics   H/R   Mfg.

FIGURE 1 In a function-based organization, people's work is narrowly defined by what they do, not the outcome or goal.

function for decades. We reinforce the functional mind-set by teaching courses in business school on accounting, marketing, and logistics. The courses develop our skills in a discipline. Then, when we graduate, we take our place in functionally structured organizational units (departments) and maintain reporting relationships to the top person of the functional area. For most of us, it is a well-entrenched mind-set, and a hard one to change. In the real world, most normal business processes cut across functions. Consider a business process like acquiring raw materials. The activity of securing the goods or services required to make a product often require the interaction of several functional departments such as purchasing, manufacturing, accounting, and maybe even logistics. Table 1 illustrates the potential roles of four

TABLE 1 Potential Roles of Function-based Departments Required to Acquire Raw Materials

Department	Role
Purchasing	Locate suppliers, negotiate contracts, place orders, monitor orders
Accounting	Process purchase orders, check invoices against purchase orders and receiving tickets, pay invoices, keep track of payments
Receiving/ Warehousing	Receive materials, prepare receiving tickets and other documentation, check for compliance with purchase orders, unload and store materials
Auditing/Inventory control	Keep track of materials on hand, audit receiving/ warehousing function, audit purchasing, audit payments

functional departments in a single process of acquiring materials. As you can see, it takes a lot of work, checking and cross-checking.

The problem with this organizational structure is that work passes through too many hands. At almost every stop, it is checked and re-checked, which adds time and overhead. It takes a lot of coordination to make sure everything passes to the appropriate next destination. What's more, each functional department will develop its own internal checks and controls for monitoring work, which can slow down the process even more. In a function-based structure, processes tend to bog down.

A process-based structure looks significantly different. As shown in Figure 2, process-based organizations take a horizontal approach to structure. It drafts people from various disciplines and places them on a team, which is given a process goal, such as acquiring raw materials.

Proponents of business process reengineering believe that process-based organizations, like those in Figure 2, are more effective because they don't have to go up and down functional hierarchies. BPR creates organizations where one person—often with a little help from auto-mation—does the job once handled by several people.

Work is arranged differently in a process based organization. It doesn't pass sequentially.

Process Organizations

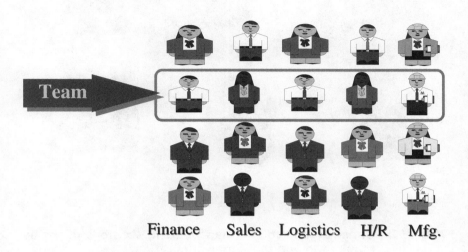

Finance   Sales   Logistics   H/R   Mfg.

FIGURE 2 In a process-based organization, the outcome is more important than the function.

Instead of developing a five-part form to process a loan application, for example, information is entered once into a computer. The computer record is updated as the approval process moves forward, through steps such as credit checking and employment verification. When all tasks are complete, the complete record can be reviewed. Processing, however, requires only one person, and the computer. There is no need to pass the work on to five or six different people.

The computer program can even serve as a monitor, rejecting approvals for incomplete records or for records which show a person's poor credit history.

Figures 3 and 4 depict how a reengineered process might work in a service organization.

Imagine the example we just discussed. You are trying to get a loan from a bank that has a function-based organization. Your

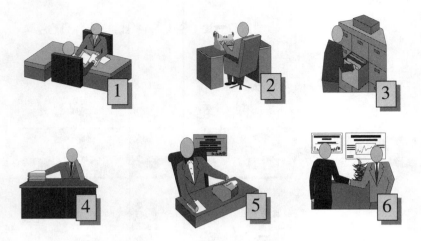

FIGURE 3 Under organizational management, six steps might be required to approve a loan application.

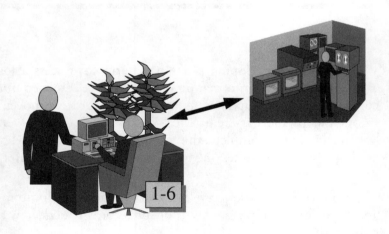

FIGURE 4 Under a functional structure, one person (with a computer) could do the work of six, faster and better.

application would be taken by one clerk, then forwarded to a series of other clerks who process the request. One clerk might check credit references, another verifies employment, and still another calculates repayment capabilities. As your request travels through multiple desks, a series of controls and checks and rechecks would be established by each department. Finally, somebody determines whether the loan should be granted.

In a reengineered process, one case worker would take the application, then let the computer validate information, and store the results. Controls, such as calculating risks and repayment capabilities, are handled by the computer. Both the time and the effort required by the reengineered process is far less than when work was passed from desk to desk.

History: How Did We Get This Way?

People are creatures of habit, and so are their business processes. If you dig back far enough in history, you'll trace the roots of many of our common business practices to the early parts of the industrial age.

The most popular way to deal with a growing business is to split up tasks among many people. Division of labor or assembly line work styles are not a 20th Century innovation—their roots go back to the days of Eli Whitney.

Technology has always been the force that moves business ahead. And computers were invented long after most contemporary business processes.

We're Stuck with Straight Pins

It turns out that much of how we arrange work today is a byproduct of work published by Adam Smith more than two hundred years ago. Smith demonstrated how the productivity of manufacturing a straight pin could be greatly increased if the process was divided up. He split the production into 18 discrete operations. Then, he measured the effects of dividing up the work among several workers versus having one worker perform each task.

The results seemed remarkable. His investigations showed that one employee alone could make from 1 to 20 pins a day. But, when the 18 steps were split among 10 employees the result was a production of 48,000 pins a day. That's an incredible increase in productivity!

Word of Smith's discovery spread throughout industry. People began to apply his principles to all kinds of activity—in fact, we still do. But Smith lived in a very different time. There were no computers and no automation.

More Ways to Divide

Management philosophy continued to support the notion that work could and should be fragmented into discrete tasks. More than a century ago, Frederick Taylor, the father of Scientific Management, performed the first empirical studies of work productivity and behavior. His research was among the first to measure the effects on time and motion.

In his "pig iron" studies, Taylor tested the effect on employee productivity of factors such as how far the worker bent over to use a shovel, how big the shovel blade was, how much load was placed in the wheelbarrow, and frequency and duration of his rest periods. Then he figured out how many workers to assign to each task, how many tasks to break a job into, and so on. From the data Taylor collected, he concluded there was "the one best way" to do this job.

Taylor's methods served as inspiration for Frank and Lillian Gilbreth to pioneer "time and motion" studies and methods of classifying elements of work. They attempt to break up a work process into small pieces, then divide the pieces among workers. They asked questions like: How much time does it take someone to handle a customer transaction or accumulate and resolve a complaint? How fast can and should maintenance work be initiated and completed to insure quality service delivery?

In each case, the process can be broken into tasks and sub-tasks. From the time of Smith and Taylor, management thinkers have been consumed with identifying and fine-tuning tasks.

No one ever stopped to ask whether the work being studied should be done at all. That's where reengineering comes in.

Reengineering versus Other Theories

In modern days, management thinkers have evaluated and adopted so many different theories that anyone would get confused.

From the humble beginnings of dividing up labor and detailing tasks, many techniques to analyze work have emerged. Techniques such as MBO, Zero-Based Budgeting, Theory Z, Quality Circles, Excellence, and Learning Organizations, have all claimed to hold the key to organizational success. Each of the theories did provide some benefit, but none was right for all situations.

Some may ask: "Is reengineering just another passing fad?" No, we see it as an integration and extension of well established theories—but with a twist. Reengineering lets you truly reinvent processes.

In many cases, people are reinventing processes simply because they can. Innovative and low-cost technology that didn't exist before can now be used. And today, management attitudes are ripe for change.

How Is Reengineering Different?

The fundamental difference between reengineering and other management initiatives is that you can choose to do something completely new—not just put a patch on what you're doing now.

Consider the options of renovating an old house against buying a new one. Using a continuous quality or total quality approach, chances are you would figure out how to fix your old house. You would recarpet the floors, repaint the walls, remodel certain rooms, and reupholster your furniture.

Using a reengineering approach, you would hire an architect and a builder, develop blueprints, and let them build a new home. Then, you would likely go out and buy all new furniture. Rather than fix what you have, you'd create your environment by buying new.

To some, reengineering may look like a quality process. Both approaches study business processes and use teams for everything from design to implementation, but there are a few fundamental difference. Table 2 lists some of the differences between approaches.

TABLE 2   Differences between Quality Management and Reengineering

	Quality Mgt.	Reengineering
Overall approach	Small improvements	Radical
Desired change	Incremental steps	Huge - all at one time
Organizational level	Micro	Macro
Belief in current processes	Basically right	Wrong

Reengineering goes after quicker, radical changes all at once. It moves over all organizational levels. And, reengineering often uses a "guilty until proven innocent" attitude when looking at existing processes. Rather than look at what you do as basically right, reengineering says it is probably wrong.

Who Is Reengineering?

By now, you may be asking: who is reengineering? Who is taking on such radical changes?

The answer: everyone. Studies of mid-sized and large organizations show that as many as 60 percent have already undertaken some kind of reengineering project. These organizations come from all sectors: public and private, product and service.

One consultant that we interviewed put it this way: "Reengineering is right for lots of companies. Anybody who is still sitting on procedures developed by Miss Nellie in 1940 ought to be thinking twice. Besides, Miss Nellie is long gone—she's either retired, dead, or both. Her procedures should be too."

We agree. Many companies still operate using rules that are ridiculous in this day and age. They under-utilize technology and apply techniques poorly. Just about every company is guilty.

Conclusion

By now, you might think that reengineering is a process that lets you make up the rules as you go. That's partially correct. It is true that reengineering lacks a formal, precise methodology. But there are several principles or guidelines which make up a set of principles.

In this chapter, we provided the definition of reengineering and a few examples. Chapter 2 presents the guidelines.

CHAPTER 2

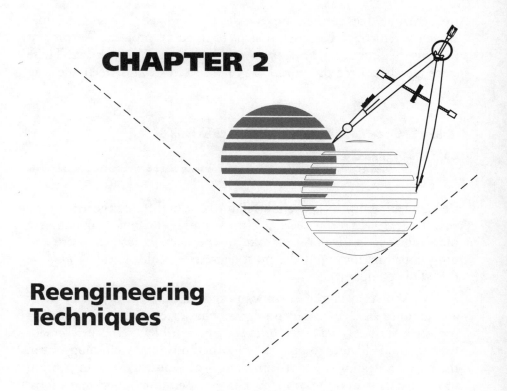

Reengineering Techniques

Reengineering isn't magic; you can't just wave a wand and make better business processes happen. As much as we can define it, we also acknowledge that reengineering is a term that means different things to different people. The trick is to apply its principles to create an environment that generates results. That takes *techniques, teams,* and *technology.*

This chapter talks about the "how to" side of reengineering. We open with a short discussion of the three levels of reengineering: how projects can *streamline, integrate,* or *transform* an organization.

Then we offer some good news and bad news about how to rearrange work by applying the actual techniques of reengineering. The good news is that most experts agree that the principles of reengineering are relatively simple, and we discuss seven of them.

But there's bad news too. There is no step-by-step methodology or procedures that will miraculously render a reengineered process.

Recognizing that there is no cookbook approach to reengineering, we've constructed a basic set of steps to organize projects. We present these as the four A's: *activate, analyze, annihilate,* and *assimilate.* These steps closely mirror the phases we've observed in most reengineering projects.

Three Approaches toward Reengineering

Reengineering projects generally fall into one of three categories. At the very basic level, reengineering efforts simply *streamline* operations; moderately aggressive projects take an approach to *integrate* work and unify job functions; and the most aggressive projects truly *transform* the whole company.

As shown in Figure 5, you can expect a different degree of effort and amount of change depending on what category of reengineering project you undertake. Each of the categories, however, can represent fundamental changes to people, work methods, and technology. Even the most basic approach—streamlining—can cause a major disruption of work activity and the complete change or elimination of many jobs.

Streamlining

Streamlining operations offers a basic, segmented approach to reengineering. It cleans up but doesn't necessarily transform a process.

For example, a streamlining approach to an accounts payable process could reduce the number of required sign-offs from 17 to 7. Another approach would be to raise the level of spending authorizations for managers. Still another attempt could maintain the current process, but add technology in the form of workflow software to electronically route documents through the organization. The approach taken is simple, functional, and makes operations go faster or better.

Purists criticize the streamlining approach because it often doesn't go far enough. It treats symptoms, but doesn't always find a cure for a bad process. It doesn't change the way a company conducts its core business, nor does it challenge whether certain processes should exist at

Levels of Reengineering

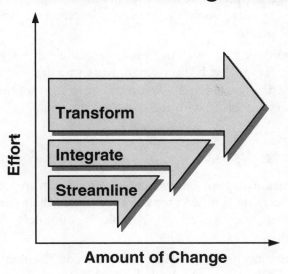

FIGURE 5 Reengineering can mean streamlining, integrating, or transforming the way you do business.

all. Streamlining is much like quality improvement processes—it makes improvements but doesn't radically change anything. It is a quick fix.

Integrating

The most popular approach to reengineering comes from projects which *integrate* discrete business processes, replacing them with a unified process that frequently cuts across functions and department responsibilities.

When Ford reengineered its accounts payable process, it took the tasks formerly performed by accountants, purchasing department staff, warehouse receiving clerks, and reordered them. The company cut through the territory of several functional departments to create a more efficient means of receiving and paying for supplies. Then, Ford implemented a computer system to support the new process and eliminate redundant work, such as keeping separate receiving logs or separate lists of prices.

Ford's change of its receiving processes didn't directly affect all functions of the company. It didn't change the way designers designed cars or the way dealers sold cars—but it did have a profound affect on the jobs of people involved with the receiving process.

Transforming

Some organizations approach reengineering by putting the whole company on the table. Those companies reevaluate their entire reason for being. They are willing to gamble a complete "enterprise transformation."

Transformation projects require complete commitment from top management. They must step back from daily activities and take a fresh, radical look at their organization's goals, skills and capabilities. They must be willing to dissect the forces of competition and customers and have the courage to change everything at once.

Examples of transformational projects are few. In our research, we came across a transcript of an excellent speech delivered by William Crain, a vice president of Chevron Corporation. Crain explains a transforming change at his company:

I have worked in the oil business for 37 years, and for about 33–34 of those years we thought our main job was replacing reserves. That's what it meant to be an oil company.

The goal was oil: find it, sell it. That was our unstated vision of ourselves, a definition of our mission. International oil companies looked for oil and gas and measured success by production volumes. And this idea worked very well for a long time. As long as prices kept moving up faster than costs, then increased volumes translated directly into increased profits.

Now, however, all that has changed abruptly. Today, the goal isn't just oil. Oil and gas are viewed as a means to an end, and that end is the success of our business. The goal is sustainable development. And cost-cutting is as important as production volume in achieving acceptable profit margins.

This change in self-concept has been required by a change in reality. Oil demand is flat, prices are weak, and there's a growing awareness that the so-called oil glut is not a temporary phenomenon. That's a fact of life.

Therefore, today, the challenge is to get revenues up and costs down.

The first sentence of my company's mission statement, the document that defines our company states, "Chevron is an international petroleum company (whose) mission is to achieve superior financial results for our stockholders, the owners of our business."

Notice it says nothing about producing large volumes—even though in North America we are one of the largest producers of oil and natural gas and the largest refiner. That was written only 15 months ago—that's what I mean about abrupt change.

Reengineering Principles

Business process reengineering places challenges on old paradigms. Practitioners put everything on the table; no process, no habit, no organization is sacred.

Among the areas likely to change are:

- ≋ Decision points
- ≋ Where data is collected
- ≋ How work is arranged
- ≋ What and where controls are placed
- ≋ Where information is created and maintained
- ≋ Roles of both workers and managers

Early in Michael Hammer's work, he defined several principles of reengineered work. Others have expanded upon and explained these principles, making them generally accepted standards for changing the way work is performed. The principles are:

1. Organize work around results, not tasks.

2. Capture data only one time—when it is first created.

3. Allow decision points where work is performed.

4. Incorporate controls into information processing.

5. Make people who use a process do the work.

6. Work in parallel instead of sequentially, then integrate results.

7. Treat geographically dispersed resources as one.

These principles should be used when reconstructing work. More specifically they mean:

1. Organize work around results, not tasks.

Instead of dividing up work into small tasks and units, determine the work's end result. As much as possible, structure the work so that one person can perform all the steps involved in a process. This accomplishes two goals: it eliminates the time wasted as a project is handed off from one person to another, and it puts workers in control of processes.

For example, an insurance firm redesigned the way it accepted new customer applications. Instead of having the application pass across many different desks in different departments, individual case managers were made responsible for handling all aspects of an application. This change shortened the time it took to approve an application and also eliminated "lost" applications. The application could be located at any time, since it didn't pass from one desk and department to another.

2. Capture data only one time— when it is first created.

Ideally, data should be entered into the company's system only once— when it is first created. All too often, organizations keep multiple lists and records of data that make it impossible to process information efficiently.

The human resources benefits system of one large company required that a complete new record be made for any incidental change. Even a simple change of address required that the employee fill out 22 different forms just to get all the records corrected. In an insurance company, multiple forms were used to process a claim. One form was required for payment of the claim, while another form was sent off to the case analysis group. The forms contained almost the same information. And what about sending Junior off to elementary school? In some school districts, parents have to fill out up to seven forms—one for each teacher—at the beginning of each year. Woe is everyone if a phone number changes during the course of the school year.

While every situation is different, we believe that redundant organizational information can be nearly eliminated by using technology. The solution for many situations is to use low-cost bar coding devices, electronic data interchange (EDI) for data collection, then database technology to store the captured data in an organized location.

3. Allow decision points where work is performed.

In many workplaces, work is separated among "doers" and "checkers." Somebody performs a task, and somebody else checks it.

This process gives managers and supervisors complete control, and fosters hierarchical management structures. The doers are assumed to lack the knowledge or responsibility to take a process to completion.

A reengineered approach to work challenges the assumption that workers are incapable of performing an entire process. Instead, it argues that the people who actually do the work should be the ones to make many of the decisions about it, and that the controls over the decisions should be built into the systems that workers use.

Such an approach to work will challenge and likely reduce layers of organizational bureaucracy. It also changes the roles of workers and their supervisors. It empowers the doers to better control their own work environment, changes the managerial role from one of controller and supervisor to one of facilitator and supporter.

4. Incorporate controls into information processing.

With a little help, the people who collect information can often process it too. Years ago, that was taboo; Work was separated as a control process and because people at lower levels of an organization were thought to be incapable of acting on information.

For example, at Ford, the receiving department creates information about goods received. It also processes this information with the help of a computer system. It is no longer necessary to send the raw data—receiving tickets—to accounts payable.

This change in responsibility is a boon to efficiency. Instead of allowing a discrepancy to pass through to several people within an organization, it can be stopped at the source. Let's say you placed a purchasing order for 12 wheels and the supplier ships 20. If the person at the receiving dock has access to the order records, he can recognize that there is a problem and take immediate corrective action. The receiving clerk can refuse the shipment, take a partial shipment, or accept the entire amount, depending on the needs. The correction won't take hours to reconcile.

5. Make people who use a process do the work.

Overly specialized processes breed bureaucracies, and cause people to spend undue time and energy following company policies rather than common sense.

Take purchasing processes. Many companies rely on purchasing departments to place orders and administer all purchasing activity, even for non-strategic items. One manufacturer found that 35 percent of its orders were for non-strategic purchases. In some cases, the cost of purchasing processes exceeded the cost of the goods purchased.

A reengineered process lets users get their own supplies or information, but builds controls into the system. If, for example, the accounting department needs new pencils, it should not have to go to a separate department to administer the process. Instead, the purchasing group should set up master accounts or a computer system and let the accounting department buy its own pencils.

Sometimes that even means pushing some tasks onto the customer, whether the customer is in a different department in the same company or in the outside world. Fidelity Investments, among other progressive brokers, offers its customers a 10 percent discount for trading stocks with a computer system hooked up to telephones. The customer need only identify herself to the system, then key in the buy or sell order. The system has become a boon to independent customers who don't want to wait for a broker to take the order.

Discount merchandiser Wal-Mart pushed this principle one step further—to its suppliers. Rather than ask its own warehouse employees to be responsible for inventories, the mass merchandiser set up key suppliers to manage inventory levels of their own products. This process took a lot of guts—trusting that suppliers would refrain from filling warehouses with slow-selling products. But it also eliminated tedious work on the part of Wal-Mart's own staff.

6. Work in parallel instead of sequentially, then integrate results.

Where possible, compress time by working the activities of large projects in parallel rather than sequentially. This challenges the old paradigm of assembly line work. It also requires that activities be linked and coordinated throughout their processes, not just at the end. Although new product development can often be accelerated by running multiple parallel sub-projects, insufficient checks during the process itself can mean that all the pieces may fail to work together properly at the integration and assembly test stage.

Information technology, as we will soon discuss, plays a key role in enabling parallel work activity. Technologies like high speed telecommunications, common shared databases, teleconferencing and workgroup support systems make possible parallel development with much lower risk of integration failure.

7. Treat geographically dispersed resources as one.

Centralize resources when it makes sense. Geographically dispersed resources should be treated as if they were centralized. Shared databases, telecommunications networks and standardized processing systems now make it possible to gain the benefits of scale and centralization (such as quantity discounts) while maintaining the advantages of flexibility and service that come from being dispersed and close to the customer.

An example of how centralization works comes from computer maker Hewlett-Packard (HP). At one time HP had more than 50 manufacturing units, each with its own purchasing department. This decentralized approach prevented HP from capitalizing on quantity discounts. The solution was to create a corporate unit that negotiated master agreements and administered the purchasing through divisional organizations. A shared database on vendors and performance linked the central and divisional groups. The payoff: 150 percent improvements in on-time deliveries, 50 percent reduction in lead times, and significant cost savings on goods purchased.

Steps to Get Started

Lacking a formal methodology, we've found that many successful reengineering projects follow a simple four-phase management approach. We've dubbed the approach the four A's and named the phases *activate, analyze, annihilate*, and *assimilate*.

We provide the details around each.

Activate

In this first phase, the reengineering project is initiated. This is the "get organized" phase of the project. The objectives of this phase are to:

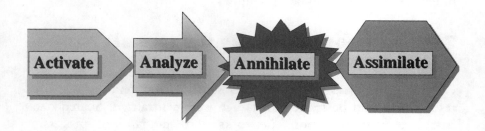

- Gain agreement that change is needed—create a mission
- Form a steering team
- Select a project champion
- Select a process owner
- Select a preliminary team
- Map core processes

Since reengineering frequently comes as a top-down activity, senior management is usually among the early participants. Company chiefs become members of the reengineering steering team. It is important to keep these high–ranking members involved as the project progresses, but the real work of the project is generally done by a team of people with skills that cross functional areas. We'll talk more about the composition of the teams in the next chapter.

Aside from basic organization and selecting of team members, the primary objective of this phase is to map out the organization's core processes. This activity doesn't have to take months and years, but it does require a little thinking on the part of organizational leaders.

The output of this phase, for many, turns into an organizational mission statement followed by a listing of activities that the company is committed to. The shorter the list, the better. That way, everyone— both those on and off the reengineering projects—knows which way the team is headed.

The final activity of this phase is for a reengineering team to be put together and assigned. Most organizations start by appointing one team to look at one process; however there can be more than one team, and more than one project.

Analyze

The second phase, *analyze*, moves the reengineering effort into gear. By this time, team members are selected and the mission is clear. This is where the team "gets oriented" with the specifics. The objectives of this phase are to:

- Select a process
- Nail down the scope

⚌ Map out current processes
⚌ Check out team members
⚌ Find breaks in the pipeline
⚌ Set goals for a new design

In many organizations, the reengineering team begins the hard work of understanding the old and designing the new. Concentration is key during this phase.

Depending on the project, some teams actually move off site to do the work. The University of Texas Health Services group rented an apartment and took its work there. American Airlines took an office behind one of the gates at the Dallas Fort Worth airport. The teams felt it best to leave behind the distractions of day-to-day business while they tried to dissect the way things are, and construct the way things should be.

Some teams use software and special methodologies to create a better picture of the current process. The software can be as simple and inexpensive as a $200 PC flowcharting package, such as ABC Flow-Charter by Micrografx or All Clear by Clear Software. Other projects implement more rigorous methodologies to track existing work. Software that supports various process identification is available from various suppliers. IDEF/0, commonly used by government, can be purchased from Meta Software and LogicWorks.

The purpose of mapping out existing processes is to find breaks or duplications in work. It is common to find four or five departments keeping the same set of records on a business process. Take, for example, a manufacturing organization we know. There were four copies of the customer master file, each maintained by a different department. The work performed on maintaining customer information was not only redundant, it was never in sync.

This is also the right time to check the composition of the team. Are the right cross-functional skills represented? If the project involves redesigning the way the company invents a new product, make sure you have both designers and manufacturing engineers on the project. Without all skills being represented, people probably will design a product that can't be built in the company's factory.

Finally, it is important during this phase to set aggressive goals for the new process. Shoot for the moon. Instead of hoping for a 10-

percent improvement in process time, try for 50 or 70 percent. Few projects ever achieve more than they try for.

Annihilate

The third phase calls for creativity. At this point, project teams need to "get crazy" and rip up as many of the time–robbing rules and regulations that they can. They need to pull out a blank sheet (or bring up a blank screen) and reinvent the process as it should be.

This phase involves:

≋ Asking crazy questions, brainstorming
≋ Finding breakthrough ideas
≋ Detailing out a new process
≋ Checking the new process—making sure it fits other systems
≋ Building a prototype
≋ Testing, refining, and testing

It is this phase where people must move from the world as it is to the world that it can be. It's not easy. Many people are not creative thinkers, but are instead prisoners of their paradigms. They can't think outside the box or invent new ways to get work done.

Certain people provide telltale signs of not adapting to a creative thinking process. Beware of comments such as:

≋ "That's impossible."
≋ "It's against policy to do it that way."
≋ "It's too radical a change for us."
≋ "We tried it before—it didn't work."

To help the creative process, some teams resort to interesting measures. We have seen teams rent motivational tapes and videos. Popular among them is Joel Barker's books and video on paradigms. Barker's book, *Future Edge: Discovering the New Paradigms of Success* has turned into an inspirational piece for more than one project that we've observed.

A large part of the *annihilate* phase involves brainstorming new ideas. Researchers at MIT recently looked into using computers and software to enhance the process. They learned that the two primary problems associated with brainstorming meetings can be avoided.

Idea blocking and evaluation apprehension are the plagues of traditional brainstorming meetings. If Sue is explaining her idea, John may simultaneously listen to Sue, think of another one, and forget it before he has a chance to speak. The process of letting only one person explain an idea at a time, while orderly, blocks other ideas from ever being presented. The other issue, evaluation apprehension, crops up when an idea is judged not on its merits but on who proposed it. In traditional meetings, ideas presented by the boss are often treated as more valid than ideas presented by the mail room clerk. Software gets around these issues by offering anonymity of ideas, and allows everyone to enter ideas at once.

Another technique for this phase consists of searching through industry literature. You might be surprised to find someone performing a process exactly the way you didn't think it could be done.

Once a new process is identified, it must be tested. Many reengineering projects build a prototype process, then test it, refine it, and test it again until team members are confident everything works. Depending on the scope of the project, the process of rolling out and supporting a prototype could take weeks or months.

Assimilate

Assuming the new process passes muster during its pilot or prototype phase, the next and final step is to assimilate it into the organization. This is the right time to "get real." Objectives of this phase are:

≋ Confirm the results of the pilot
≋ Determine the needs of widespread implementation
≋ Document the benefits
≋ Install and implement
≋ Look for on-going support (continuous improvement)
≋ Make it a part of the culture

Check and double-check everything. Does the pilot or prototype perform as desired? Will it scale to the organization as a whole? What is required for widespread implementation?

At this point, the reengineering project team must assess the organizational impact of the new process. Will it change jobs? How will it be accepted? Will major changes in staffing be required? If an organizational development or human resources professional is not already on the project, solicit the services of one at this time.

Many organizations come up with great ideas for reengineering, perform successful pilots, and see implementation fail miserably because they didn't figure the human factors of major changes. It is important to consider these factors now and seek professional help.

Also, it is important to estimate on-going support needs of the new process. Should the company buy a new computer system? Do they need to hire additional staff to support it? How will integration issues with existing technologies and procedures be handled?

The final phase of the reengineering effort can bring on as much work as the first three combined. It is important to keep the team together and work through issues as they surface.

Conclusion

Throughout this chapter we have discussed techniques and phases of reengineering projects. Our review of hundreds of projects tells us that no two are alike. It is important to understand the phases and approaches, but it's even more important to tailor activities to the needs of the organization.

In the next chapter, we will discuss the most critical element of reengineering: people and teams. Good people and well–structured teams make reengineering work. Poorly contrived organizations ruin projects.

CHAPTER 3

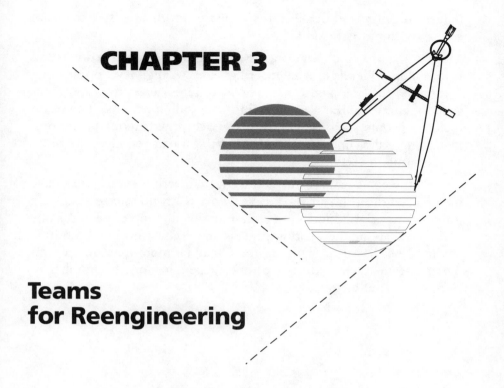

Teams
for Reengineering

The success or failure of reengineering projects often boils down to one simple component of the ToolKit: the team. In our studies of companies that have successfully reengineered business processes, we found that the proper composition of teams, followed by effective executive sponsorship of the reengineering effort, turned out to be the most important factor of success.

In this chapter, we examine the components of the reengineering team and talk about how to put reengineering teams together. We introduce the concept that most successful reengineering efforts require teams at two levels: an executive level and a knowledge worker level. Also, we address who should be on the teams.

Admittedly, team selection is tricky. Getting the right members with the right skills and the right attitudes is as important as getting the right tools and technologies. This chapter explores the options and suggests how to construct team membership, specifies the positions that people play, and finally, gives some tips for making sure the team continues to move forward.

Most companies find that a successful method for constructing teams is to build two levels of reengineering teams. A high level or "steering committee" or "steering team" consists of senior executives and managers of the organization's operating and staff functions. This team includes people such as the executive vice presidents of operations, marketing, sales, finance, manufacturing, human resources, logistics, and information services.

The second team is the actual "reengineering team" itself. The members of this team are the people who actually do the reengineering project. They should include a cross-functional group of people, some who know about the existing process and some who know nothing about it. As shown in Figure 6, there may be more than one reengineering team assembled at one time, depending on the number of reengineering efforts afoot.

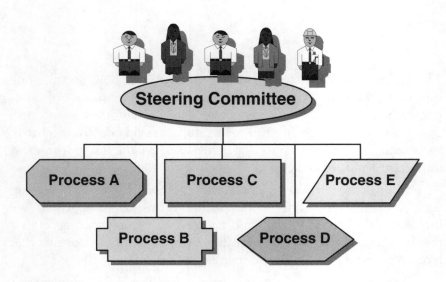

FIGURE 6 The Steering Committee can oversee several reengineering process teams at one time.

Team Number One— The Steering Committee

The primary focus of the reengineering steering committee is to provide overall guidance to a company's reengineering efforts. This committee or team is generally comprised of highly placed senior executives of perhaps traditionally function-based roles.

The steering committee should not do the work but should lead, support, and approve new processes and organizations as they are formed. This team takes on different activities during the course of the reengineering work, but in most cases turns into a "hands-off" team. They should not over-manage the activities of the actual reengineering teams unless they seriously doubt its recommendations.

The most important prerequisite for a membership on the steering committee is the desire to see change for the better happen. These individuals must be willing to cut through their traditional roles, find a way to fund projects, and feel comfortable that the reengineering activity is in the best interest of the company. They must be willing to lay down their old jobs and organizations to the new organization that the reengineering teams will bring them.

In one company we studied, the reengineering effort led to dissolution of the marketing department. The marketing function was broken up and put within the domain of two processes: new product development and product fulfillment. Of course, the initial reaction of the vice president of marketing was not favorable, since he would lose his power base in the new organization. In fact, he wasn't sure that his own job would remain intact. This type of dilemma is not unusual.

Roles for the Steering Committee

In many cases, the steering committee acts as leaders and coaches, but, once again, they don't do the work. They should provide leadership and counsel during phases of the projects. Their involvement is especially important during the first phase of a reengineering effort, as projects get off the ground.

Depending on the individual organizations, our studies have concluded that the steering committee may either work closely with the reengineering team or it may not provide much more than a rubber stamp.

At McKesson Water Company in California, the steering committee only met for a total of eight hours for the entire two-year period that the reengineering efforts were going on. Rather than burdening the reengineering teams with many meaningless meetings, the steering committee confined meeting time to important decisions and allowed the project team members to invent new concepts and processes with little encumbrance or close supervision.

In other companies, especially where great change is about to take place, the steering committee may take on a more active role. The decision is generally based on the culture of the company.

Membership in the steering committee is generally flat. All members have an equal say and equal vote. There are, however, two more active roles that emerge from the steering committee: the champion and czar.

The Champion

From the ranks of the steering committee, someone is generally identified as the Reengineering Champion. This particular role is for someone who has taken responsibility for the success of individual reengineering projects. He is highly visible in the organization, willing to cut through politics and problems, and considered to be a mover and a shaker.

The Champion is generally assigned one reengineering project at a time. Although he may not work on a day-to-day basis with the reengineering team, the Champion is only a phone call away. He is the person that is frequently credited with success or failure of the project, since he has the closest view of what's going on.

In many organizations, the Champion is self-appointed. That is, the Champion learns to become very involved in the reengineering process and understands that he or she has a stake in the success of a productive and successful outcome.

Most important, the Champion must be willing to make the hard calls and do whatever is necessary to communicate—both up and down the organization—what's going on or what's about to happen. Generally speaking, the Champion is very articulate, with excellent persuasive speaking and writing skills.

The Czar

In organizations where a lot of reengineering work is going on at one time and there are multiple teams working on multiple projects, the company generally selects a Reengineering Czar. The Czar oversees many projects. She is more less a "Super-Champion." The Czar is responsible and accountable for the progress of all the reengineering activity going on in an organization and makes sure that projects do not conflict with one another.

In one company we studied, three different reengineering projects were about to tackle the accounts payable process. They had no clear charter as to which group should be taking on the activity, so all three teams decided to reinvent accounts payable. A Reengineering Czar would have spotted the duplication and determined who should ultimately do the work.

The Czarship is a full-time job. It may be a vice president-level position reporting directly to the CEO. In many cases, the Czar stands in for the CEO as a tie-breaker or as the person to set priorities and on reengineering projects. This very important position must be staffed with someone strong enough to break through organizational hierarchies.

Sometimes, the ideal Czar turns out to be an outsider. When an outside person directs the projects, she is more likely to cast aside previously held beliefs of how the organization should run.

Team Number Two—
The Reengineering Team

The people who do the actual reengineering work are members of the reengineering team. Most companies select a cross-functional team— people coming from many different occupations, persuasions, activities, and backgrounds. The members of the reengineering team are almost always dedicated to the team, with all their previous work responsibility relieved. In some cases where it is not possible to pull people on a full-time basis, reengineering experts recommend that you dedicate at least 75 percent of the person's responsibility to the reengineering team.

Another key component is that team members are empowered to make decisions. The teams must be fully capable of making their own decisions on a day-to-day basis, without fear of encumbrance from senior management or their previous functional managers.

The reengineering teams that are successful are successful because they have the power to run their day-to-day activities. Ultimately, the reengineering team reports to the champion, the czar, or the CEO. This team is generally very small in size—frequently with fewer than 10 people. In fact, in some organizations, the teams are so small they consist of only four or five people.

Teams are frequently self-managing, although they may have a team leader. A good way of understanding how important it is to have a reengineering team with just the right people and the right background comes from the following story about Pacific Power and Light.

The Honey Pot: A Lesson in Creativity and Diversity

A number of years ago, Pacific Power and Light (PP&L), which serves many customers in the Cascade Mountains, was faced with solving an on-going problem that resulted in an unsafe job situation for the PP&L linemen.

In the Pacific Northwest, there are a number of ice storms in the fall and spring. These storms result in the accumulation of a significant ice load accumulating on the power lines. If not removed, this ice accumulates until the lines break.

The method used to remove the ice was to send linemen out into the field, have them climb the poles and towers and shake the lines with long poles hooked at one end. The linemen hated this job. A number of them were hurt when they fell from the icy poles and towers.

PP&L had, in the past, conducted a number of "brainstorming" sessions with no positive results. They then turned to a professional resource to organize still another session. He suggested that a diverse group be assembled to look at this problem. Rather than assembling just linemen and their supervisors, the resource insisted that people with a large variety of job functions be convened to look for a more creative way to get the ice off the power lines. In the session that followed were linemen, supervisors, accountants, secretaries, and people from the mail room.

Several hours into the meeting, the professional resource was beginning to become concerned that this effort would be as unproductive as previous ones. Then, during one of the coffee breaks, he overheard two of the linemen talking. "I hope we can finally figure out a better way to skin this cat." said one. "I really hate this job. Why, just last week, I was coming down from a pole, and, when I hit the ground, I was looking eye to eye at one of the biggest, meanest black bears I've ever seen. That bear, apparently, was not happy that I had invaded his territory, and chased me for well over a mile before he was satisfied that I would not return."

Trying to stimulate the group, the resource retold this tale to the rest of the session. "Why don't we train the bears to climb the poles," quipped one of the linemen. "They are so big and so heavy that their weight would probably be enough to shake the wires and knock the ice off."

After the laughter died down, the group thought of hundreds of reasons why that was a silly idea.

Then another of the linemen suggested that although training the bears seemed foolish, perhaps by placing honey pots on top of the poles, the bears would naturally climb the poles to get the honey and, in the process, shake the poles sufficiently to knock the ice off the lines. After another period of laughter followed by more objections generally centered around the fact that the bears might choose to empty the honey pots in fair not foul weather, one of the more senior, more sarcastic linemen said, "You now should have the executives put all those fancy honey pots on top just after an ice storm. That way the honey will be there when we need it, and, besides, it will do those fat executives some good to walk for a change."

Still another period of laughter followed. Then one of the secretaries spoke for the first time. "I was a nurse's aide in Vietnam. I saw many injured soldiers arrive at the field hospital by helicopter. The downwash from the helicopter blades was amazing. Dust would fly everywhere. It was almost blinding. I wonder if we just flew the helicopter over the power lines at low altitude, would the downwash from those blades be sufficient to shake the lines and knock the ice off?"

This time there was no laughter—just silence. She had come up with an answer. By valuing diversity and by encouraging divergent thinking, the resource had enabled the group to come up with a possible solution to a problem all wanted solved.

By the way, ever since that meeting, PP&L uses helicopters to fly over the power transmission lines after ice storms. It works beautifully. Linemen are no longer required to climb up ice-covered poles to shake the lines. The brainstorming session was a success. But remember, if they hadn't found the bear, they may never have found the helicopter.

As you can see, it was the person perhaps least likely to come up with the solution that actually did come up with it. In fact, reengineering experts generally recommend that the reengineering team be composed of both insiders—people who know how the existing processes work—as well as outsiders, who know nothing about the process, the industry, or any of the activities under scrutiny (Figure 7).

Roles within the Reengineering Team

The best reengineering teams come from a team of equals. People, no matter what their previous job, salary, or level, all should be equal team members. The members should possess cross-functional skills so that all important issues of a process can be seen from the vantage point of a variety of disciplines.

In most teams, however, people do take on specific roles. There is a Team Captain, a Process Owner, a Team Member, an Outsider, and an Insider.

The Team Captain

The Team Captain is generally appointed when the reengineering team takes shape. The Captain is not necessarily the team's manager, but she

FIGURE 7   It is best to include people from a variety of disciplines on the reengineering team.

is the person to call when someone wants an update on the reengineering activity. As a result, the Captain turns into the secretary, the treasurer, and the person with the administrative responsibility. The Captain needs to be a diplomat, a facilitator, and someone who is politically savvy about the organization.

Like the Champion on the steering committee, it is important that the Team Captain have excellent speaking, writing, and communications skills. This person must be persuasive and well-regarded in the organization. In most cases, the Team Captain must be an insider.

The Process Owner

The Process Owner is the person who will likely be responsible for the process once the reengineering efforts are over. This can be a little confusing at times because, in the beginning of the reengineering activity, people don't know how the process is going to end up. Therefore, how can one assume who the Process Owner is? It turns out that the Process Owner is frequently known in the beginning, though sometimes it does not become a formal activity until after the team is underway.

Sometimes the Process Owner is the Team Captain. Sometimes it is the Champion. Ultimately, during the reengineering activities, someone is going to have to step forward and be responsible for the process when it is all over and done with.

Team Members

As previously mentioned, the Team Members themselves are generally best selected from across functional groups. Some people should have general business knowledge, some people should have expertise in the process, and certainly someone on the team must be savvy about information technology and what it can do, though not necessarily a member of the information services department.

The Outsider

In most reengineering activities, it's important to bring in an Outsider. The Outsider might be someone from outside of the company, or someone just inside the company but outside the organization. Some more innovative reengineering teams have actually brought in a customer as an Outsider. These teams seek someone who would be unbiased, yet might have a stake in the success of a reengineering effort that improves customer service.

The Outsider is an important part of the team because he brings a perspective that might be different from the internal organization's, and untainted by "the way we have always done it." The Outsider is generally not knowledgeable about the organization's policy, so doesn't worry about whether people end up with the same number of people reporting to them. Those issues need to be dealt with later, but not considered during the reengineering effort.

The Outsider also doesn't have any turf to protect. There is no more unbiased person than an Outsider who really doesn't care whether there will be thirteen people in a process or three.

Another role of the Outsider is just to keep the team focused and on track. In some cases, that requires a professional facilitator, someone who has been through reengineering activities before and can keep the team going. Outsiders are important and always necessary in one form or another.

Choosing the right outsider is generally the job of the reengineering steering committee, not necessarily the reengineering team.

The Insider

The role of the Insider is to represent the process as it currently exists. This person is the knowledge expert. Most teams staff the reengineering effort with more than one Insider—usually people who are rated very good to excellent at their jobs.

The Insider must come with an open mind. It helps to include at least one Insider who is unhappy with current processes. The unhappy Insider is most likely to be receptive to change.

Conclusion

The reengineering teams are important, but as we study companies, we realize there is more than one way to build a good team. Our recommendation is to choose team members carefully based on a combination of skills and cross-functional attributes.

You should be able to name key roles on reengineering teams, such as Champion, Czar, Team Captain, Insiders and Outsiders. With everyone in place, your teams are ready to tackle business processes.

Don't forget to include that information-savvy person on the team. Without someone there who understands what can and can't be done with information technology, the teams will never come to some of the conclusions they might otherwise find.

Starting in the next chapter, we explore the uses of innovative technologies and how they support the seven principles of reengineering.

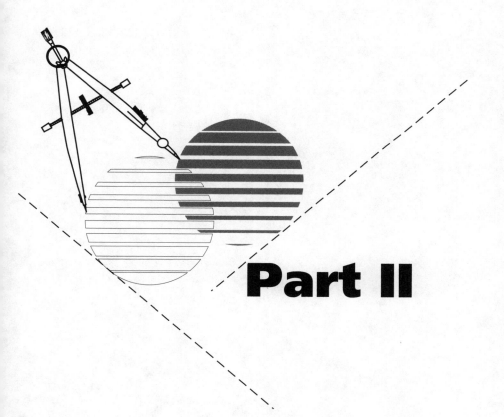

Part II

The 15 Enabling
Technologies

Now the identification process begins. Where are your problem areas and what are the technology tools available to accomplish your improvements? So far you have learned what the term "business process reengineering" is and what it really means. You have seen several examples of businesses in trouble and how BPR helped them out of the quagmire. You have read about the teams and techniques.

Now you will learn of the information technology tools that are available to you. The chapters in Part II are the hammers, saws, and screwdrivers. The typical bag of tools carried by any carpenter, plumber, or electrician contains tools that they use frequently as well as tools that hardly ever see the light of day. The frequently used tools are usually clean and shiny; the others are dirty and dusty—and most likely have some rust here or there. But all these tools have a purpose. All are needed.

The tools described in these chapters need to be part of your bag. Although you will keep some of these information technologies bright and shiny because they are necessary to your reengineering, some of these technologies—as in any toolkit—will slip to the bottom of the heap and go unused. Don't feel that it is all or nothing. You may need only a few of these tools to accomplish your task. Then again, you may need them all.

CHAPTER 4

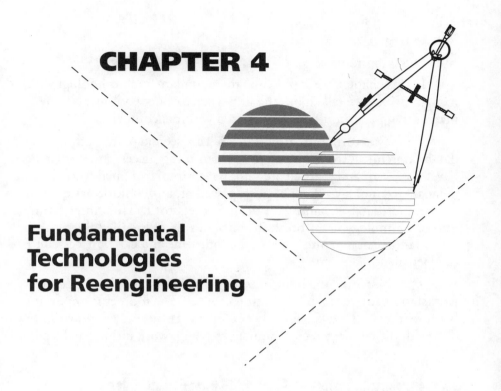

Fundamental Technologies for Reengineering

For years, organizations have tried a simple method for automating work processes: they threw computers at people. But if we've learned anything from the trillions of dollars spent on technology in the 1980s, we've learned that just adding technology to business problems simply doesn't work.

In all of our analysis and study of reengineering projects, we found that technology counts, but not just any technology. And no technology works when people just throw it indiscriminately at business problems. That said, we believe that certain core technologies are important, if not fundamental, to the success of reengineering projects. We've constructed a list of important technologies and present them in the chapters that follow.

However, for the purposes of getting started, there are basic building block technologies that are fundamental. We have identified three distinct technologies that provide the foundation for other information technology to add value. Those three technologies are:

≡ Networking

≡ Databases

≡ Desktop tools

In this chapter, we explore the three fundamental technologies for reengineering. We talk about the importance of networking and how a networking plan should be constructed within a company.

Then we turn our attention to the second core technology: database architecture. Many of the reengineering success stories that we have observed and participated in have simply applied very basic database technology. These projects placed organized information into a computer database, and gave people access to it. This simple computing technology helps break the ancient rule of the file folder—that information exists in only one place at one time and can be accessed by one person at one time.

The third fundamental technology is that of building a desktop workstation environment, a desktop tool set. The tool set is important because it gives knowledge workers tools to act on information and to deal with the connected environment that a network ultimately brings.

Networking—First Stop to the Information Superhighway

It is absolutely critical that a company pursue a network vision, to connect all of the company's computers no matter where they exist. A good network computing strategy connects a lot more than the company's computers, though. It connects the company's people. It creates electronic paths so people can collaborate across functional lines, geographic boundaries, and time zones.

The vision of a connected environment must stand beyond simply connecting a workgroup, a department, a process team, or even an enterprise. The connected environment must allow for stops and access paths both inside as well as outside the organization. It must include suppliers, customers, or any other interested party that may have business to conduct with the organization. It can be accomplished not only by connecting the company's infrastructure of computers, but by allowing a hook-up to a public service or information highway provider. Today, plenty of business is being done across the Internet and CompuServe, a private network that provides a connection to over 133 countries and several million users.

Begin at the Beginning

Even if your company has a network architecture in place, it's a good idea to review that architecture in light of technology's expanded role in the business organization. The key objective is complete networking capability; that is, a one-to-one relationship between wherever the workers are and a network connection. That doesn't just mean a network jack in every office. It should expand to include people at home and people on the road, as well as remote or branch offices. Beyond the enterprise, it includes items such as connections to customers and suppliers.

This network infrastructure can often start with local area networks. It is not uncommon for companies to find that by placing all of the network computers on a simple topology base, such as Ethernet or Token Ring, they can build a solid platform. It turns out that these simple platforms work just fine to begin a company's global technology infrastructure for networking.

Planning for the Information Superhighway

Over time, most networks will needs to grow to accommodate people wanting access from their homes, hotel rooms, or branch offices, or from suppliers and customers. Figure 8 shows how a simple infrastructure can be extended and expanded. A little advance planning for extra-network connectivity goes a long way.

It is possible to build a very robust network and infrastructure without spending a lot of money. It will require, however, that the people responsible for technology in your company be acutely aware of new technologies such as mobile and wireless computing, dial-in and remote-access vehicles such as Internet connections.

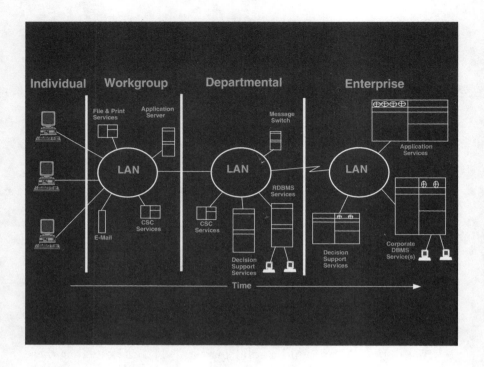

FIGURE 8 A simple and inexpensive base can grow into an enterprise network infrastructure, if you plan early and carefully.

A Technology Checklist for Networks

Networks provide many flexible options, and sometimes all the options create confusion. Rather than list all the possible combinations of technologies, we provide a checklist of technology features you should have in your network:

≋ A stable wiring architecture for all local area networks

≋ Use of intelligent hubs and/or routers to connect and interconnect local networks

≋ A stable network operating system (NOS)

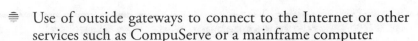

≣ Use of outside gateways to connect to the Internet or other services such as CompuServe or a mainframe computer

≣ Monitoring tools to check changes in network traffic

≣ Management tools to distribute software or check network devices, such as nodes, printers, and gateways

≣ Administration tools to help add, delete, change, or maintain network users

Databases

The second infrastructure technology critical for reengineering efforts is a database. Because of the many options available with database technology, it is important for an organization to settle on one or two standard products.

Database technology lets you store information in an organized fashion. A database will help you break the ancient rule of the file folder and let multiple people access information at different times and from different places. This capability can do more to end sequential processing of work than almost any other technology.

Think of how an airline system works with a shared database. Many people can access records as travel is planned, then commences. The travel agent plans the trip and creates the original record, the ticket agent checks in the passenger and confirms the seat, and the gate agent can access the record in case any change is needed upon boarding. All along the sequence of events—from planning the trip to getting on the plane—several people can access or modify the record. Also, depending on how the reservation is booked, the passenger may be able to skip some steps and simply go from reservations to taking a seat on the plane. Without a shared database, however, it would be impossible to move many people smoothly from making a reservation to arriving at a destination.

Database Technology

Databases can be based on a number of different technology architectures. There are three popular models: host-terminal, file server, and

TABLE 3   Processing Locations Based on Standard Activities

Activity	Host-Terminal	File Server	Client/Server
Create screens	Host	Client	Client
Prepare query or update	Host	Client	Client
Process query or update	Host	Client	Server
Prepare result (sort/format)	Host	Client	Server
Process update	Host	Client	Server
Store data	Host	Server	Server

client/server. Each model delegates the actual processing in a slightly different manner. Table 3 shows where processing is performed for standard database activities.

As Table 3 shows, the host-terminal model places all the processing activity on the host, the file server model put most activity on the client, and the client/server model divides up activity. As such, client/server is the most flexible architecture.

A Technology Checklist for Databases

Networks and databases provide many flexible options, and sometimes all the options create confusion. Rather than list all the possible combinations of technologies, we provide a checklist of technology features you should have in your network. While arguments can be made for technologies not on our list, we believe that standard technologies are the best and safest buy:

☰ A database based on the SQL (structure query language) standard

☰ A database that conforms to the client/server architecture

☰ A database supported by numerous third party development tools

≋ A database that allows for stored procedures to maximize operations for complex transaction

Desktop Tools

Finally, our third infrastructure set of technologies covers the desktop interface. There are seven components to the basic tool set. They include:

≋ Spreadsheet
≋ Word processor
≋ Presentation graphics
≋ Filing system (database or personal information manager)
≋ Calendar
≋ Electronic messaging
≋ Access to external data

Some people prefer to purchase these basic tools from one vendor. This adds to the consistency feature and often lower overall software costs. Three popular choices for software suites are: Microsoft Office; Lotus' SmartSuite, and Borland Office, which combines products from both Borland and WordPerfect. Buying a suite won't give you all the necessary desktop tools, but it will get you started.

There are a few rules for giving people an adequate set of tools so they can create, manipulate, and share information. The tools must be consistent, able to multitask, and able to share data with other programs.

Consistent Tools

The first rule is that software products must be consistent. People don't want to spend all their time learning which keys to push; in fact, they don't want to spend time learning the mechanics of software at all. A popular selection for the business office is to create a desktop environment based on Microsoft Windows. Windows provides a graphical user interface (GUI) that is consistent among different software products. A Windows-based word-processing program will have a good bit of consistency with a Windows-based spreadsheet. The same goes for a Windows-based e-mail package.

Multitasking Tools

Another rule is that desktop tools should allow people to quickly switch from one task to another. This is sometimes called multitasking because people can have more than one application running at one time. For the most part, people use multitasking as task-switching. Say, for example, that you are working on a spreadsheet and the phone rings. Within an instant you want to check your calendar, add an appointment, then return to your spreadsheet.

This type of task-switching is built into most Windows applications and provides a major advantage over older DOS-based applications which would require you to: save your spreadsheet file; exit the program; load the calendar program; update the records; save the calendar file; exit the program; then reload the spreadsheet program and bring up the worksheet.

Data Sharing of Tools

The final rule of a desktop tool set is that it must allow for data sharing. Often people want to add information they created in a spreadsheet into a report created by a word processor. Older DOS programs allowed this capability, but only after a series of complex commands.

A Word about Hardware and Quality Components

Although hardware selection is not one of our infrastructure technologies, we feel it important to cover the issues of hardware selection. Simply put, we believe that the best laid plans of a technology architecture can be easily derailed by buying the wrong hardware.

Several years ago, it was a popular notion for technology buyers to purchase inexpensive, no-name personal computers on the belief that PCs had become a commodity. The penalty for saving a few dollars on the purchase order was often severe. No-name PCs turned out to be the leading cause of network glitches. Since all computers are *not* created equal, users found that certain programs and applications did not run exactly the same on all computers. Inconsistencies created trouble calls, network down-time, and general dissatisfaction with technology. Some companies quickly learned that the cost of "cheap" computers actually ended up costing more in support and labor than the savings achieved over brand name computers.

R&D is another argument supporting the selection of brand name hardware. Most major hardware and software companies have development arrangements, so that new types of software are tested with hardware and inconsistencies are spotted before products ever see the general market. The time and energy to integrate and optimize hardware and software configurations is borne by the vendors and not the end user.

Conclusion

Infrastructure technologies are important building blocks for the Reengineering ToolKit because they provide a solid base for other, more tailored, technologies. Although you can indeed start a reengineering project without fixing the infrastructure, we strongly encourage you to set aside some time and effort to make sure that proper infrastructure technologies are in place.

In this chapter, we outlined the technologies, made suggestions on what to look for, and gave you a check list. Next, we expand the tour of technologies to the "Fabulous 15." We explore, chapter by chapter, 15 different technologies and relate their value to the principles of reengineering. Throughout these chapters, we offer you definitions, rationales, case studies, and ideas for using these technologies to change the way work is performed.

CHAPTER 5

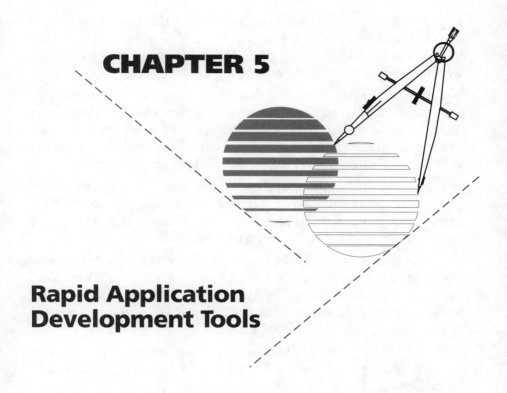

Rapid Application Development Tools

Remember how it used to be when you wanted to change a computer system or develop a new one? You phoned the Information Systems group and asked to get together to discuss your plan. Instead of being able to move forward with a meeting this week or next, you learned that you were the latest to be added to a lengthy queue.

Other people also had plans for improvements or changes, you see, and they had beaten you to the punch, calling in last week or, to your horror, as long as 18 months earlier! You learned that systems being updated or in some stage of implementation had been in the works for up to two years or more.

Two years later, you would get a call telling you that the IS department was finally ready for you. You'd have a meeting and lay out your plan in detail. You answered their myriad of questions to the best of your ability and then sat back and waited for months until they returned with something for you to look at. The long delay wasn't because the IS folks didn't like you. No, the methods they used really were that cumbersome and time-consuming.

It would be nice to say that that doesn't happen any more and that new technology has let IS departments complete their various tasks in months instead of years. Well, it hasn't happened yet. However, the transition is beginning to occur, as more and more IS groups become familiar with Rapid Application Development (RAD) tools and methods.

All IS groups would probably sell their Aunt Alice up the river if they could speed up their application development processes. But many paradigms of the past have been around forever, and any attempt to change them will likely be met with firm resistance.

The description of RAD is very simple: RAD helps get systems out faster, using a combination of data modeling, fast design iterations, teamwork between users and developers, and automated development tools. Some proponents have estimated that RAD methods can speed systems delivery by up to 1,300 percent.

 Please note that we are talking here about "methods," not just neat tools. A critical element is the rethinking of development methodologies and management techniques, and the acceleration of developers' learning cycles. Most companies trying to utilize RAD will experience no increase in delivery speed unless they recognize the need to rethink their processes.

Four Points to RAD Success

For a company to have any hope of succeeding in its application of RAD, there are four points it must keep in mind:

≋ Deliver system components one at a time, but keep rolling them out. Don't ever try to deliver everything in one package. It is impossible to begin using new tools in an existing environment and expect any productivity increase. Plan to deliver the first component in no more than four months and all successive components in three-month cycles. Implement a firm rule that says no component will take more than five months to deliver.

≋ Build a team. Develop cohesiveness among developers and their business users. It is imperative that they work closely, meeting frequently as a team, to ensure that the work is proceeding smoothly towards the pre-established set of goals and objectives. These goals and objectives, contained in the project plan, must be agreed to by the team.

≋ Set reachable goals. The team, not management, will agree on the delivery schedule and insure the schedule fits the project plan.

≋ Leverage and maximize your work. The developers must seek to eliminate unnecessary activity. That means that a fresh new approach to developmental tasks must be encouraged. There is always a better way to get the job done. Seek it out. Perhaps there is a way to leverage something that has already been done, and restructure it only slightly to fit the new task.

How You Can Benefit from RAD

An oil company in Texas broke its pattern of changing requirements and extended delivery schedules by altering the rigid ways it managed projects. Instead, it adopted RAD and its management technique of delivering systems incrementally.

The IS team set initial goals in which developers finished core applications, such as a tax subsystem for natural gas accounting, early. The developers could then focus on creating remaining pieces of such a system more quickly—pieces that contained important functions, such as interfaces to the general ledger and accounts payable system.

This project, which was slated to last one year from the start of construction, took seven months—four months for the first core systems, with remaining pieces released three months later.

What is most striking about this example is that developers did not use cutting-edge tools. The fanciest that IS got was an applications generator that made code production easier. Otherwise, developers worked with conventional technologies such as COBOL. The change came by understanding business requirements, applying database technology, and learning how to work effectively in teams.

Developers at the Virginia Department of Taxation opted to keep things simple, too. They created the organization's imposing tax accounting system—a synthesis of 1,500 programs and 40 databases—by coupling conventional third-generation language and database technology with RAD management techniques. Users now wait no more than a year for any new functionality.

In one of the insurance divisions at Travelers, IS was under extreme time pressure to deliver business applications. Because delivery took an average of 18 months using traditional development methods, the group turned to RAD, hoping to capitalize on automated development tools. In the long run, the tools became incidental; the group came to rely heavily on teamwork, involving its business partners and instilling team-based decision making in IS.

Today, this group is using RAD to help enhance applications, and is delivering pieces in three to six months. While the company is still not using such methods for its mainstream development activities, acceptance of RAD techniques appears to be growing steadily.

The Deadline Pressure

IS continues to be under pressure to deliver systems ever more quickly, and many companies turn in desperation to RAD to satisfy critical business needs. As a result, RAD has sprung up in small pockets in many organizations, even though the companies haven't openly embraced it. It is in these renegade groups that RAD gets its best public relations; if it works there, it is more likely to find a home in the organization at large.

RAD Tips for Success

- ≋ Split up very big applications into small pieces.
- ≋ Apply the RAD methodology to each piece.
- ≋ Finish each piece in three months.
- ≋ Create a team of developers and clients for each piece.
- ≋ Make the work highly visible using GUI prototyping.
- ≋ Don't use conventional development methodologies.
- ≋ Let go of old, worn-out tools.
- ≋ Get trained on new methodologies.

Computer-Aided Software Engineering (CASE)

Although RAD is essentially a technique for rethinking how application development gets done, you may find that you also need some new tools. As corporations delve into client/server computing, CASE tools are evolving to combine the best of mainframe-like management with rapid PC-style prototyping.

Traditionally, CASE has provided developers with analysis and design tools based on structured methodologies. While that worked well in mainframe environments, the demands of client/server applications call for a new set of features. As a result, CASE tools are combining the RAD of PC tools with the model-building of larger systems for fast, stable development. The new CASE market also will provide interoperable tools that programmers can mix and match.

Alliances are forming to create big client/server packages. CASE tools vendors are rushing to team up with back-end database vendors to create total integrated development environments. For instance,

Gupta Corporation, makers of SQL Base and the development product SQL Windows, recently signed agreements with CASE vendors Bachman Information Systems Inc., Burlington, Mass.; Intersolv Inc., Rockville, Md.; LBMS Inc., Houston; Logic Works Inc., Princeton, N.J.; Popkin Software, New York City; and Visible Systems Corp., Waltham, Mass. The client/server development tools that are strong in RAD need to complement their strengths with a design strategy that makes sure there is a maintainable and sustainable architecture behind the flashy screens that users want.

CASE products will represent one-fourth of the $5.6 billion market for software-development tools this year, according to CASE Associates Inc., a consulting and market-research firm in Clackamas, Oregon. By 1997, CASE products will own about 35 percent of the market, which will have reached $16.3 billion. The increase is due partly to the market's continued demand for software that will manage complex applications in client/server environments.

As we move in the direction of client/server computing, the development management process becomes more important than ever, because client/server requires many pieces of applications running in more than one place over complex networks. Such complex networks often include a mix of computer platforms and multiple application programming interfaces. CASE tools often are the keys to understanding and managing these diverse elements.

The Old versus the New

How can it be that technologies from the mid-1960's are coming back? Sometimes the value of an old idea is best realized through longevity. It turns out that many application development technologies didn't realize their true potential because supporting structures and tools were immature or unimagined at the time.

The willingness to revisit existing application development technologies can offer many benefits. Because the tools and products are already around, the corporate budget, the IS staff, and the end-user community all win. Many companies have used Object-Oriented Programming (OOP) for some time, and they are on intimate terms with the C and C++ programming languages. But applying them in a multi-user client/server environment has been difficult.

Using What You Already Have

The sluggish economy may have helped foster the re-examination of existing technologies in the application development market. With less money to spend, IS managers have looked for new ways to use technologies already on hand. Vendors responded accordingly, and the rate at which new concepts are hitting the market may have slowed.

One of the older technologies to undergo re-examination is 4GLs (Fourth Generation Languages). Because 4GLs allow developers to address the task a computer should perform, instead of worrying about how the computer executes the task, application development is faster and data access is simpler. With so many corporate sites expecting developers to act as bottom-line business managers, 4GL technology makes sense.

CASE tools also are experiencing a renewal. Where 4GLs are well suited to prototyping and creating quick solutions, CASE tools employ a more diagrammatic approach appropriate for complicated applications. The maturation of CASE technology provides more power to the development staff.

With the proliferation of CASE and 4GL tools, some sites may have trouble determining the best strategy. Although 4GLs are known for providing quick solutions and CASE tools are better suited for professional IS personnel, midrange sites may not benefit from choosing one or the other. Many companies should go with both technologies to address different sets of users and applications.

Transition Time

The reengineering of IS processes can be a trial. Managers must understand that there will be a period of transition, because technologies must be integrated and supported while people change the way they approach their business and IS. Managers will need to support a variety of configurations while they move to decentralized structures in a more network-based, client/server environment.

Once an IS department decides to reengineer, it needs to leverage the distributed nature of its systems by using technologies that can help build applications in a distributed environment.

Not all technologies are appropriate for all environments. Midrange sites need to consider which technologies are best suited to their use of OOP techniques. Application vendors that produce objects need different tools than IS departments that use objects developed for IS consumers. Very few users require high-powered tools like C++; most of them would probably be content with an application development environment like Microsoft's Visual BASIC.

Many users mistakenly think C++ is going to be useful for them. Considering the objectives and skills of a typical midrange development organization, a move to C++ would probably be a disaster. C++ is sophisticated and complex, and it is well suited for the mass production of objects. It is not for use by midrange development staffs. It can leave developers exposed to the risks of memory violations and other pitfalls that are endemic to C and C++.

RAD has long been a standard at mainframe sites that need new applications quickly without the process of analyzing requirements, defining the application, and designing prototypes.

RAD allows sites to iterate the application development process, so working prototypes quickly are produced and deployed, often with the end user's input. While initial skeptics cautioned that quick development could lead to faster disaster, the application of proper methodologies to RAD over the last five years has created solid structures suited for producing commercial results.

Remember Your Repositories

Another mature technology that is rarely used to its full advantage is the repository. Once a storehouse for lists of information, repositories warehouse a site's reusable application objects as well as the information needed by developers. The use of repositories is gaining momentum because of the need to manage distributed application development.

The complexity of applications has increased to the point that one piece of code is often meaningless without information about how it is being used as an object. IS sites need some central point to draw upon. A repository can store reusable application elements critical to the development of complex applications.

Why You'll Have Trouble with RAD

The goal to all software development is to get end users the information they need to make decisions. If the application development tools to do that don't exist, your users don't get served and the rest of your technology doesn't get used.

Although the re-emerging application development technologies are mature, they often fall short in the areas of portability and scalability. Application portability is more critical than ever, as IS staffs link discrete corporate systems. The need to switch platforms or to run applications across different platforms forces IS managers to build applications that can be ported from machine to machine. Although vendors are pondering how to help, none have a complete answer.

Also still evolving are application development tools that can be scaled to meet various development organization needs, from sites who only are interested in RAD to those who need enterprise-scale development. Some of the most popular and inexpensive tools, which offer short learning curves and are widely available, are most limited by the number of platforms they can run on, the way they access databases, and their lack of support for repositories. At the other end of the scale are mainframe-style tools designed to readily handle application definition, analysis and design.

Who's Confused?

Considering those problems and the ongoing confusion in the application development field, what is a system buyer to do? Before committing to a platform or product, investigate each vendor's approach carefully. Some large vendors are not committed to the application development market, while some small vendors lack expertise in the field. Other vendors promote products and platforms that are not quite available

There is plenty of hype in this market, and users tend to overlook that vendors still have to solve problems and deliver applications that provide a competitive advantage for customers. The strategic decision to be made is not what client package is the hottest or what database has the most features, it's how to serve your clients. If you can't show a measurable increase in productivity, you're on the wrong track.

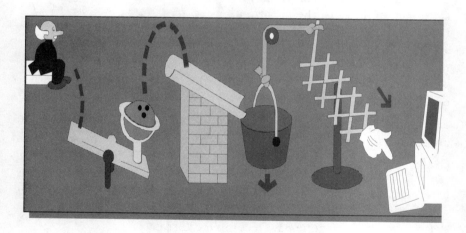

Above all, make sure your vendor can address all your needs. With most application development technologies only in their first or second generation, the future will bring significant change to both the products and operating environments.

Often, however, sites need to live with what they already have. Those sites typically are not leaping ahead but are quietly incorporating or revisiting technologies that can make them more efficient. That trend may not be exciting, but it is real.

Choosing the Right Tool

Using two or more technologies may help get your company on the application development fast track, but speed is less important than fitting your strategies to your goals. At Goodyear Tire and Rubber, the need for rapid application development capabilities led one IS manager to reject CASE technology and select a 4GL.

Goodyear uses Business Computer Design's ProGen 4GL product to create applications for non-manufacturing activities such as metal scheduling, payroll systems, and plant downtime. Ninety percent of the IS staff workload is the development of small systems requested to track various aspects of production.

With ProGen, the staff creates help screens and pop-up windows for the major manufacturing programs, as well as the tracking systems. The tool helps developers incorporate data integrity checks such as table look-ups, which often are omitted when coded by hand. The staff estimates that development productivity has increased tenfold. After using the 4GL for 18 months, the quality of application programming had also improved.

Although Goodyear considered moving to a CASE environment, it would have involved too much money and effort. The benefit of automatic program generation far outweighed the big leap into CASE and its anticipated learning curve. The BCD product is not everything Goodyear may have found in a CASE product, but the return on investment has made it worthwhile.

Supporting the Seven Principles

RAD tools and methodologies support all seven principles of reengineering:

1. Organize work around results, not tasks. The tools and methodologies are geared to produce results in a very timely manner.
2. Capture data only one time—when it is first created. The implementation of the RAD concept is founded on this principle.
3. Allow decision points where work is performed. Because of the close working relationships of the project teams, and the constant flow of information and status, decision points are built in throughout the process.
4. Incorporate controls into information processing. Due to the piecemeal systems delivery and the project team's hands-on approach to setting goals, controls are integrated easily.
5. Make people who use a process do the work. By incorporating the team development approach, users are deeply involved in the work.
6. Work in parallel instead of sequentially, then integrate results.
7. Treat geographical resources as one.

Conclusion

The reengineering of systems is by no means simple. There is no blueprint for you to follow. No one else has ever been where you are right

now, and no one else has ever gone where you need to go. In this chapter, we have discussed many of the issues that you will face along the journey, and many of the methodologies and tools available to help you. You should now be better prepared to deal with the difficult questions that will need to be asked, and with the many decisions that you will have to make.

In the next chapter, we show you how your users and customers can benefit by tying your computer systems in with your telephone systems. It's yet another way to use technology to serve your corporate goals.

CHAPTER 6

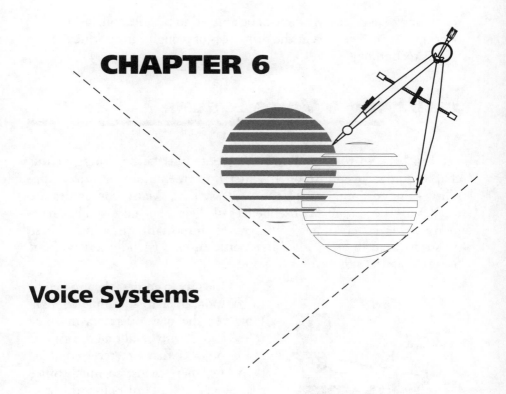

Voice Systems

When was the last time you called up a company—any company—to get some information about their products? Were you faced with a response that sounded something like: "GoodafternnXYZcompanpleasho...."? After that hurried, unintelligible greeting, you probably heard a click and, then, nothing. Did you actually have the patience to wait for someone to come back and find out what you wanted? And, did you remember the reason you called in the first place?

Fortunately, technology is helping to make those inhospitable greetings a thing of the past. Today, there are systems that let a machine do all the phone-answering work quickly and efficiently. Some even let you talk to a living, breathing human being if that's what you really want.

In this chapter, we discuss voice systems, focusing on computer applications that are linked to the telephone. We also touch briefly on voice mail, business audio, and voice recognition—each an important example of the marriage of voice and computer. After we look at the technology, we discuss how it can be applied to business process reengineering. Finally, we look at the principles of reengineering which apply to this technology.

Justifying a Voice System

Let's go back to the situation we presented at the beginning of this chapter and concentrate on the first implementation of voice capability—the computer/telephone voice system. Many companies are faced with the very real consequences of their own success. They have many potential customers calling with important questions. These prospects need to be handled in an efficient and friendly way without overloading the system.

 One way to address the problem is to get more operators. Simple enough. However, the new operators must be trained on how to handle all the various kinds of calls that are received. Furthermore, there is just so much office space you can build or rent and just so many people you can hire.

Many companies are turning to technology for help. For example, one major computer company had 24 operators to handle incoming calls. Its PBX ("Private Branch Exchange"—it's an old telephone company buzzword for "switchboard" or "phone system") processed about 5,000 calls per hour, both incoming and outgoing. After it installed a voice system and with approximately the same number of outgoing calls, the company employs only four operators. But the system handles 25,000 calls per hour! Fewer than 35 percent of incoming callers actually need to talk to an operator. They can get to the extension they want without intervention, and can leave a voice mail message without an operator's help.

To make a voice system operate, you need a PBX or some kind of intelligent telephone switch to become the control point for the system. Next, you need a device called a voice response unit (VRU), which can either be integrated into the PBX or added on as a separate box. And lastly, you need some software.

Of course, it is not that easy. These are very powerful, sophisticated systems that have taken years to develop. Here are some of the things a voice system can do for a company:

- Voice mail and messaging
- Interactive voice response
- Fax-back

Voice Mail

How did the world survive without voice mail? We no longer need to spend hours playing phone tag. We don't need to stay chained to our desks to catch that important call. That customer who calls in to provide a purchase order number doesn't need to waste time waiting for a sales person to come on the line. And, the boss can broadcast a message, with all the power of voice, to all employees in the company who have access to a phone.

The naysayers would have us believe that what we really need is a living, breathing human being on the other end of the line. While it is true that a real person is best, experience has shown us that voice mail is better than no answer at all. And now, instead of getting frustrated with playing phone tag, we get to address all our vituperative comments to the voice mail system!

A clever implementation of technology to leverage the use of voice is provided by Norris Communications Corporation in their product called Flashback. This product is a totally digital voice recording device that plugs into a PCMCIA slot on a personal computer. It's very small and light—about the size of three credit cards stacked together and weighing about 2 ounces.

Using the Flashback, the boss can prepare a broadcast voice mail message at his leisure and download it into the voice mail system to be broadcast whenever he wants. The reverse is also true; if you have voice mail messages that you need to hear, you can download them to your PC and listen to your voice mail at your leisure.

Interactive Voice Response Systems

Interactive voice response (IVR) systems are becoming much more commonplace as their cost goes down and their sophistication goes up. An IVR system can supplement the work of a telephone operator. When you call up many companies today, you get a pleasant voice that wishes you a good day and provides you with a list of options from which to choose. By making a few simple keystrokes on the number pad of your telephone, presuming you didn't make the call on an old-fashioned rotary phone, you can get to the right person in the company to help you. That's an IVR.

There are many examples of how service organizations use IVR systems to process their services. You can call the Internal Revenue Service and pay your income taxes using a telephone. In New York, you can claim unemployment assistance from a Touch-Tone telephone. In California, you can get information from the Secretary of State's office regarding a corporation. Many financial institutions provide for bank-by-phone services, and many brokerage firms let you get stock quotes from a Touch-Tone phone. Some even allow you to buy and sell stock. All of those are IVR applications.

Unfortunately, we have all gotten caught in the endless loop of a poorly designed IVR system. We get a recording which tells us to do something, but the menu we hear doesn't include the service or information we want. There is no way out of the system to talk to a real person. You wind up screaming at a machine, and you hang up, vowing never to call that company again. Badly implemented IVR systems frustrate your employees, anger your customers, and cost you money.

A good example of a voice response system is available from WordPerfect Corporation. The company offers a product called Telephone Access Server (TAS). TAS lets users access their WP Office mailbox remotely without using a computer. Many systems today allow remote modem access to the office computer. But, many users may not be at their computers when they need information from their office. Using IVR technology, these users can now get the required information. Here's how it works.

The user calls the system, enters his or her password and ID number and listens to a menu of options. If the user wants to hear new voice mail or e-mail messages, the system plays or reads them. If he or she wants calendar information, TAS asks for the day for which the information is needed and then gives the user the option to listen to appointments, notes, tasks, or all three.

The system requirements are fairly straightforward. The user needs a Touch-Tone telephone. TAS software needs to be running on the system, preferably on a dedicated machine. You need an interface to the telephone lines. Finally, you need a WP Office Message Server to provide message routing services to the network.

There is still some work to be done to improve the quality of voice from the text-to-voice conversion module, but that will come with time. The point is, this system provides an excellent example of how voice systems can be implemented to improve basic business processes.

IVR systems can be enhanced by another telephone service that is becoming more available each month—Caller ID. Caller ID is a service available from local telephone companies in almost all states of the United States and in Canada. It lets the user see the number of the caller as the telephone rings.

There could be many different uses for such a service. You won't need to repeat your telephone number three times to the guy at the pizza delivery shop—he can read it on his telephone. More important, caller ID can automatically route an incoming call to a selected agent or service based on the caller's telephone number. It can provide higher levels of security in bank-by-phone and pay-per-view TV applications. This technology is just beginning to become available. New applications tools are being developed and announced daily.

Fax-Back

One of the menu selections in the IVR systems mentioned earlier can be fax-back. This service allows a caller, using a Touch-Tone phone, to get information faxed to a specified number. This is particularly useful for callers looking for product information or for any data that is easily stored and retrieved. There are many vendors offering products with this capability. It works something like this:

1. You call a company and get the normal menu as described earlier.

2. If you select the fax-back option, you enter the code number for the document you want faxed to you.

3. If you don't know the number, most companies will fax you the catalog.

4. Once you have selected an identification number for the document, you enter your name and fax number.

5. Within a matter of minutes, the document is faxed to you.

Because there is no person at the other end of the phone to operate this type of system, it can run 24 hours a day, 365 days a year.

Inside the system you called, there is a database that contains all of the service's available documents. When the customer taps in a document's code number, the system retrieves the file and transmits it with

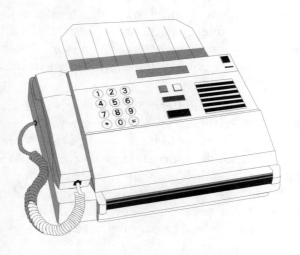

a fax-modem. There is no need for human intervention in this process, which is routine and frequently repeated.

Of course, all of this is done using the Touch-Tone number pad. Letters are identified by tapping the appropriate key the correct number of times to identify the desired letter. For example, to enter the letter "A", tap the "2" key once; to enter the letter "K", tap the "5" key twice, and so on.

There are many other variations of interactive voice recognition systems, but the point is made. This is exciting new technology that has every chance of busting old paradigms. It is no longer necessary to hire, train, and support more and more people to do routine and boring work. The proper application of technology can do the drudge work for you.

Business Audio

If there ever was a technology that was oversold, it was voice recognition. We have all seen *Star Trek* episodes where Captain Kirk merely speaks and some really neat thing happens. Great fiction, bad expectations!

However, we are not very far away from realizing the fantasy. Today, there are many vendors shipping products that support an extension to Microsoft Windows called Windows Sound System. These systems will recognize simple voice commands spoken to the computer—commands like, "Open file" or "Print." This facility may be useful to a novice user but they are a long way from replacing the keyboard, a much less natural but more developed input device. Further, the voice recognition algorithm is not very advanced. The system gets confused when you change tone or pitch.

Another feature of business audio is the ability to annotate files with voice messages. For example, you have prepared a complex spreadsheet. You need to tell the user to go to cell H12 and begin data entry; after filling in the next five cells, move over to cell Z27 and fill in the right ZIP code. Using business audio, you can give these instructions by speaking into a microphone. The message is stored as a file on the disk and associated with the spreadsheet file. When the user opens the spreadsheet, an icon will appear that indicates there is a voice message. Clicking on the icon will play back your instructions.

Voice Recognition

The next real payoff for voice recognition technology comes when you can speak into a microphone, dictate a letter, and have the computer generate a word processing document. In fact, IBM has a product called Personal Dictation System priced at under $1,000. Even at the beginning of its life cycle, the system has a 95 to 98 percent accuracy rate. This is very acceptable performance.

The system is simple to operate—just speak and it converts spoken words to text. The specifications say that it will accept about 70 words per minute. It will probably do better than that, but most people, who speak at a rate of 100 to 120 words per minute, will have to slow down a bit. As the technology is developed, that rate will surely go up.

As in the past, the real challenge is to "train" the system to recognize the user's voice. This is accomplished by reading to the computer until it learns your dialect, pitch, and voice fluctuations. After training, the application actually converts words into text by using a series of algorithms to identify your individual voice patterns.

IBM, Verbex, and Dragon Systems have introduced new products that eliminate the requirement for training. They are called "user-independent continuous-speech" recognition products. These products get around the training issue by using advanced digital signal processors (DSP's). In addition, through the use of feature extraction and modeling, the computer analyzes each phoneme—the smallest unit of speech that distinguishes one utterance or word from another. For example, the *m* in *mat* and the *b* in *bat* are phonemes. By analyzing each phoneme and using statistical modeling, the phonemes can be put together to create an entire word.

After the document has been dictated, you just go into your word processor and edit it as you would any document. This application works with such desktop tools as WordPerfect, Microsoft Word, Lotus 1-2-3 and Lotus Notes. More applications will follow as the product is developed.

Supporting the Seven Principles

The entire area of voice systems has the unlimited ability to provide real benefits. Some, like IVR systems, have been around for a while. However, we are just scratching the surface of the potential of the technology. Applications that link the computer to the telephone will soon become much more pervasive, and we will get into that classic regenerative loop—as more people use them, the cheaper they get; and the cheaper they get, the more people will use them. All of these applications—IVR, voice mail, business audio and voice recognition—support many of the principles of reengineering.

≋ They capture data only one time, when it is created. Whether it is selecting an option from a menu or providing instructions for a spreadsheet, you only need to perform an action once for it to be entered into the network.

≋ You allow decisions to be made at the point where the work is performed. When the customer decides he needs a certain product description, he can ask for it. There is no need to have someone write down the request and pass it on to the clerk in the fax room to send the document.

≋ Make the people who use the process do the work. Why use an expensive stock broker to tell a client what XYZ stock is selling for? Make the customer do the work by inputting the right information to get the answer.

Conclusion

We told you about voice systems that link the computer with the telephone, voice mail, business audio, along with the ultimate computer that recognizes your voice. This union forms the marriage between the voice and computer. We encourage you to try some of this technology. You may be surprised how powerful it is in supporting principles of reengineering.

In the next chapter, we look at another set of devices that help in the input process. Automated input devices go a long way towards streamlining worn out processes in the world of the global business.

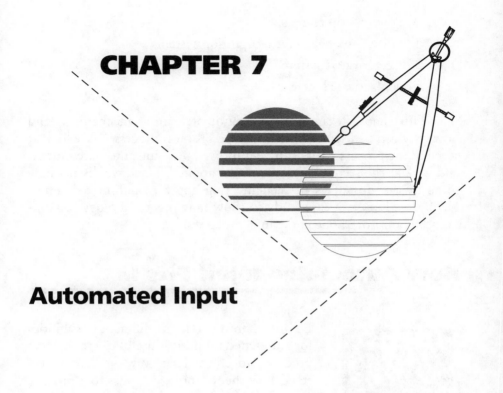

CHAPTER 7

Automated Input

During the election campaign of 1992, President George Bush went into a grocery store. He was intrigued by a device that shone red beams of light from under the surface of the checkout counter, and was amazed to learn that it was hooked into the cash register and could identify products and record prices.

How often do you think a president or vice president drops into the grocery store for a gallon of milk? Although Mr. Bush was derided for not knowing about bar-code scanners, he probably hadn't been shopping in about 12 years. During that time, tremendous advances were made in the technology of automated input. Today, automated input devices are everywhere:

≋ Bar-code readers
≋ Optical-character readers
≋ Document and image scanners

- Magnetic-strip readers
- Magnetic-ink character recognition systems
- Voice-activated systems
- Touch-activated screens

This chapter examines these automated input mechanisms and how they can be used to better manage business processes. We look at some of the processes that can be improved by using automated input, and look at the technology that can be applied. Next, we discuss how some of the principles of reengineering apply to automated input. Finally, we look at a case study to show how this technology has dramatically improved one company's processes.

How Automated Input Fits In

Because there are so many different possibilities for automated input, it is useful to group some processes together. That way, we can understand how the technology applies to a process, regardless of where the process appears. For example, let's look at the retail industry.

It wasn't very long ago that the typical grocery store had many people keeping track of the flow of products through the store. Most of these processes were very tightly interrelated but almost never automated. Errors were frequent because of multiple manual input into the system:

1. The store manager predicted the needs for various products. Sometimes, if he was good, he would get it right.
2. The purchasing manager issued purchase orders to vendors for the products required.
3. The receiving clerk unloaded trucks through the back door.
4. Someone counted the boxes and checked them against the purchase order.
5. The boxes were transferred into inventory.
6. The stocking clerk would then swing into action:

- Check the floor to see what shelves needed restocking.
- Go back to the storeroom and get the right box of products.
- Get the gizmo that stamps the prices on the individual packages.
- Fill it up with ink. Spill the ink.
- Look at the price list to see what the right price is.
- Apply the wrong price.
- Put the products on the shelf.

7. The customer strolled through the store, selecting products to purchase and putting them in the basket with the bum wheel.

8. At the checkout counter, a clerk or the customer would take products out of the basket and put them on the counter.

9. The checker, who spent a long time memorizing prices, would either remember the price or look at the price tag (which might be wrong), then enter the price into the cash register.

10. Once the total was determined and the arguments about how the price didn't match the newspaper ad were concluded, the customer would write a check.

11. The checker called the manager to approve the check.

12. With the check approved, the transaction was complete.

You can readily see that this whole process—simply getting the right product into the hands of the customer so he could buy it—is very cumbersome. In addition to requiring a lot of checking and double-checking, the only thing the store manager knew after the transaction was complete was that some stock was gone and some money was in the till. There was no other information about the sale.

Grocery stores have very high volume and very low margins. Anything that can decrease costs is good.

Suppliers of grocery stores are starving for information about products they sell. Which store location sold what? What day of the week and time of day did the sale take place? Did the newspaper ad have any impact on volume the day it hit the street? There are hundreds of questions a vendor can think up to ask a store manager.

The drive for cost savings and the thirst for information have both been addressed by technology. In the grocery store of today, many of those processes described earlier are either changed or eliminated by automated input devices. Let's look at a few.

The store manager and the purchasing manager are communicating through a network, which has accurate data on which to base the forecast. The purchase orders are automatically generated. All this is done through a workflow system like those described in Chapter 9.

When inventory arrives at the back door and the boxes are moving down a ramp from the truck, a bar code reader counts them and includes them into inventory. The shipment can automatically be compared to the quantities on the purchase order, which is already in the system and accessible.

Virtually every package has its own printed bar code that complies with the Uniform Product Code (UPC) standard. Each product, with its unique UPC code, has a price associated with it in the store's database. The scanners at the checkout counter are tied to the database. Therefore, there is no need to stamp prices on the packages (unless state or local law requires it). The storeroom floor will look a little cleaner without all those purple ink stains. The checker doesn't need to memorize all those prices.

At the checkout counter, products are scanned and the price and quantity are registered. Besides adding up all the items purchased, the printer at the checkout can generate a coupon from a vendor that encourages the customer to buy another product related to the one that was just scanned. And, to make the vendors happy, data about the sale—time of day, day of week, location—are recorded. Some stores with frequent-buyer plans can even associate a product with a type of buyer. And as products get sold, the manager—or the network itself—can decide what to restock and how many to order.

Not Just a Cash Register

Sticking with the retail example for a moment, let's look at another device that illustrates the movement towards automated input: the cash register, now more commonly called a point-of-sale (POS) terminal.

The original POS terminals were closed, proprietary systems. They were based on microprocessor technology but were very specific to a manufacturer. Typical vendors, like NCR, IBM, Omron, and Fujitsu, would provide the entire system—the POS terminals as well as the "back-office" system. These products were expensive and hard to modify to a specific customer's requirements.

With the advent of PC technology, POS terminals are now fairly inexpensive—around $3,000. Not only can large retailers install thousands of units, but "Mom and Pop" stores can also afford the benefits.

Here is what a typical retail checkout counter now looks like:

- ≡ An industry-standard personal computer
- ≡ A cash drawer
- ≡ A bar code reader
- ≡ A keyboard
- ≡ A monitor
- ≡ A printer
- ≡ Local storage (a hard disk)
- ≡ A network interface card
- ≡ A credit card reader
- ≡ A MICR printer for checks

The automated input devices in this kind of system—the scanner and the credit card reader—have made fundamental changes to the retail industry. For the large retailers, they provide speed, efficiency, and detailed information that was not available before. For the small shop, they provide the kind of services previously available only through very expensive devices.

It didn't take very long for IS managers to realize that the suppliers of products sold by their stores wanted as much information as such systems could provide. They have played a key role in creating a new industry: selling data to providers of consumer products.

Today, retail outlets routinely sell their data to vendors, usually through a broker like Information Resources or A.C. Neilson. This revenue helps offset the cost of the systems which are required to run the business. In some cases, it even generates profit for the company.

Touch-Activated Screens

A variation on the POS terminal that is growing in importance is the touch screen. It is particularly popular in restaurants and bars. It's easy to use, requires very little training, and is essentially impervious to food and drink.

As touch screens become more pervasive, their price drops, so they are beginning to find their way into grocery and convenience stores.

Magnetic-Strip Readers

There are many variations on the magnetic-strip reader. One implementation that we have all seen is the automatic teller machine, which is described in more detail in Chapter 13.

Another example is the credit card reader. This is a magnetic strip reader hooked up to a telephone line. The clerk no longer dials a telephone number to give a person at the other end of the line your credit card number and the amount of the purchase. Now, the card reader reads the number, the clerk enters the amount of the purchase on the number pad and the system checks a database for your credit limit. Approval is granted by the system, provided the purchase amount is in line with your available credit.

You can see another credit card reader when you pull into your local gas station. You no longer need to go inside the station to pay for gas; you just insert your card in the slot. The system checks your credit automatically, records the transaction and prints a receipt for you. An interesting addition to this island on-line system is a TV screen. As you stand there pumping gas, wasting dead time, Shell Oil Company plays its latest advertisement for your viewing pleasure. Talk about a captive audience!

In Japan there is a clever variation on the magnetic reader: the phone card. For ¥500 ($5), you buy a card to put in a slot in public telephones. As you talk, the phone subtracts the appropriate charge from the remaining balance on the card. The cards are cheap to make and easy to carry. The phone company doesn't need to send a person around to empty all the coins out of the phones. And, even better, you don't have to carry around heavy coins. A similar system has been in use in Europe for several years, and another is being tested in New York City.

Companies have their logos and slogans printed on cards to be given to customers and prospects. Golfers have them printed to memorialize their holes-in-one. Cards are printed as collectors items, representing pure profit to the phone company. The phone card is a very efficient automated input device that will certainly grow in importance around the world.

Mass transit companies have been using magnetic-strip readers for years. The commuter buys a card and, as it is used, the turnstile subtracts the proper fare from the remaining balance on the card. Commuters don't have to carry tokens, transit companies gather trip data, and fares can be changed according to trip distance, time of day, or even frequency of travel. That means we don't have to kill all those trees to make those useless paper tickets. It also means we don't have to pay those maintenance people to sweep up all the used tickets off the sidewalks. And, it means we don't need all those people to stamp and collect tickets.

Scanners

We have briefly touched on the retail application for bar-code readers. But that's just one variation on scanning technology. Bar codes also are used very effectively in many manufacturing processes. A computer manufacturer may use a bar code to identify a specific serial number of a unit being built. The bar code is usually put on a pallet at the beginning of the assembly and testing process. As the unit moves through the manufacturing process, readers along the line not only track where the unit has been but can tell it where to go next. Test data on a specific unit can be tracked, recorded and analyzed. And this can all happen without manual intervention.

That same bar code is linked to a record of the computer's configuration. It assigns the computer to a specific inventory location in an automated distribution facility. As customers order that configuration, the system picks the computer and routes it through the facility to the right truck bay to be picked up for delivery. The same bar code can be linked to a delivery transaction and invoice.

There are hundreds of variations on the scanner. Hand-held scanners take inventory. Business card scanners record an image of the hundreds of cards you used to file. The system supporting the business card scanner provides indexing, storage and retrieval capabilities as well.

Optical-Character Recognition

Optical-character recognition (OCR) has been around for a long time. OCR readers are essentially scanners that use software to recognize typed (or sometimes written) words. Once recognized, the characters are converted into text.

The US Department of Commerce uses OCR systems in granting export licenses. Before the systems were installed, a company's typed application for an export license was manually input into the database. A typical application for exporting high-tech products took 45 days to process. Using OCR to input the data not only cuts down on input errors but also reduces processing time to four days.

Magnetic-Ink Character Recognition

We have all seen magnetic-ink character recognition (MICR) being used. Virtually every check issued by a bank has various data—bank number, routing codes, account number—printed in magnetic ink at the bottom.

Although this technology has been around for some time, significant improvements have been made in the printing process for checks. Many companies now use specialized laser printers and toner with ferrous oxide to increase the speed at which checks are made. This, of course, drives production costs down.

Voice-Activated Systems

Voice has been a part of the computing process for a long time. We have all seen examples of how this technology has been implemented. Using Microsoft's business audio extensions to Windows, you can issue your PC simple voice commands like "Open File" or "Print." The marriage of voice and the computer is more extensively discussed in Chapter 6.

A Case Study

United Parcel Service is a great example of how to effectively use automated input. We know them as "The delivery company that most companies count on." But what does that really mean to the customer?

UPS was founded almost 90 years ago and is today the world's largest package delivery firm. Revenues for the company in 1993 were $17.8 billion because UPS delivered almost 3 billion parcels and documents to customers in more than 185 countries around the world. The company employs 284,000 people and operates a fleet of 119,700 ground vehicles and more than 200 airplanes.

All UPS does is move 12 million things a day from one place to another. To put that in perspective, that means UPS could deliver a package to every man, woman, and child living in Sweden *and* Norway every day of the year!

Just thinking about numbers like that will lead you to the root of the problem: what do you do with all the paper generated by moving 12 million packages a day? Imagine matching 12 million tracking labels with 12 million packages with 12 million signatures.

Historically, UPS viewed itself by its literal name. Because they were—and still are—the world's largest package delivery firm, their belief was that they delivered packages. They concentrated their energies on creating an efficient and dependable service.

But their customers told them otherwise. Some said that information about their shipments was becoming just as important as the shipment itself. They wanted advanced package tracking, which required top-flight information technology. And if UPS didn't provide this service, other companies would.

UPS set out in 1986 with a five-year, $1.5 billion information technology investment plan. It is now able to track overnight air deliveries and direct its air and automotive fleets around the world.

A key result of this investment is an on-line tracking system, called TotalTrack, which provides immediate delivery information for all bar-coded ground packages and documents, as well as all air and international shipments that UPS delivers. It is a very elaborate, sophisticated system. For purposes of this discussion, however, we focus on the automated input portion of the system.

TotalTrack uses an electronic data collector, a series of scanners, one of the largest relational databases in the world, and connections to more than 70 cellular carriers.

The system's predecessor was a paper system, in which all deliveries were hand-recorded on sheets of paper held together by a clipboard. That clipboard was as much a part of the driver's uniform as were the brown shirt and pants. If the manual system were in place today, UPS would be storing 77.6 million sheets of paper containing 1.9 billion delivery records.

That old clipboard has been replaced by an electronic data collector called the DIAD (Delivery Information Acquisition Device), the primary information-gathering component of the entire system. The DIAD records pickup and delivery information; it also captures an exact image of the receiver's signature when the customer signs the DIAD signature pad with a special stylus.

When the driver plugs the DIAD into an adapter mounted inside his vehicle, delivery information is uploaded over UPSnet, a private data telecommunications network, and into DIALS (Delivery Information Automated Lookup System). The information is stored for 18 months and can be accessed through UPS Customer Service or through package-tracking software that is available on the customer's computer.

Supporting the Seven Principles

By applying the basic principles of reengineering to the delivery process, UPS has created a competitive advantage that is hard to beat:

≣ It has organized the work around the *result*—delivery of a package—not around the *task*. The work flows through all the tasks that are involved.

≣ There is no redundant input of data. Once information is entered into the system, it is available throughout the process without having to be re-entered. The package gets into the system when it is scanned at the transit hub of UPS. There is no need for anyone else to re-enter the same data on a piece of paper that travels with the package.

≣ All the geographical resources are treated as one. Data in the database can be used anywhere in the world by anyone who has a need to use them.

Conclusion

Because automated input devices are useful tools that fully support the principles of reengineering, the industry will continue to provide new input devices, and innovative companies will continue to use them to reengineer their business practices.

In the next chapter, we discuss Geographic Information Systems and Global Positioning Systems, two emerging technologies that will have an tremendous impact on the global enterprise of the future.

CHAPTER 8

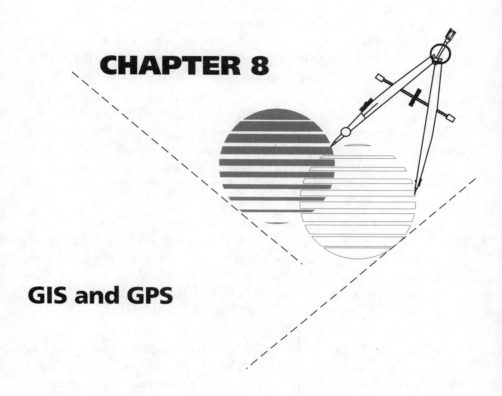

GIS and GPS

Sally is the top salesperson for a global manufacturing company. She is not having a good morning.

She has just been reassigned to a new territory on the East Coast, in an area she's completely unfamiliar with. After her plane arrived late, she checked into her hotel; in her rush to get out to the client, she left her portfolio behind. Both her directions and her background on other customers in the area are now 30 minutes behind her in her hotel room.

Fortunately, she left her laptop computer in the rental car. She quickly pulls over to the side of the road, powers up her PC and pops up a mapping application. She turns on her Global Positioning System (GPS) card to find her current position on the map. Then she types in an address of the client from a business card and a stick pin appears on the map showing the customer's location.

She pulls down a menu and requests the quickest route from her current position to the customer. A new window pops up that gives the instructions, including distance, direction, and road names for getting to her destination. On the map, her route has been traced in color.

Now to solve the final problem. Who are the other customers in the area? She turns on her cellular phone and dials into the home office's Geographic Information System (GIS). After a few moments she has a different map displayed on screen. She locates the customer, drags a circle in a 20-mile radius around the customer's location, and requests customers in the selected region. After a few seconds, out pops the answer.

Sounds like it might be a really interesting set of technologies when it gets here in 10 years? With the exception of the Geographic Information System (GIS) back at the home office, all of the technologies Sally used are available today as off-the-shelf software and hardware. What's more, all of it can be had (including the laptop, cellular phone, GPS card, and software) for less than $4,000.

To demonstrate the point, we've included both the hypothetical map and the directions for Sally's trip. Let's assume that Sally was trying to reach the town of Honey Brook, Pennsylvania, from Philadelphia International Airport. Using a $99 software package called Automap Road Atlas (from Automap, Inc.), she maps her trip (see Figure 9 and Table 4).

Geographic Information Systems

A Geographic Information System (GIS) can be thought of as a means of tying a map to any other type of data that we might want to associate with a particular location. These data might be demographics, like the number of households in a region with a mean income above $40,000, or convenient grouping information such as streets, area codes, or ZIP codes.

A GIS usually consists of two forms of data: graphical object and mapping data manipulated by the GIS software, and databases which contain the attribute information related to the maps. Although the database alone might contain the information you are interested in, a

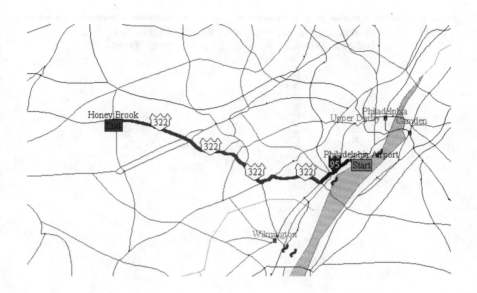

FIGURE 9 Roadmap from Philadelphia International Airport to Honey Brook

GIS is capable of rendering data into two of the most easily accepted human terms—pictures and places. When information is arranged visually, it is simpler to pick out patterns that might otherwise go unnoticed. It's also easier to ask questions about specific regions by visually selecting them.

Problems with GISs

In the past, GISs were restricted to users who could afford to collect the data and build proprietary systems. GIS applications require tremendous amounts of data, and early systems required the processing power of mainframes. As such, many of the early developers of GISs were government agencies, gas and power utilities, and other large organizations that possessed both the strong need for the information and the resources necessary to develop the system.

TABLE 4   Automap's Directions from Philadelphia International Airport to Honey Brook

Time (min.)	Distance (miles)	Instruction	Road	For	Dir.	Towards
00:00	0.0	**Depart** Philadelphia Airport (PA) on the	S-291	2 miles	W	Collingdale
00:03	2.3	At Collingdale turn left onto	I-95	2 miles	S	Wilmington
00:06	4.3	At Ridley Park stay on the	I-95	1 mile	S	Wilmington
00:08	5.7	At Chester stay on the	I-95	2 miles	S	Wilmington
00:11	7.9	Turn off onto	U-322	16 miles	NW	West Chester
00:30	24.4	At W Chester stay on the	U-322	9 miles	NW	Downingtown
00:40	33.0	At Downingtown stay on the	U-322	1 mile	NW	Coatesville
00:42	34.4	At Coatesville stay on the	U-322	12 miles	W	Honey Brook
00:56	46.3	**Arrive** Honey Brook (PA)				

Broad acceptance of GISs has been hampered both by costs and by a lack of standard methods for integrating data spread across multiple systems and platforms. While there are industry standards now available—such as SAIF (Canada), DIGEST (USA), and SDTS (USA)—they are not yet widely embraced by developers and users. Proprietary implementations of early CAD-based GISs or applications that even today command sizable market share have to some extent prevented acceptance of industry standards.

However, as more and more applications appear for the personal computer market, industry mapping standards are becoming more prevalent. We are seeing more products that support access to SQL, dBASE, Paradox, and ASCII databases.

The Cost of a GIS

A GIS can range from the multi-million-dollar proprietary systems with privately acquired data all the way down to PC based systems for less than a thousand dollars. In 1992, the market for GISs was estimated by Datatech Research Inc., Cambridge, MA, at $378 million, representing 20 percent growth from the previous year.

While the market is growing, the cost of GIS has been driven downward. Commercially available GIS software packages and development tools now run on nearly any platform you can think of. In the midrange, there are a growing number of off-the-shelf products that come packaged with mapping data and limited overlay data. Some of the more popular systems include Atlas GIS for Windows, TerraView 4.0, GPS MapKit SV, Hipparchus 2.2 for Windows NT, ArcView for

Windows, Atlas GIS, MapInfo for Windows, SPANS GIS 5.0 for OS/ 2, and Tactician 2.3 for Windows.

The gotcha in GISs is the cost of maps and overlay data. Prices for maps and overlays range from free to hundreds of thousands of dollars, depending on the amount of information and the source of the data. Doyle Frederick, Associate Director of the U.S. Geological Survey, conservatively estimates that the federal government spends more than $100 million per year simply gathering GIS data. Frederick says the collection and management of data alone accounts for 80 percent of the cost of a GIS.

Fortunately, many of the agencies who developed large-scale GISs have tried to recoup some of their costs by making the data publicly available. In doing so, they are driving down the cost of GISs.

Research companies including A. C. Nielsen, Dun & Bradstreet, and Equifax have made tremendous amounts of demographic business data available to vendors of mapping data. These vendors in turn, shape, filter, convert, divide and otherwise add value to the data and sell it on the commercial market.

The U.S. Census Bureau made 19 gigabytes of U.S. Geological Survey maps and 1990 census data known as the Topographically Integrated Geographic Encoding and Referencing (TIGER) data files available to the private sector. These databases contain digitized maps of streets, railroads, pipelines, and rivers, as well as geographic information about the tracts and blocks that make up urban communities (subdivisions) for all states and counties in the U.S.

Reportedly, the cost for TIGER data in machine-readable form is around $10,000. However, companies like Wessex Corporation have taken the $1,600, 16-volume CD-ROM set that comprises the Census Bureau's "short form" data, massaged and compressed it and have made it available with navigation software for $95. In addition, the "long form," 40 gigabytes of data is available from Wessex on a four-volume CD-ROM set for $395.

Etak, Inc. of Menlo Park, California, one of the world's renowned developers of digital mapping data, combines aerial photography, U.S. Geological Survey maps, local municipal maps, tax assessor information, ZIP code data, and field surveys into street and address maps which cover 3.5 million miles of U.S. and European roads. Etak recently made an agreement with Core Software Technology and

Digital Equipment Corporation to provide access to Etak maps through the Internet, where users will be able to select and download maps for an annual fee of $500.

Uses for GIS Technology

Geocoding, thematic mapping, and spatial analysis are three of the most important processes that a GIS facilitates. Probably the most important for the business user is geocoding.

Geocoding is the process of taking data that have inherent value to you—such as customer lists, trade routes, service areas and the like—and placing it into coordinate space on a map. More than 75 percent of the corporate databases in use have positioning information, such as addresses, ZIP codes, and phone number prefixes. Geocoding takes the data out of tabular and list forms and converts them into a format where it is easy to see patterns.

Thematic mapping is the process of creating and defining maps through geocoding to meet particular needs. Using a sales database, you might create a map that displays sales regions and concentrations of sales personnel. You might use the same software to create a map that shows the distribution of your customer base. While each of these maps has a different theme, the real value comes in being able to overlay one map on another. In this example, it might indicate where holes and weak spots exist in your sales strategies.

Finally, spatial analysis is a means of graphically representing three-dimensional data such as terrains, topologies, land formations, and fault lines. For many engineers, scientists and civil planners, these are the tools of the trade.

Here are some ways you might want to use GIS tools:

≡ **Site selection.** Opening a new location for business? With GIS tools, you can use data you probably already have about your current customer base to help select new locations with demographics that meet your business criteria. You might want to reach the greatest number of potential new customers without affecting current retail outlets. Or you might want to place a new store to provide maximum competition to other vendors.

≡ **Marketing research.** There is a tremendous amount of demographic data available for use with a GIS. These can be used to identify patterns in your current customer base. The inventory of a grocery store or retail outlet, for example, might be heavily influenced by the mean income and ethnic makeup of a neighborhood.

≡ **Sales support.** GIS systems help salespeople answer questions that might be critical for closing large accounts. A company investing in copiers for locations in several cities might want to know how many service centers in those regions have a 24-hour turnaround policy. In the past, a salesperson might have plowed through reams of paper to find the answer; today, a GIS could provide it quickly and efficiently.

≡ **Management of delivery routes or service fleets.** GIS tools can help organizations identify the most efficient distribution of service areas or delivery routes by analyzing their customers based on location and volume, type, or frequency of business.

≡ **Disaster management.** Our research has shown that this is one of the fastest growing areas for a GIS. A GIS enables insurance companies, health care providers, fire, police, and numerous other organizations to predict the effects of natural disasters and to determine the best way to deploy limited resources.

≡ **Regulatory monitoring.** Wherever regulations govern the operation of service providers—such as health care, banking, telecommunications, and utilities services—a GIS provides tools for assessing the performance and behavior of these organizations.

The concept of a GIS is not new—far from it—but the market-place is only now responding with tools that can be used by mere mortals. The most robust products on the market are usually general-purpose systems for analysis or toolkits for those who want to "grow their own." In most cases, business people are not interested in learning cartography or mapping; what they want is the information that a GIS is capable of deriving. To that end, expect to see greater specialization in the GIS market.

As standards become more prevalent and the general availability of demographic and statistical data grow, more and more software products targeted at special markets will appear. We've already seen that the power of PCs, combined with readily available information from Etak maps and TIGER data result in what Keith Hendricks, the President of Road Scholar Software in Houston calls, "maps for the masses." Consumer-level mapping, GIS, and personal navigator products are becoming more common all the time.

Eventually, we might expect to see GIS and mapping function-ality transparently embedded into applications we use daily, just as database and spreadsheet technologies are transparently imbedded in the personal information managers and financial tools we use today.

The Global Positioning System

The Global Positioning System (GPS) is a set of 24 satellites placed in orbit by the U.S. Department of Defense. These satellites orbit at an altitude of nearly 11,000 miles, and their coverage of the earth is com-plete. The primary purpose of the GPS is to identify the location of a GPS receiver at any point on or above the face of the earth—or under water—in terms of latitude, longitude, and elevation.

We saw a graphic demonstration of the GPS's capabilities during Operation Desert Storm. The GPS enabled the precise navigation and targeting of many of the weapons used during the Gulf War. With the sophisticated systems used by the military, the GPS is capable of placing a location to distances of less than a meter. The effects were devastating. It's worth noting that civilian GPS receivers can only pin-point locations to within 50 feet; military receivers can resolve to about 1 meter.

How Does the GPS Work?

 The GPS satellites are arranged in orbit such that at any given location on the earth, a GPS receiver can pull in radio signals from at least four of the satellites at any time. Each of these satellites broadcasts a unique code.

Two-way communication between the receiver and the satellites is not necessary. GPS receivers simply monitor the continuous transmission of the GPS satellites, decode them, and use triangulation to determine the precise location of the receiver.

Receivers Are Becoming Abundantly Available

There is no cost associated with receiving GPS transmissions; once you have a GPS receiver, the system is free. Because GPS devices are only receivers, they are moderately inexpensive to build. Add low cost to free service, and it's not surprising that they are becoming readily available.

GPS receivers for the marine and aviation industries have been available for several years. They come in many forms, but most are embedded into navigation systems or installed on the instrument panels of boats and planes. More recently, though, there have been several GPS receivers designed as navigation systems for cars and even hand-held personal units.

We found hand-held GPS receivers from Garmin, Magellan, Micrologic, Panasonic, Sony, and Trimble. Most of these devices are designed as personal navigators. They contain integrated displays that indicate current position, direction, waypoints, and course variance. Some support graphical displays with moving map indicators—your current position is superimposed onto a map—while others merely present textual data. The price for these devices depends on their intended purposes but range from just over $500 to nearly $2,000.

Perhaps the most useful form of GPS receivers we've seen are those that can be incorporated with standard PCs and laptops. Both Rockwell and Trimble have developed GPS receivers that are based on the Personal Computer Memory Card International Association (PCMCIA) type II slot standard. If you've purchased a laptop within the past year, chances are good that it has a PCMCIA slot.

Taking Mapping and GIS Mobile

When combined with PCs, GPS receivers become the perfect companion to mapping and GIS applications. Consider that these receivers are small enough to be carried and powered by a laptop, and you have a mobile navigator, data collection unit, GIS, and fleet management unit all wrapped up in a neat little package.

The Rockwell GPS unit is called the MicroTracker. The Trimble unit, co-developed with Socket Communications, is called the Mobile GPS Sensor. Both cards sell for less than $500, about the same as the cost for a high-end PCMCIA modem or LAN card.

When combined with inexpensive mapping software like Road Scholar Software's City Streets for Windows or Horizons Technology's Sure!MAPS—both of which sell for less than $100—these systems are easily within reach of both the light commercial and consumer markets. Companies that could not afford to invest in expensive navigation units or fleet management systems can now use general purpose PCs with GPS cards and low-cost software to accomplish the same results.

Manufacturers and market research firms are optimistic about the growth of this market. According to Technologic Partners, New York, revenues from the use of GPS technologies with mobile computing will grow from $17 million this year to over $57 million in 1995. Whether you're an early adopter or a cautious veteran, this technology is worth looking into.

GIS and GPS Success Stories

GISs and the GPS are proving to be successful technologies for a wide range of uses. To illustrate, let's take a look at a few case studies.

Continental Insurance of New York

Continental Insurance of New York used Strategic Mapping's Atlas GIS software to develop the Catastrophe Management Information Network (CatMan). This tool is designed to help Continental predict the extent of insurance claims that will arise out of a natural disaster. It can be directly connected to real-time weather services and can track hurricanes, earthquakes, floods, and other such events.

Continental hopes these tools will help limit its exposure in the event of catastrophic events. It gathers information about the insurance coverage in a particular area, down to the level of individual policies, and uses this information to examine existing risks before writing new policies.

Federal Emergency Management Agency

The Federal Emergency Management Agency (FEMA) is using a number of GIS- and GPS-based tools to predict and adapt to the effects of natural disasters. Using ARC/Info GIS software, FEMA developed a damage prediction model for hurricanes. The All-Hazards Situation Prototype-LAN (ASAP-LAN), was built in response to the unexpected damages caused by Hurricane Andrew. ASAP-LAN receives information directly from the National Weather Service and runs simulations to determine the probable extent of hurricane damage. This type of information helps FEMA better deploy resources in the event of an emergency.

FEMA also is testing pen-based computing systems combined with GPS receivers as possible tools for helping relief personnel locate buildings after a disaster has wiped out street signs and addresses.

Sylvania

Sylvania uses geographic information—addresses, ZIP codes, and phone prefixes—from its corporate database to support its sales staff. Using a custom version of Tactician, Sylvania sales representatives can compete for shelf space in retail outlets by showing the stores their potential customers and buying habits overlaid on a local map. They can then show the store owner hot-spots within the customer base for particular types of bulbs or buying habits.

Crime Prevention

The University of Virginia and the National Center for the Analysis of Violent Crime (NCAVC) are teaming up to use GIS tools to track patterns in serial rapes. NCAVC is using MapInfo to study the patterns involved in 119 solved serial rape cases to see if there are recurring patterns that might lead to the solution of new cases. So far, they have been able to identify patterns that could help identify where a rapist lives and where the rapist might strike next.

The Illinois Criminal Justice Information Authority is a state agency that develops information systems for law enforcement. In an effort to identify patterns in violent crime, they developed the Spatial and Temporal Analysis of Crime (STAC).

STAC is a set of analytical tools based on MapInfo 2.1 for Windows. The system accounts for several hundred variables relating to all of the homicides that have occurred in Chicago since 1965. Chicago police use the system to identify hot spots of gang activity and violent crime, and then target those areas. More than 80 law enforcement agencies nationwide have begun using or experimenting with the system.

Conclusion

Although GISs and the GPS cover all seven of the principles of reengineering, two stand out. First, organize work around results, not tasks. Second, capture data only one time—when it is created.

More than anything else, GIS tools organize work around results. What once took a team of statisticians and clerks poring over reams and miles of paper can be translated into an instantly available source of information. What's more, in doing so, the process has been converted from a static one to an organic one.

Both GISs and the GPS also aid in capturing data only once. GIS tools can take data from sources you already have and translate them into usable information. GIS representations are intuitive and more efficient than tabular representations. Similarly, a GPS in the hands of sales, field, and disaster personnel can prevent errors in data entry, provide automatic logging details, and provide a means of tracking and guiding people in real time.

In the next chapter, we look at workflow systems, software that automates sequential processing of work.

CHAPTER 9

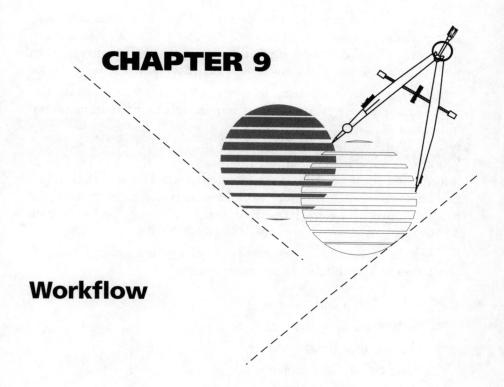

Workflow

Imagine this: You get back from a trip and need to do an expense report. You sit down at your PC and fill out the electronic form. When you are through, you click on the "Complete" icon and go on to your next task. The report is sent to your boss; he approves it. The report goes to your boss's boss; she approves it. A payables clerk gets it and makes a direct deposit to your bank in the right amount. You get electronic confirmation that the money is there. No pens, calculators, erasers, no copies to get lost on your boss's desk, no inter-office mail to lose the report.

Sound a little different from what you are used to?

This example shows how workflow can be creatively managed to make the grueling experience of filling out an expense report much easier and more pleasant.

This chapter examines how workflow management is used to make business processes better, faster, and more efficient. We look at an example of the old way versus the new way. Then, we discuss how technology makes improvement possible. Next, we tie this back to some of the principles of reengineering to illustrate their applicability. Finally, we look at a case study to show how effective workflow actually works.

Let's first get a working definition of workflow. In any organization, there are certain tasks that require information from several individuals. Information is collected, compiled and communicated as work moves through the organization until the task is completed. Workflow management is simply the automation of that movement of information to make the process more efficient. Think of it as industrial engineering for the office. Workflow management is fundamental to all processes and workflow software is ultimately going to show up on your network. You might as well get ready for it.

There are four basic elements associated with a successful implementation of a workflow management system:

≋ Work design and processing
≋ A database (or many databases)
≋ Communications capability
≋ Application development

By incorporating these pieces, you can implement a workflow computing model without disrupting existing work processes—assuming that the current process doesn't deserve disruption. A user will be able to fill out forms, obtain critical information, add important information to the database, and send the results along the prescribed path to completion of the task, all in an efficient, organized fashion.

Now that we have some idea of what we're talking about, let's dig in a little deeper to understand the whys and hows of workflow management.

Workflow Management

Managing Your Workflow

Pick a process—any process—and ask "why?". Don't just accept a workflow as being right or efficient. Dig. Probe. Get to the heart of the matter. Why does the accounting clerk have to plow through piles of source documents to select the right data necessary to issue an invoice? Why do the sales people fill out endless paper reports and then forward them to a regional office for input into a central computer system? And why can't invoicing or sales information be downloaded to a desktop or mobile PC and made available on the spot and at the time it's needed?

To illustrate the point further, let's dig into the expense report example a bit deeper. Think about what happens today. How does the expense report system in your company work? It might go something like this:

1. You gather up all your receipts and get a form. Better get several forms because you'll need them.

2. You grab a pen and a calculator to fill out the form, in triplicate. Press hard so the ink will show on the last copy.

3. After you have added up all the expenses and cross-footed the report, you make copies of your report and receipts.

4. You send it on to your boss for approval.

5. It gets lost.

6. A week later, someone finds it. Your boss signs it.

7. It goes to Accounts Payable.

8. The accounting clerk re-adds and re-cross foots all the rows and columns, checks all the receipts and compares to all the entries on the form.

9. Oops, where's the receipt for that $36.50 dinner? Back to you.

10. You attach the receipt and send it back.

11. Sorry, the pay-for-view movie is disapproved. Back to you.

12. You take it off, re-add, re-cross foot, and send it back to the boss, who approves it and sends it on.

13. Back to the accounting clerk. See Step 7.

14. Sorry, it exceeds the limit. Your boss's boss needs to approve it. Back to you.
15. You send it to the boss's boss. She signs it and sends it back to you.
16. You send it back to Accounting.
17. The completed, approved report is now checked, re-added, and cross footed.
18. It gets approved.
19. The accounting clerk makes an entry into your Accounts Payable ledger to issue you a check.
20. A payables clerk issues the check and puts it in inter-office mail. It gets lost.
21. You get your check.

OK, so maybe this is a little overstated. Yes, there are some manual systems like this that work very well. However, technology can help make this process better.

A lot of this can be eliminated with some creative thinking about how the desired results can be best achieved:

1. You open the expense report form on your PC.
2. You fill in the appropriate cells with the right numbers.
3. You scan in the receipts using the scanner down the hall.
4. You sign it electronically.
5. You close the file and e-mail it to your boss.
6. Your boss's PC beeps and says there is a task to be done.
7. He opens and reviews the report, "signs" it and sends it to his boss.
8. She opens, reviews, and "signs" the report and sends it to Accounting.
9. Accounting opens, reviews, approves the report, and issues the journal entry to credit your bank account.
10. You get confirmation that the money is in the bank.

Again, the point is exaggerated here. Networks do crash, and PCs lock up and need to be re-booted. But, eliminating wasteful steps in a process and automating those that remain does improve the process dramatically.

By applying some of the principles of reengineering, the process is simplified and expedited:

≋ The desired result is to have you reimbursed for your expenses incurred on that trip, to make sure the expenses are within the rules of the company, and to create a record of each transaction.

≋ Capture the data at the source. You have the required information. Fill out the form once. Let the spreadsheet do most of the work: calculate, flag mistakes, indicate where receipts are required (you can scan them into the system), highlight the names required for approval.

≋ Move the form *electronically* from place to place where approval is required. Let the system initiate the action and require the decision makers, the approvers, to use the system.

≋ Create the permanent record for purposes of control.

That is how the expense report process can, and should, be managed.

What does a workflow system do? It converts many manual or electronic work processes into a system of electronic processes that flow in an orderly fashion through the organization. A workflow system is either structured or ad hoc, depending on how the work is directed to flow through the system.

A structured system provides a very specific framework that makes all the routing decisions for work entered into the system. Those decisions may be based on some finite number of possibilities based on a pre-established set of rules.

At the other end of the spectrum, users make routing decisions in an ad hoc way. Here, the routing decisions are more complex, and depend on human evaluation and professional knowledge not available from a machine.

What do you need to make all this possible? We have been assuming all along that you have a network, but you don't need much more hardware to make a workflow system work. The components of a workflow system are:

- 🔁 Application software to create the work
- 🔁 Routes and tasks to direct the work
- 🔁 A tracking mechanism to know where work is in the system
- 🔁 Workflow servers to manage the process in the network
- 🔁 A filing system—a database

Of course, the real trick is to get the right software and apply it properly to the issue at hand.

Loans in an Hour: A Case Study

A very good example of how workflow management can help make dramatic productivity improvements can be found at one major banking establishment with more than $15 billion in assets.

In 1987, the State of Texas changed its laws to allow branch banking for the first time in more than 100 years. Instead of conducting business as separate entities, banks could consolidate operations and eliminate duplicate effort and resources. The change helped expand the consumer lending market. Our case study was already a very well-established leader in the commercial banking field, and it wanted to duplicate that performance in the consumer lending arena.

To that end, the bank implemented a program that allowed customers to merge all their checking, savings, and financial transactions into one comprehensive account. Since 1988, the bank has attracted more than $4 billion in deposits from this program.

The bank installed a network of hundreds of PCs running state-of-the-art proprietary workflow management software to help streamline its business to better serve the consumer. This system consolidates all of the labor-intensive, time-consuming "back office" activities into a single site.

The bank replaced its antediluvian approach, having highly paid loan officers deal with piles of paper, with a system that uses personal bankers, who devote almost all of their time to selling financial products, to deal with the customer.

When a consumer applies for a loan, he fills out a loan application. It takes about 10 minutes. The rest of the process is highly automated. The application is faxed to the operations center. As it is received, it is automatically scanned into the network. Then the application is electronically sent on for analysis, including contact with the appropriate credit bureaus, and approval. After approval, the final closing documents are completed and sent to the originating bank to be printed on a laser printer and signed by the customer and the bank. What used to take a day or two now takes three hours—one hour on a priority basis.

The image-processing software allows clerks, lenders, and analysts to capture, store, retrieve, and process applications, along with all the supporting documentation, right from their desktop PCs. There is no paper.

All the departments at the operations center—mail room, loan origination, underwriting, funding, closing documents preparation, collection, and customer service—are hooked to the Ethernet LAN using PCs. Of course, there is an on-line link to the minicomputers and mainframes in the bank's home office.

As you might imagine, this was not a quick and simple system to implement. Getting into the consumer loan business provided the bank an opportunity to address two strategic issues. How should business be structured? What technology should be used? Both issues were fundamental to the way the bank conducted business and deserved serious consideration and a lot of work.

The consideration was given and the work was done. The bank added to its traditional business and entered the consumer business. The results have been above expectations. In the largest market in the state, the bank's loan volume more than doubled in less than one year.

Most customers today have no idea what goes on behind the scenes. They only know they get better service and quicker response.

The internal benefits to the bank are even greater. Because of the focus on customer service, the loan volume has doubled. Yet, there are fewer people processing and underwriting loans than one year ago. There has been a dramatic reduction of paper. Documentation now gets passed from place to place electronically. No more thick file folders to get lost. No more file cabinets. Better service to the customer which, after all, is the most visible thing a bank uses to differentiate itself from competition.

Supporting the Seven Principles

This is an excellent example of the results of reengineering. The bank has done an excellent job in restructuring its workflow management to create a system that truly responds to the needs of the business.

- ≜ The bank organized work around the desired result—a quick and expeditious review and decision of a loan application.
- ≜ The data created by the consumer was captured once and used throughout the process.
- ≜ Because that data and the credit bureau reports are on the PCs of the decision makers, there is no duplication of effort.
- ≜ The fact that the location of the source of the data is different from the location where the decision is made has no impact on the process.

Conclusion

In this chapter, we saw questions you need to consider when approaching the application of workflow technology.

- ≜ Study the application thoroughly—there is more to it than you think. Completely question every step of the process, and don't just make a bad process go faster.
- ≜ Be prepared to change things. Redefine jobs. Bring together fragmented departments. Kill some sacred cows.
- ≜ Understand and use technology to make the process better.

In the next chapter, we examine document management and imaging, two technologies that are closely linked to workflow management.

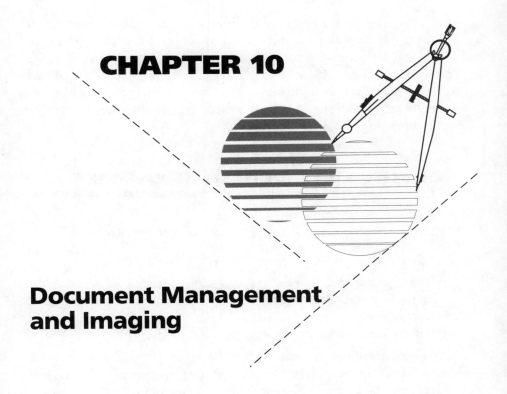

CHAPTER 10

Document Management and Imaging

Now that we have discussed workflow management, we now turn to document management and imaging—two key ingredients in a workflow system.

Remember the expense report process discussed in the last chapter? Let's say that while you are filling out that expense report, you remember a memo the CFO wrote about something unpleasant happening to the next guy who tried to slip a pay-per-view movie into an expense account. You sit down at your PC and enter "John Doe" (the CFO) and "pay-per-view." The document appears on your monitor and is ready for review. You read it carefully and learn that the penalty for reporting a "pay-per-view" charge is immediate dismissal. So you put the $15 charge in the "Meals" column and move on.

This example gives a hint as to how you can ensure continued employment (at least until your next trip) by using document management.

This chapter studies how document management systems can help you use information much more easily, and can even let us do things that we otherwise couldn't. We make some comparisons of life before and after document management. Then, we discuss the role of technology. We survey some examples of how effective document management can improve business processes. Finally, we show the applicable principles of reengineering.

Defining Document Management

Document management is often tightly tied to workflow. What is flowing through a workflow system can almost always be described as a "document." As we show in Figure 10, a document can be text, graphics, spreadsheets, voice, images—any intellectual asset of the company. Document management moves those assets, stores them, creates indexes for them, and makes them immediately accessible by many users at any time, any where they are needed.

There are some basic attributes that must be present to make a system useful for workflow or document management. The system must integrate several different facilities—word processors, spread-

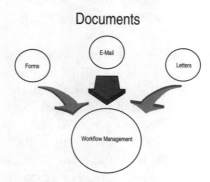

FIGURE 10 A "document" can be pretty much anything—a pre-printed form, e-mail message, or a letter, and workflow management involves making sure that people can get at any document they want at any time.

sheets, graphic systems, multimedia. It must be easy to use. It must have a powerful search engine. It must have extensive security mechanisms.

Managing All That Paper

Just look at what it would take to create the paperless office. Consider the Group of Seven (G-7) nations, the economically developed countries that have the most impact on the world's economy. They are the United States, the United Kingdom, France, Germany, Italy, Japan, and Canada. They have a total of 325 million workers. If you assume each worker generates five pieces of paper a day—letters, purchase orders, shipping acknowledgments—then the G-7 countries alone generate 1.6 billion pieces of paper a day. No telling how big the number would be if you add the 1.05 billion workers in China, India, Indonesia, and Russia. These are numbers even Carl Sagan can enjoy!

Paper has many advantages over the so-called alternative media. It's easy to read (most of the time). It's cheap. You don't need electricity to read it. It's everywhere.

But there are many drawbacks to paper. Only one person can read it at a time. The right piece of paper is not always easy to find. Searching for the right set of words is very labor intensive. Storage of all those paper documents is expensive.

Because of these and many other drawbacks, we are driven to minimize the use of paper as the medium for transmission, review, and storage of information. Inexpensive, pervasive PCs hooked up to a network do a much better job. In the future, a document management system will be a part of every LAN.

There are other reasons why document management will be pervasive. When you are working with hundreds or thousands of documents, remembering their nondescript file names and locations can be a problem. This problem is particularly important when you move to a network with dozens of servers and you're saving documents in several different directories.

With today's speedy word processors and desktop publishing software, the question of "Where is my document?" is not just for large companies. As you produce more documents day after day at home or in the office, you take longer and longer to find that document you wrote just one month ago. Even a telecommuter or a small organization of three to ten people can easily generate hundreds of documents each month.

The need for sophisticated document management procedures becomes even more important as the number of networked nodes, desktop or mobile, grow. If you waste five or ten minutes searching through a Microsoft Word index for a document, your productivity nearly evaporates. A well-designed document management system will make all documents, regardless of where they came from, immediately accessible.

Document management systems can take on many forms, depending largely on the way the document gets into the system. The information may have been created within the network, with the document management information an integral part of the file. Or the information may have been generated inside the network but before document management was an issue. And finally, it may have been created outside the network.

Let's go back to the original example. You need the guidelines to fill out your expense report. You don't know, and don't care, what the file name is, where it is or what the format is. You could go searching through those 357 feet of file cabinets to look for the right piece of paper. If you ever found it, which is doubtful, you would probably be so frustrated that you would not remember why you wanted it in the first place.

For documents that are generated within a LAN using a document management system, there are two ways the system can work: front-end or a back-end. The front-end design forces the user to comply with rules for file names and extensions. This design leads to more consistency. It places each class or type of document in its own electronic folder and makes document retrieval from word-processing, spreadsheet, and desktop publishing applications quicker and more systematic.

The back-end systems don't require users to learn a set of file naming rules. You will access your documents as usual, and fill out a profile card as you exit the application you're using. The profile card lets you identify the subject, key words, author, and any other information you might use in searching for the document tomorrow or a month from now. You easily could forget an eight character name with a .DOC or .LTR or .WK1 extension.

The method for dealing with electronic documents created before the document management system is put in place is only marginally different. They can be put into the system by using a front-end tool that helps index and describe the document.

But what about all those documents created outside the network? Imagine you're a lawyer in the depths of the discovery process in a large product-liability suit. You walk into the defendant's office and he shows you three tons of paper with the guts of the case spread all over it. There are words, there are engineering drawings, there are hand-written notes, there are coffee stains.

How do you get through all this stuff? And, more important, how do you make sure you only have to do it once, and still find that one tidbit of information that will make or break the case?

How Can Technology Help?

Fortunately, technology can help. The documents can be scanned into a system.

Scanners act like fax machines, except that output is directed to a computer rather than a telephone line. As with fax machines, there are many scanners available. You can buy small, personal devices and you can buy large, departmental machines that scan a page per second.

The scanner creates an image file that is compressed and stored on a disk. Each document needs to be described——to whom, from who, what drawing number, and date. Then, an index needs to be created. Indexing is the most difficult and time-consuming part of the process, but it is key to the success of the project.

But once all that is done, you will have all the information in a system that will provide you with the immediate access you need.

What does a typical user want out of such a system? The requirements are fairly simple and straightforward. The system should:

≋ Be easy to use. It should be intuitive, with little training required.

≋ Provide immediate access to information. Users should be able to get to any document, anywhere and at any time.

≋ Be secure.

≋ Be able to do something with the information—e*dit it, print it, or cut and paste it into another document.

≋ Be dependable.

What do you need to make all this possible?

Proper planning of the document management system is an indispensable step to the system's eventual success. As with any planning effort, you need to consider the basic parts of the plan and manage their interrelationship:

≋ A document server is where you store documents themselves and keep information about them in a database.

≋ An index structure is the blueprint for the database, accommodating the storage and retrieval needs of the user. It contains the hierarchy of how documents are related as well as the indexes, templates and attributes of the documents to be managed.

≋ Database partitions allow the easy distribution of data on different platforms. They also help with flexible data management, easier administration and increased performance. The definition of the partitions is one of the key strategic planning issues to be decided. They can be divided by chronology, application, volume, geography or in any combination of these.

≋ Optical storage devices save space. If you use paper, you can get about 120,000 pages in 80 linear foot of file cabinet. With optical storage devices, you get the same amount of data in about the space of a pizza box.

When you apply document management to your network, you need to make sure all the plumbing is unclogged. There will be lots of stuff flowing to and fro across the LAN.

A typical text document runs about 5K per page. A scanned and compressed document runs about 75K per page. What does that do to the LAN of a company, say an insurance company with lots of claims to process, that handles 10,000 pages of stuff a day? Even if all pages were 100K scanned images, which they won't be, that still only means 1GB per day: 10,000 pages times 100K per page. Some simple calculation—1 GB of data transmitted at a constant rate during 8 hours per day times 3600 seconds per hour—translates this traffic load into 35K/sec, not a big dent in a 10MB/sec Ethernet network.

Of course, transmission is never at a constant rate and testing is always in order to get through the peaks and valleys of network utilization. But a 10MB/sec bandwidth is not even close to being challenged by a load of 35K/sec.

But there is a dramatic need for the next piece of technology: a storage device, a very large storage device. One GB of data is a nontrivial amount of data. You are immediately led to an optical disk, most assuredly one with a jukebox. If you think about getting 650 MB on a 5¼-inch disk and getting a 16-disk jukebox for under $10,000, the problem becomes much more manageable. Much larger juke boxes with up to 144 disks are available, too What this allows you to do, in addition to all the benefits of access and manipulation, is to get rid of 350 of those 357 feet of filing cabinets. If you are renting office space in New York or Tokyo, think of the money you'll save!

Next, you will need a scanning facility. If you need to record something like 10,000 transactions a day, the best solution might be to go to a single vendor like IBM, ViewStar, or FileNet to get an integrated solution.

Lesser requirements can easily be satisfied by readily available devices from normal sources for PC and LAN hardware. That is not to say that the temp you hired during summer vacation from high school last year can set up your system. It will take a good network administrator. But it is fairly easy to do.

If you have a huge requirement for document management, you probably have already considered outsourcing the task. If there are millions of pages of documents to be managed, setting up the system and inputting the documents is probably a one-time problem, and you don't need to buy the equipment necessary to complete this task. You can out-source the project to a company like Docucon, Inc. (San Antonio, TX).

Then, of course, there is the software. Many workflow and document management packages are shrink-wrapped and on the shelf of PC dealers. Most workflow packages include a document management capability. Some vendors who provide shrink-wrapped software are SoftSolutions Technology Corporation (Orem, UT); Delrina Corporation (Toronto, Ontario, Canada); PC DOCS, Inc. (Tallahassee, FL); FileNet Corporation (Costa Mesa, CA); and ViewStar Corporation (Emeryville, CA).

How Will Standards Help?

Whenever there are different vendors providing pieces to a solution, standards are an issue. So it is with workflow and document management. In the PC world, these systems are fairly new, so there is no clear body of standards to be applied.

One clear need for a standard is at the interface between the workflow and document management system and the database that lets users locate the documents they need. The Open Database Connectivity (ODBC) standard, shown in Figure 11, is currently emerging. Many database vendors, like Sybase, Oracle, and Borland, have ODBC drivers available. And there are many tools that can help: SQL Access Tool, Visual Basic, Excel 5.0, Q+E, FoxPro, and more.

Because standards are still emerging, and because most systems will be department-wide or enterprise-wide, users may be likely to buy an integrated system. But as workflow applications become better understood, standards will evolve and become an important part of the overall concept.

Document Management in Banking

A major Australian bank needed to provide its legal staff with a Client/ Matter Information Storage/Control system. It had to include a seamlessly integrated suite of applications that supported all aspects of

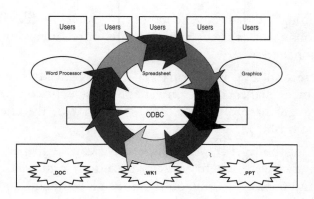

FIGURE 11 The emerging Open Database Connectivity standard promises to simplify access to documents within a document management system.

their day-to-day business. These aspects included word processing, spreadsheet, client information, legal matter information, legal resident references, hard copy files, hard copy communications (correspondence) and electronic communications (fax and e-mail). The most important aspect of all these processes was the control and maintenance of any relationship between client and subject matter.

The application, developed in Microsoft's Visual Basic and Soft-Solutions 4.0's document management system, establishes the controlling relationship among client, subject matter, and resources. These relationships are then passed on with the permanent record which is stored, retrieved, managed, manipulated, and sent to on-line optical disks or, finally, to archive tape.

The system is designed so any application software package can be replaced by another similar functioning product without requiring a change in the solution. Any additional function, such as voice or business audio, can also be included as needed.

Users have to deal with only two levels of information. The first is new or unprocessed information. That can be a document generated within the system—a word-processing document, a spreadsheet—or an external document—a fax or a scanned letter. A user reads the new document through e-mail and chooses to either profile it through SoftSolutions against a client, subject matter or resource, or to maintain it as a personal item.

The second level is information that has already been profiled. The document management software provides tight control and easy access through the profile index, full-text index or the client/subject matter relationships.

Most of the legal staff had little experience with personal computers, but they were used to dealing with letters, legal briefs, diagrams, pictures, and books. By using SoftSolutions Document Desktop, they need not be concerned about which application belongs to which document. The software handles that for them.

Supporting the Seven Principles

Document management strongly supports the seven principles of reengineering.

≋ Building the document management system properly will organize the work around results, not tasks. A document database is not limited to the marketing department, for example, but is available to the product development team. Information from a single source is available to every user that needs access to it—at the same time, if need be.

≋ At the point of input, whether from a word-processing application or a scanner, we capture data only once. It is stored, managed, and retrieved many times but captured only once.

≋ Decisions can be made by the staff from their desk, where the work is performed.

≋ Controls, such as security, are incorporated in the document management system at the time of design.

≋ The people who use the process, the legal staff, use the system and do the work.

≋ Since there is an electronic copy of a document, it can go anywhere in the world where there is a node on the network. Geographic resources get treated as one.

Conclusion

We hope this chapter has enlightened you to the benefits of document management, especially in reengineering your business processes. We know that many organizations are plagued with poor document management procedures. Be sure to check out the current technology to find the cure. Document management is a valuable tool for reengineering.

In the next chapter, we look at collaborative systems, often called groupware, which allow many users on a LAN work together in a variety of ways.

CHAPTER 11

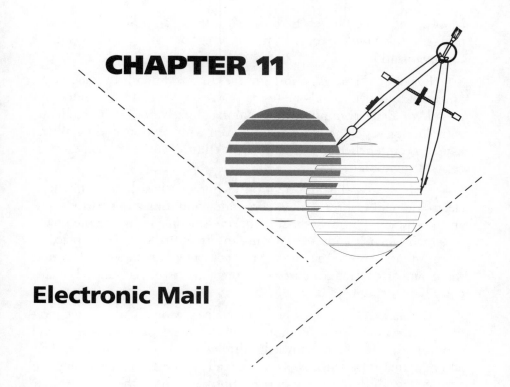

Electronic Mail

News announcement, June 2, 1993:
"The White House announced today
that for the first time in history it is
directly connected to the Internet. Con-
stituents may now correspond with
White House executives via electronic
mail. President Clinton's new Internet
address is president@whitehouse.gov,
while Vice President Gore can be reached
at vicepresident@whitehouse.gov."

Most people would have a hard time imagining an office without telephones. How would people communicate, both inside and outside of the organization?

For us at Currid & Company, it is just as difficult to imagine an office without electronic mail (e-mail). We have become dependent on e-mail for daily communication among ourselves, with our clients, with colleagues in the industry, and even with vendors and suppliers. E-mail is entrenched in our company's culture, and our business processes depend on it.

Perhaps no other information technology has done as much as electronic mail to break down corporate communication barriers and arcane reporting processes. Astute business people recognize the power of e-mail when it comes to moving information easily from place to place. What's more, e-mail users find they can go up, down and around the chain of command, cutting through layers of corporate bureaucracy with a couple of keystrokes.

E-mail has changed many corporate lives. More than other technologies, electronic mail combines the power of computers and communications to pass knowledge throughout an organization, and we all know that knowledge is power. E-mail is an essential technology to both enable BPR and to support new processes once they are in place. Even the US federal government has recognized the importance of "getting connected" in the Clinton administration's push to reinvent government. (Although electronic mail is received by the White House, it is immediately printed out and distributed on paper, and all constituent e-mail is answered via the US Mail. Reengineering takes time.)

In this chapter, we explore some of the ways that electronic mail changes an organization's culture. We look at e-mail's role in reengineering projects and in newly designed business processes. We discuss some of the capabilities of e-mail systems and products, and reveal the issues of implementing and using e-mail.

Just What Is E-mail?

E-mail is best thought of as an electronic method of moving information from one person to another. Information is usually generated by a person, but sometimes by a computer itself. E-mail is like conventional mail, but its potential reach is much broader.

Sometimes there is confusion about where e-mail starts and stops. There are actually several technologies that get caught in the definition web: *E-mail*, which is person-to-person(s) messaging; *Groupware*, which lets many co-workers (or workgroups) share information with each other in an interactive or collaborative effort; *Public forums*, which are like computerized bulletin boards for different people to share information; and *On-line databases*, which let people communicate directly with data stored somewhere on a computer.

We'll stick to person-to-person e-mail and public forums or bulletin boards in this chapter. We will spend time with groupware and on-line databases in later chapters.

From a mechanical standpoint, e-mail closely follows the metaphor of regular mail. E-mail is written, addressed, sorted, and delivered. With e-mail, though, computers (instead of people) do most of the work.

Each person on an e-mail system will have his or her own address and mailbox. Messages intended for that person are delivered to the mailbox and are held there until collected. The e-mail system, in essence, forwards and stores messages.

Many of the newer e-mail products provide expanded features. Besides simply receiving and passing on messages, these newer products let you attach files to messages. The files can be common data

files such as spreadsheets, word processing documents, or can even contain voice or video clips.

Other conveniences have become popular, including the ability to forward mail to other people; courtesy copy someone on a message; get a return receipt when someone opens mail you sent; or the option to store mail in folders after you've read it.

E-mail's Role and Promise

E-mail's purpose is to pass information, and its promise is to do so efficiently. It lets people share thoughts and  ideas without having to be in the same place at the same time. Some frequent e-mail users carry on complex conversations and delicate business negotiations without so much as a piece of paper passing between them, or without their ever having to lift the phone or engage in a real-time conversation.

E-mail is sometimes a preferred method of communication, especially if you need a little time to think and digest information before acting on it. Many multinational or global organizations have found e-mail to be a boon because it lets people think and/or translate before they have to answer. It also lets messages cross time zones without forcing people to get up in the middle of the night to talk to a colleague in Japan or Europe.

E-mail's capability is powerful, but its benefits are not always instantly understood. It is difficult to explain the more far-reaching effects of e-mail–empowered organizations until you live in one. Frankly, many people simply have to use it to believe it.

E-Mail versus "The Old-Fashioned Way"

Let's look at the difference between the old way of doing business and the reengineered, electronically empowered way. If you are a corporate citizen in a large organization (or even some small ones) and you want to get a piece of information to the guy down the hall, you might have to go through hoops and loops to do it.

Take, for example, the official procedure one Fortune 100 company dictated for sending a report to a co-worker down the hall. Believe it or not, this policy existed up until just a short time ago. It involved a 16-step process that went something like this:

1. Business person handwrites a memo or report on a yellow writing tablet and gives it to his or her secretary.

2. Secretary proofs the document and edits for spelling, grammar, and correct use of company trademarks.

3. Secretary walks the memo and deposits it into the wire basket in front of the word-processing center.

4. The center clocks in the document, assigns a job number to it and puts it in the queue for the next available word-processing specialist.

5. The word-processing specialist types the document in draft form and places it in the out basket.

6. Secretary collects the document, proofs it, places editing marks on it, and returns it for approval to the business person.

7. Business person reviews the draft, edits it if necessary and returns it to the secretary.

8. Secretary copies the marked-up draft, returns it to the word-processing center for final edits, corrections and printing.

9. Word-processing center clocks in the document, assigns a job number to it and puts it in the queue for the next available specialist.

10. Word-processing specialist retrieves the file, makes the appropriate edits, prints it in final form, and places it in the out basket.

11. Secretary picks up completed document, proofs it again and gives it to the business person for signature.

12. Business person signs document and returns it to secretary.

13. Secretary copies document, files it, addresses an inter-office envelope and sends it to the mail room.

14. Mail room receives envelope, sorts it, and distributes it in the next mail run.

15. Secretary of the recipient down the hall receives mail, opens envelope and places it in appropriate folder, and delivers mail.

16. Recipient down the hall gets the message.

Total elapsed time: 3 days to 1 week.

This is not a joke, or even a slight exaggeration. It was company policy—the rules, the law. The same procedure was followed for everything from a one-page memo to a 200-page report. No exceptions allowed. There were even administrators employed in each department to make sure no one violated or short-circuited the ordained company procedures. (In fact, when the first personal computers came into this company, there was a major management and political confrontation trying to stop people from using PCs to write their own memos.)

Now contrast the 16-step procedure with the way things are done today with electronic mail. Today, the process of getting information to the guy down the hall can be as few as three steps:

1. Business person drafts document in a word-processing program, or directly in the e-mail software.
2. Business person sends electronic document to guy down the hall and electronically files a draft copy.
3. Guy down the hall gets the message.

Total elapsed time: 3 minutes to an hour (depending on the length of the document).

And today's approach doesn't cost more than the old system, even when you consider all the costs for computer hardware and software.

Changing Corporate Culture

Most types of information technology are brought into a company and are molded to fit the pervasive corporate culture—the way employees interact with each other. That's because most technologies simply automate the old way of doing business. The technology itself has little bearing on how people communicate.

Electronic mail is different. While the original intent may be to automate communications throughout the organization, e-mail actually changes the way people interact. We use the term "empowerment" to refer to the cultural shift. Rank-and-file workers are empowered to communicate freely and broadly.

E-mail is a great tool for reengineered companies, because it is a method for communicating lots of information quickly. Let's take a look at some of the ways that e-mail enables (or forces) cultural changes.

E-mail Is the Great Equalizer

No other technology has as much power as e-mail to equalize everyone in the organization. Anyone in the company can send mail to anyone else. There is nothing inherent in the technology that forces people to observe the entrenched corporate chain of command. The lowest-level employee can send mail to the company president. Of course, some business decorum might be needed here, but the point is, the technology allows the communication to happen.

Even the federal government is jumping on the bandwagon. Ordinary mortals can send e-mail messages directly to the White House or to some members of Congress. While we certainly wouldn't expect President Clinton to read and respond to every piece of e-mail that comes his way, it still gives citizens a sense of importance, just knowing we can send our opinions to the President with the touch of a keystroke. (For the record, we understand that Vice President Gore is an avid e-mail user, so you just may get a message directly from him some day!)

E-mail Changes Expectations for Communication

Electronic mail changes our expectations for how quickly we can communicate with fellow workers. While we don't necessarily expect to have a real-time on-line conversation with someone (although that *is* possible), we certainly do expect that our correspondents acknowledge and respond to our mail within a day, perhaps even sooner.

Contrast that with the traditional hard-copy means of correspondence. Even for interoffice correspondence, we generally allow several days for the recipient to receive and respond to mail. What's more, it seems more acceptable for the recipient of a hard-copy letter to give the excuse, "I haven't seen it."

With e-mail, we expect that the recipient checks and reads his mail often, and that he will respond as soon as he reads the note. (The response may well be, "I'll look into this issue and get back to you," but at least he has acknowledged the note.) E-mail sets up the expectation for much quicker communication. Even the White House responds to its e-mail by the end of the day, although it's not likely to be the personal response that you might like.

When e-mail takes the form of electronic bulletin boards, it can provide information to large groups of people almost instantaneously. As a follow-up to President Clinton signing the Government Printing

Office Electronic Access Bill in the summer of 1993, the federal government now makes all types of government records available over on-line bulletin board services. To set the example, the White House strives to provide an electronic version of all speeches, press releases, and other public information within 30 minutes of its original delivery. Now we can watch a State of the Union address on television, and read it on the Internet electronically a mere half-hour later.

E-mail Extends Our List of Correspondents

When we send out a hard copy of a letter or document, we tend to limit the distribution list to only those people who really need the information. After all, it's such a hassle to make all those copies and send one to everyone on the distribution list. And, how will we know when everyone gets the mail and has a chance to read it?

With e-mail, there's no hassle to adding "just one more" person to the distribution list, just to make sure that everyone who may need a copy gets a copy. Moreover, it's so easy to attach a file—even a long one—that we tend to share more information than we would with hard copies. And, with a simple option like an automatic acknowledgment, we know who has read the mail, and when.

Public and private electronic bulletin boards also make it easy to communicate with many people at once. Some bulletin board systems (BBSs) provide for one-way communication—posted notices only—while others allow for interactive conversations.

On January 13, 1994, we took part in an unprecedented electronic town meeting, hosted by CompuServe and U.S. News Online, that featured a real-time conversation with Vice President Gore. More than 900 people nationwide (and a few internationally) joined in. The electronic medium made it possible for so many people to enjoy this conversation from the comfort of their own homes and offices.

E-mail Extends Our Reach

In keeping with the reengineering principle that says "Treat geographical resources as one," e-mail extends our reach in many ways. Experts estimate that the worldwide list of e-mail users contains more than 30 million people and is growing daily. That's a lot of people that you can reach electronically! Of course, you can't reach everyone with just a few keystrokes—yet. Today's technology requires complex gateways to connect disparate e-mail systems, but the impending arrival of the information superhighway may change all of that.

Certainly some of your customers and other important contacts are among those 30 million users of e-mail. Can't you imagine ways to improve communications with them via technology? You might use the international e-mail system called the Internet to instantly transmit a proposal to a prospective client in Europe, saving time and money, and perhaps even beating a competitor to the punch.

Another way that e-mail extends our reach is by freeing us from the bounds of our offices and the restriction of a specific set of hours for our workday. Without e-mail, you are likely to be dependent on paper-based communication and the telephone. With e-mail, you are free to collect, read and respond to your mail, any time of the night or day, virtually anywhere you travel. Your mail is ready and waiting for you, when and where you want it.

New e-mail products are widening the prospects for mobility. Today, there are products that support remote access to central e-mail systems, so you can check your mail from home or from a hotel just as easily as if you were at your desk. Some e-mail systems will even find you, no matter where you are. For example, the wireless e-mail system from Ericsson/GE called Viking Express, transmits mail messages into an exceptionally convenient notebook-sized unit that can be taken virtually anywhere.

Going a step further with mobility, WordPerfect Corporation has a product that allows you to use your computer-based e-mail through an ordinary telephone. Now you can check your office e-mail, including the day's calendar and list of tasks, from your bedside telephone without having to connect via a PC modem.

E-mail is especially effective for communicating with business contacts around the world, eliminating the problem of dealing with different time zones. No more getting up at 3:00 AM to call that client on the other side of the globe! You can transact business at a time that is convenient for you.

By now, you can see not only the benefits of e-mail, but some of the ways that it will likely change your corporate culture. Messages and documents will move quickly throughout the organization. People can share information much more readily. Barriers to communication, such as line organizations, are broken down. All of these results of implementing e-mail can help to move your company toward a more responsive, "make-it-happen-now" attitude. And isn't that the real purpose of reengineering?

E-mail's Role in Reengineering

Whether e-mail is new to you or whether you already use it, you should begin to see ways this technology can support new or improved business processes. Let's look at a few examples of the power of e-mail for achieving results much more quickly.

Currid & Company Vice President Thomas Howard recalls a very effective use of electronic mail from his days as international business development director at Compaq Computer Corporation in Houston, Texas. In the early days of Compaq's expansion into worldwide markets, 25 subsidiaries around the globe needed to provide manufacturing forecast information to the home office in Houston. These forecasts were instrumental in planning manufacturing run rates and acquiring parts and supplies.

Prior to Compaq's implementation of worldwide e-mail, the forecasting process went something like this:

Each month, the home office developed an electronic form with all the possible types of supplies and part numbers on it. The form changed monthly due to the nature of the rapidly developing PC market. The home office sent the form on diskette via courier to all 25 subsidiaries. The subsidiaries made their forecasts and sent the forms back to Houston. The total elapsed time could easily be two weeks or more. If changes needed to be made, the process took even longer.

Then the company deployed electronic mail. Finally, the whole company was connected and communication became almost instantaneous. The new procedure for developing manufacturing forecasts goes something like this:

The home office attaches the forecast form to an e-mail message and sends it out to all subsidiaries. The remote offices get the forms within minutes, fill them out, and send them back via e-mail. Total elapsed time: just a few days. Compaq eliminated the time wasted by having the electronic forms in transit. Now the subsidiaries have more time to prepare more accurate forecast numbers.

Currid & Company is another firm that is absolutely addicted to e-mail. We can't imagine running our business without it. Since the company's inception in 1991, we have depended on an internal e-mail system as well as external services provided by CompuServe, MCI Mail, and the Internet. Yet we continue to improve the way we use e-mail. Here are just a few examples of how new e-mail technology changed the way we work.

As the head of a dynamic consulting firm, I like to be in touch with my colleagues at least several times daily, even if I'm on the road. In the early days at Currid & Company, I found my way to a phone as often as possible to check in with people at the home office for messages and other important news. The problem was, phone calls are expensive and not always convenient.

I sought a better way to stay in touch, and found it with Radio-Mail—wireless e-mail. Now I carry a lightweight unit that combines a subnotebook PC with a wireless modem. When my colleagues have news or messages to pass along to me, they send an e-mail message via CompuServe or MCI Mail. The messages are automatically forwarded to me on RadioMail, and I can receive my e-mail almost anywhere I travel. I've been known to check my e-mail in taxi cabs, in rental car waiting lines, and even in restaurants. But RadioMail isn't one-way e-mail; I can send messages, too. Now I can keep in constant touch with coworkers, clients, and anyone else that is an e-mail devotee.

And now, the company is getting ready to take another step forward with WordPerfect Office TeleMail (described later in this chapter). Once we get this system up and running, we won't even need a PC and modem to check our e-mail (and calendar) back on the home office network. All we'll need is access to a telephone, which will connect us to our communication server. You can't get much simpler than that!

E-mail Features and Capabilities

We mentioned earlier what some of the basic capabilities of e-mail are, including person-to-person messaging, group messaging (or bulletin boards), document attachment, message sorting and storage (folders), and message printing. These are the barest necessities of e-mail. Most products today, particularly for LAN-based systems, have many more "office organization" features. In our opinion, these organization features—calendaring, task assignments, and so on—are as important as the messaging features to the enlightened, empowered, reengineered organization. Let's take a look at some of those features.

Electronic Calendars and Scheduling

Many e-mail packages can do more than keep track of your conversations; they also keep track of your time with electronic calendars and automatic scheduling features.

You probably manage your own daily calendar. You schedule appointments and keep track of activities. You can view your calendar in various formats—daily, weekly, monthly, or even yearly. That's nifty. However, you'll realize the real power of collaboration through e-mail when you give others in your organization access to your calendar.

You can let others view your appointments (at least those that you haven't marked "private") and see when you are available for meetings and other activities. Taking this a step further, you can choose to give others the right to place appointments on your calendar. Here's how

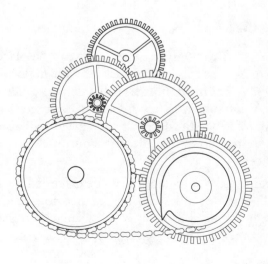

Currid & Company uses the full power of the calendar and scheduling features of our e-mail system:

1. A person who wants to schedule others in the office for a meeting gets into e-mail. He brings up the automatic scheduling feature, tells the system who he wants in the meeting, and gives the computer some parameters such as when the meeting should take place and how long it will last.

2. The e-mail system checks all the attendees' calendars, finds out when everyone is available, and suggests a possible meeting time and date.

3. If this time is acceptable to the person doing the scheduling, he has the system send a meeting notification to everyone. The e-mail system also places a tentative appointment on the attendees' calendars.

4. Each meeting attendee can then accept or reject the tentative appointment.

5. The original scheduler gets notified of who plans to attend his meeting.

This powerful system places the burden of optimizing schedules on the computer, rather than the meeting sponsor. Moreover, it all takes place within minutes instead of the hours that might otherwise be needed to check everyone's hand-written appointment books.

Task Tracking

Appointments aren't the only activities that can be placed on an electronic calendar. You can also keep track of your major milestones and task-due dates. A gentle reminder will tell you when a deadline is approaching. A not-so-gentle reminder (usually a red flag) will tell you when you have missed a due date. Of course, you can also mark tasks as "completed" so the computer doesn't continue to send you nasty reminder notices.

Once again, the task metaphor can be extended to an entire workgroup, so tasks and deadlines can be assigned to a project team. The project manager will be able to easily see what activities are completed, what is yet to come, and who is assigned to what task.

Message Routing

Many e-mail packages are adopting some of the traits of electronic workflow systems. WordPerfect Office 4.0 is one package that has incorporated message routing, which ensures that an e-mail message follows a very specific distribution pattern. For example, a message first goes to Mary, and when she's done with it, John sees the message, and then Bob gets it after John. Each person can add his or her comments as the message moves along. Imagine how this feature can be put to work:

Brian has just taken a business trip and wants to get reimbursed for his expenses. He uses his spreadsheet software to lay out all his costs. Brian attaches the spreadsheet to an e-mail message and sends it along the chain of approval. His project leader, Tamara, is the first one to get the message. She reviews the spreadsheet and approves all expenses. Tamara sends the message on its way to Barbara, the department head. Barbara looks over the spreadsheet and notices that Brian forgot to add mileage to and from the airport. She makes a note on the spreadsheet, and the message moves along its way to Kenneth, the company accountant. He reviews the expenses and gives his approval for reimbursement. Kenneth sends a message back to Brain that he will cut a check for the expenses by the end of the day. This can all take place in a matter of minutes. What's more, no paper documents were involved (other than the reimbursement check).

Under the old fashioned way, Brian would send a stack of papers routing from desk to desk, hoping they don't get lost under someone's piles of other "important stuff."

Remote Access

More and more e-mail products are incorporating some way to check your mail from a remote location. The most popular method is to provide dial-in capabilities, so you can use a PC and modem to log in to your network and view your mail. You have access to the full range of e-mail features that you have when you are directly connected to the network.

WordPerfect Corporation recently announced an innovative new approach to remotely access your WordPerfect Office electronic mailbox. Called Telephone Access Service (TAS), the product lets you check your messages and your calendar via telephone. No modem and no PC are required.

Through TAS, you can send and respond to e-mail messages; accept, decline, or send meeting or appointment requests; listen to and update your calendar; accept, decline, or send tasks; and also listen to and send notes. Almost anything you can do with WordPerfect Office at your desktop, you will be able to do from the phone. This opens up whole new realms of possibilities for remote computing for the keyboard-phobic.

E-mail Gateways

Most e-mail products are like little fiefdoms—they have a proprietary file format that keeps you from easily communicating with other e-mail systems. Gateway products, or translators, have been growing in popularity. Whether you have disparate e-mail systems within your organization or whether you want to communicate with others outside the company, a gateway could be the solution to opening up your electronic world.

At Currid & Company, we use a Message Handling Services (MHS) gateway on our WordPerfect Office server. This MHS gateway communicates with a Novell NetWare Global Messaging (NGM) gateway on our NetWare server. The two gateways, or translators, give us the capability to send and receive mail to and from outside services such as CompuServe, MCI Mail, and the Internet, directly from our local WordPerfect Office desktops. This allows us to exchange mail with people outside the company, but it appears as if they are on our own internal e-mail system. The whole gateway system is inexpensive and quite convenient.

Filtering Agents

As the popularity of e-mail grows, so does the amount of information coming at you electronically. Depending on the number of distribution lists you are on, and the number of correspondents who want to keep in touch with you, you may find yourself buried in e-mail. The solution? Use an electronic agent to screen your mail and categorize it for you. President Clinton does.

To help volunteers sort and forward the electronic mail that has been pouring into the White House since Clinton and Gore went on-line, MIT is developing software that will scan the e-mail and look for specified words, such as "health care" or "NAFTA." By identifying a certain number of words, the software will guess at the letter's gist and decide who should see it and what kind of response to generate. This is artificial intelligence at work.

Most filtering agents aren't quite so sophisticated. Instead, most agents let you identify specific names or words that appear in the "From" or "Subject" fields of your e-mail. You can design rules that tells the e-mail package what to do with mail that meets the specified criteria. For instance, you might direct all mail for a certain project into a specific folder. Or, you might have all mail from your boss be identified as "urgent" and placed at the top of your in-box listing. Conversely, you might choose to toss all mail from someone, saving you from having to read frivolous mail.

Filtering agents are like electronic secretaries who sort the mail for you. The more dependent you become on e-mail, the more useful you will find them.

And Coming Soon...

E-mail technology is advancing rapidly. Soon we will see facsimile services merged with e-mail. You will be able to send and receive faxes (including binary files and other types of messages) directly through your preferred e-mail system.

The Issues of Implementing and Using E-mail

For all our talk about how great e-mail is for universal communication, there are some issues that need to be worked out to make the technology truly effective. Many of the issues involve technical problems that vendors are trying to solve with new products. Some issues, however, are simply cultural.

Achieving Critical Mass

No electronic mail system can be fully effective unless it has achieved critical mass among the users in an organization. That is, everyone has to have access, and everyone has to use it. What would happen if only some of the people in your office had access to a telephone, or if people had telephones but wouldn't use them? You couldn't call everyone, so you would develop procedures outside the system. You might walk down the hall to talk to the guy who has no phone. The same is true for e-mail. Unless everyone has it and uses it, you will have to go outside the system to communicate.

End-user training on the e-mail system is critical to gain acceptance and to get everyone to use it. Remember that technology can be intimidating to some people, and they will avoid using it unless they know how, and understand how they can benefit from it.

It only takes one time for a coworker to miss out on something very important, such as the boss's staff meeting, before he becomes an e-mail believer. Suppose the department secretary sends out an e-mail message saying that the boss has scheduled a meeting for 2:00 Tuesday. Everyone but Bob (who avoids e-mail) reads and acknowledges the message. Tuesday rolls around, and Bob misses the meeting. At 4:00 on Tuesday, the boss asks Bob why he didn't show up for the meeting. Bob says he didn't know about it. The boss says, "go read your e-mail." You can bet that Bob will begin to check his e-mail on a regular basis from that point on.

Electronic Etiquette

There's a protocol for using electronic mail that many people simply don't follow. For example, it's not appropriate to send e-mail to someone far above you on the chain of command, unless you would ordinarily communicate with this person. Another etiquette rule is to keep your messages brief, meaningful, and to the point. Express one idea per message, rather than a whole list of ideas in one message. (This facilitates storing an idea in a folder for later use.)

Every office has its own protocol for what is appropriate use of e-mail. It's a cultural thing. Some offices are very formal, and it shows in the e-mail. Other offices are more casual, so the e-mail messages can be more relaxed. Whatever your organization's style, be sure to observe the unwritten rules of etiquette. Remember, e-mail creates a permanent record of your actions. You don't want to be remembered as the person who sent "flame mail" to the boss (that is, mail with LOTS OF CAPITAL LETTERS for emphasis).

Interoperability

Many companies use several different products for e-mail, particularly for departmental LANs. One company we know uses Lotus Development Corporation's cc:Mail on the Accounting Department's LAN, Wang Office on field locations' minicomputers, and IBM Office Vision on the corporate mainframe. Each e-mail system works great for its own little group of users, but it's nearly impossible to send messages across the various systems. Does that mean that Accounting shouldn't talk to employees in the field? Of course not. It just means that technology has to bridge the gap between e-mail products.

Interoperability is a big problem with e-mail. Soft-Switch Corporation has made a handsome profit over the years by building gateway products that translate e-mail messages from one system to another. While gateways do work to get the basic messages delivered, they can lose a lot in the translation. Attachments such as spreadsheets or documents aren't likely to cross over the e-mail path.

There are communication standards, such as X.400, that help promote interoperability among disparate e-mail systems. And vendors are getting better at making their products cooperate with others on the market. Since there is no clear winner in the e-mail marketing war, we have to look to technology to solve our intercommunication problems.

Distributed Directories

A problem that is closely related to interoperability between e-mail systems is the synchronization of distributed user directories—that is, the names of people who are authorized to use the e-mail systems. In order to use e-mail, you must be identified to that system. The list of all authorized users is called the directory.

If you are a user on more than one e-mail system, you must be identified to them all. This is where synchronization becomes a problem. More than likely, the task of updating each e-mail system directory belongs to more than one person. It's easy to see how the various directories can get out of sync.

For example, Kathy, Julie, and Jerry are all network administrators who oversee e-mail directories on their respective networks. Patrice is a new employee who will need access to all three systems. Kathy and Jerry update their directories with Patrice's account information. Julie is on vacation this week, so Patrice won't get put into that system until next week. In the meantime, Patrice's mail can't cross over to and from Julie's network (and to all the users on it) because Patrice's name isn't recognized there.

Right now, the solution for directory synchronization is largely procedural. Technical challenges abound as well, especially when the e-mail systems are from different vendors.

Network Traffic

The typical network is quite capable of handling the short, "bursty" kind of traffic generated by textual e-mail messages. However, with more and more e-mail products supporting the attachment of all kinds of files—including audio, video, graphics, and images—e-mail traffic is likely to cause network capacity problems. There's a quick but not very attractive solution to this situation, and that is simply not to send attachments with your messages. The alternative is to increase your network bandwidth to accommodate the multimedia files. This is an expensive proposition, but probably quite necessary for other uses beyond e-mail. If your network is getting bogged down by e-mail messages, it's certainly time to upgrade the network.

Conclusion

Although electronic mail isn't yet as pervasive as the telephone, it offers an excellent means for communicating ideas and information. We have seen how it can be used to support communication in business, and how it can shape a new corporate culture. We looked at an example or two of e-mail as a reengineering technology, following the principle of simplifying how a process is done. We discussed some of the features

and capabilities of today's e-mail products, as well as the issues surrounding the implementation and use of e-mail.

In the next chapter, we continue our look at electronic communications, but we go a few steps further with how information is exchanged and transactions are completed. We call the next topic "electronic commerce."

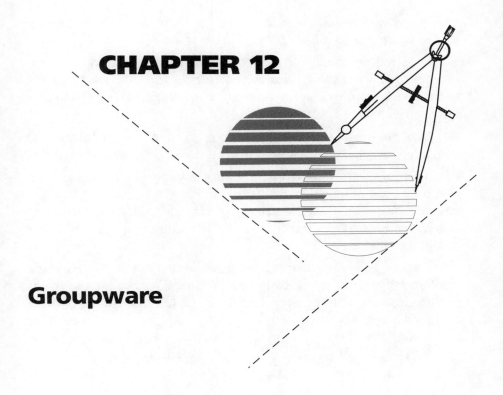

CHAPTER 12

Groupware

Steve, the vice president of finance for a large real estate investment firm, was looking for ways to reduce the company's travel expenses. He asked each of the company's regional managers to participate in a brainstorming session to come up with a few innovative ideas. With all 10 of the managers comfortably seated, Steve said, "OK, let's get started."

Within an hour, the group had come up with more than 50 ideas, and had evaluated and prioritized the most promising suggestions. They all had minutes from the meeting, with action items assigned. Unbelievably, all this was achieved without any bickering or political positioning. In fact, it was achieved without any of them even speaking to each other, or, for that matter, even being in the same city.

Steve and the managers used electronic conferencing to hold their meeting. Using software on the enterprise's network and their own desktop PCs, all of the participants could submit ideas simultaneously and anonymously. The best ideas were built upon, until the group gained consensus on a few potential plans of action.

The results? Plenty of ideas to implement right away or investigate further. Cost savings, for minimizing the time and travel needed to meet. And esprit de corps among the managers, who had solved a serious problem.

By the way, the number-one suggestion for reducing the company's travel expenses was: "Hold more meetings electronically."

If your goal is to reorganize the way people work together, groupware technology may be just the ticket. Groupware can support your mission with shared databases, electronic calendars, messaging systems and other services designed to streamline business tasks that involve groups.

In this chapter, we define the elusive term *groupware* by assigning attributes to the quality of work that it enables. We explore the effects of using groupware technology, and present a few case studies of organizations that have reorganized their work using groupware. We look at a few specific groupware products and categories. Finally, we offer a few "do's and don'ts" for working in a groupware-enabled office.

Groupware? What's That?

The term *groupware* was coined in 1978 by researchers Peter and Trudy Johnson-Lenz, although the idea has been around for more than 30 years. The concept became a widely available product when Lotus Development Corporation introduced its Notes product in 1989. Even so, the concept of groupware suffers from being hard to explain, hard to understand, and worst of all, hard to sell to the boss.

Groupware doesn't refer to any one product or solution. Rather, it refers to a set of technologies that can be applied to improve the productivity of people working together in groups. These technologies include:

≣ **Group scheduling/calendaring.** All members of a workgroup can share their personal calendars with each other; multiple resources can be scheduled at one time.

≋ **Information sharing.** Freeform or structured databases hold information vital to an entire work team.

≋ **Electronic conferencing.** Through a computer network, groups of people can "meet" and exchange information and ideas, with permanent meeting notes being stored on-line.

≋ **Desktop videoconferencing.** Almost like two-way live television, groups of people can "meet" while viewing each other through their desktop computers.

Some industry experts include electronic mail, workflow, and document management in the realm of groupware. We consider those technologies to be more "point-to-point" communication than "many-to-many" communication, so we chose to cover them outside the discussion of groupware. Chapter 9 covers workflow extensively, Chapter 10 is all about document management, and Chapter 11 has information about e-mail.

The Currid & Company test for products that claim to be groupware includes meeting the criteria or having the attributes listed below:

≋ They should let people work in groups while sharing different types of information to get their jobs done.

≋ They should include the rapid and broad movement of information across boundaries.

≋ They should allow people to access, track, share, route and organize information.

≋ They should allow communication among many people simultaneously, not just a "one-to-one" burst of communication.

≋ They should enable real-time collaboration, where participants correspond, view changes as they happen, communicate ideas and decisions immediately and simultaneously review information by project teams.

How Groupware Gets Used

Since the concept of groupware is so broad and so hard to define, we might best approach it by talking about how some companies have implemented it to improve team communication. In some cases, a commercial product was the platform. In others, the companies designed their own systems, piecing together applications based on commercial products and home-grown links.

More and more commercial groupware products are coming to market. We continue to see breakthrough technologies being introduced in the areas of rapid communications and data compression. One hot area to watch is videoconferencing.

Let's take a look at two innovative approaches to workgroup computing.

Vennet: A Comprehensive Communications Network

When three U.S. engineering firms undertook a massive oil refinery expansion project in Venezuela, communication among the partners and with the client became paramount. The companies—M.W. Kellogg, Bechtel, and Foster Wheeler—developed their own communication network, which they dubbed Vennet. The $6 million system combines voice, fax, data, electronic mail, and videoconferencing into a totally integrated system.

The home-grown system was driven by the need for constant communication among all the parties, despite the wide geographical dispersion of the companies in the U.S. and Venezuela. Moreover, the existing communication facilities in that part of Venezuela were poor, at best. Vennet incorporates transmissions via the Intelsat satellite, providing almost instantaneous communication among the Maraven refinery in Punta Cardon, the Kellogg office in Caracas, the headquarters of Kellogg and Bechtel in Houston, and the Foster Wheeler headquarters in New Jersey.

All of this high tech wizardry provides benefits that far outweigh the costs. The companies have been able to cut down on travel costs by holding "virtual meetings." These electronic meetings have also brought more people into the information-sharing and decision-making processes, regardless of where they are. The result has been a dramatic change in the way work is performed and professional relationships are built, particularly among the highly competitive engineering firms.

How might the work have been done without a network such as Vennet? There would be a lot more travel required between the two countries. Documents and other important papers would probably have been shuttled via couriers. Meeting attendance would have been limited to those with critical input, with little or no opportunity "on the fly" comment. And, realistically, there would probably have been a few political battles among the contributing companies.

With Vennet, design documents and other important documentation can be distributed and exchanged quite easily. Ongoing discussions can take place via electronic mail. Best of all, any participant can call an impromptu meeting when necessary, quickly pulling together technical and management personnel to address the issues of the day.

Compaq's Worldwide Data Repository

Compaq Computer Corporation has turned its Lotus Notes groupware application into a set of vital tools in its worldwide business operations. Compaq has used Notes to host several strategic databases, including its wealth of technical support information, reseller and product availability information, and sales and marketing information.

Compaq's original goal for groupware was to make business communication within the company more effective. The company learned, however, that communication could also extend to product resellers, authorized systems engineers, and customers.

For example, Compaq has a technical information system, called Techpaq, hosted on Notes. Techpaq is made of 14 Notes databases. Information held in the databases is easily accessible to resellers, and includes up-to-date technical information and software fixes. Distributing software this way could mean the end of shipping disks via courier. Instead, software can be downloaded from a Notes database anywhere in the world. The databases also provide software solutions and tools, as well as technical information in reference and bulletin format with new products highlighted.

David Clarke, marketing director at Compaq, says the business benefits are "immense." The company has had a huge reduction in telephone calls and faxes from resellers since it implemented the groupware application. Says Clarke, "Our resellers find it much easier to get information from their own computers, making their service faster and therefore better. A reseller can solve a problem there and then, when previously it might have taken days to get the information. It's the end, we hope, of the 'We'll get back to you' syndrome. And maybe the days of the six-inch-thick technical manuals are numbered too."

The Notes applications are especially useful in places like Australia, where real-time communication with Compaq's headquarters is difficult because of the time difference. Mike Wells, systems engineer manager in Compaq's Sydney office, laments the short time window available for telephone calls to folks in Compaq's home office in Houston. The Notes databases have virtually eliminated the problem.

Says Wells, "As it stands, we have about a two-hour overlap in the business day between Houston and Sydney. Using Lotus Notes has transformed our business contact with the head office from a telephone system where we had a tiny window of opportunity to communicate, to a full day window. When we have problems to escalate back to Houston for resolution, we can log them at the end of our business day, which is just the beginning of theirs. When we come back in the morning, quite often we find that the problems have been assessed and resolved overnight, which translates to an improvement in productivity for us, and a tremendous benefit for our clients."

Types of Groupware

Practically every vendor with a product that runs on a network bills his product as "groupware." However, our definitions narrow the products and technologies in the groupware category. There are a few examples worth mentioning here.

Shared Information Bases

Some groupware products are collections of databases that can be sliced and diced many different ways to yield meaningful information. Lotus Notes is the most popular product in this category. It is also the most venerable product, having defined the genre more than five years ago.

Notes itself is not an application. Rather, it is an application development environment and tool. Notes uses a client/server configuration; part of the application resides on a central server or servers, and part resides on the users' workstations. Data can be dispersed among the servers and workstations.

Most Notes applications are freeform databases. That is, the information is unstructured, unlike a traditional database where specific data types and lengths are predefined. Notes is ideal for variable length text, as well as alternate data types such as audio and video.

Undoubtedly, the strongest feature of Lotus Notes is its data replication feature, which assures that anyone using a Notes database has the most up-to-date data possible. Replication is the facility that sends data out over a communication network. It doesn't matter where in the network the data was updated—on a server or on an individual's workstation—Notes updates anyone and everyone who has access to the data. Thus, information version control is not an issue, even for applications like Compaq's Techpaq, where users are spread all over the globe.

Notes databases are not like traditional transaction processing applications, which automate a discrete step-by-step process. Rather, the databases revolve around people working together. The applications are "business-process oriented." By our definition, a business process has nothing inherently to do with computers. It is what you have to do to run the business. Customer service is a business process. Order fulfillment is a business process. Entering orders into a computer system isn't. Notes serves the former type of application well, while a relational database serves the latter.

Three prime areas for Notes applications are customer service, product development, and sales and marketing. The type of information that is shared to meet these business processes is usually freeform and is sometimes unpredictable.

Let's use product development as an example. The cross-functional team involved in developing a new product—such as a pair of athletic shoes—includes people from research, marketing, engineering, and so on. Each team member needs different information to make decisions. However, the information is all related in some way: it is all about the new product. The research folks may want to know about new space-age materials for developing the soles of the shoe. The engineering people want access to design information. The marketers are interested in customer opinions about new styles. The accountants want to know how much all of this is costing. No traditional database can keep track of this type of information. A Notes database, however, is able to keep the unstructured data as well as a running dialogue of everyone's comments about the new product as it takes shape.

Meetingware

The example at the opening of this chapter demonstrates a new category of groupware: electronic conferencing, or "meetingware." This type of technology attempts to overhaul that paragon of corporate time-wasting, the business meeting. Meetingware does more than simply automate the meeting process; it eliminates the aspects of a meeting that are inherently unproductive.

In a traditional meeting, all the participants need to be in the same room. Only one person can (or should) talk at a time. Participants must not speak out of turn. Good ideas may be forgotten while someone is waiting his turn to speak. Politics play a part in who speaks and for how long. Someone must record minutes, and transcribe and distribute them at the end of the meeting. Emotions and politics may play a role in the outcome of the meeting. In the end, not everyone may agree on the ideas discussed and the action items assigned.

Sounds pretty unproductive, doesn't it? It usually is. Meetingware changes the ground rules.

First of all, people don't need to be in the same location at all, as long as their network permits access into the electronic meeting. Everyone may "speak" at once, with the computer keeping track of the volley of ideas. Participants can be anonymous, which eliminates political power plays that so often disrupt the progress of a meeting. The computer also filters out emotions and, of course, body language. Finally, the computer keeps track of everything that's discussed, records them as minutes of the meeting, and distributes them to all participants.

Meetingware is most effective for brainstorming sessions, where you want the group to generate as many ideas as possible without stopping to discuss each idea as it is proposed. Meetingware lets people build on other ideas as they are proposed.

Obviously, electronic meetings don't fill every need. Sometimes you *want* politics, emotions, and body language as part of the meeting. For instance, an interview of a prospective employee wouldn't work very well via computer.

Videoconferencing

If meetingware isn't for you, but you still want to "meet" electronically, think about desktop videoconferencing. It's like having a two-way television right at your PC. With a bit of special equipment, you can call other people on your network and meet as if you were face to face even though you might be a world apart.

Until recently, desktop videoconferencing was expensive and jerky. The technology only permitted the exchange of about 15 frames of video per second, which made for a distracting picture. Since mid-1993, though, the technology for videoconferencing has been improving rapidly and getting cheaper by the day.

Intel Corporation is leading the charge. In January 1994, Intel announced capabilities for "personal conferencing," which initially addresses the need for one-on-one communication. Later, the capability will expand to allow personal conferences among groups of people.

Intel's view of desktop videoconferencing includes all the best of personal computing. You can work on documents, spreadsheets, presentations and other information stored in your PC—simultaneously viewing, editing and annotating the information while you discuss it. You can also share live and recorded video on your PC screens, either seeing each other simultaneously or sharing information that is not stored in your PCs. What's more, Intel is projecting prices in the $500 range for each personal conferencing-equipped PC.

Group Scheduling

Electronic calendars and scheduling systems are another class of groupware. These types of products help people use each other as resources on a project by keeping track of tasks and scheduling each other as needed. Group calendars may or may not be a part of an electronic mail system. For instance, WordPerfect Office incorporates scheduling into its overall e-mail package. It's easy to see, at a glance, how your co-workers have scheduled their time and projects.

The Effects of Using Groupware

Most organizations that have implemented groupware have done so to get people to work together more efficiently and/or at a lower cost. But there's more to groupware than simply the products; it is also an approach to computing. With groupware, people tend to do things differently. Computing goes beyond the typical process of "speeding up the mess." Perhaps more than any of the other technologies we present in this book, groupware supports the seven principles of reengineering.

There are residual effects of implementing groupware technology. For one thing, "work" tends to be more collaborative in nature, rather than a product of individuals. As people contribute their part, the end result becomes a team effort. Moreover, using groupware tends to reduce redundancy—that is, multiple people doing the same work. With a central "clearing house" for information, workers can see what has been done already and make use of the results.

This "technology-enabled teamwork" cuts across organizational boundaries. Instead of separate departments working on sequential portions of a project, we now find process teams collaborating on the work.

Groupware has been known to inspire "virtual companies," whereby the resources for a project come together from different companies to work as a team. The Venezuelan engineering project is a good example. Workers from three different engineering firms become a virtual single company, especially in the eyes of the client.

Another far-reaching effect of groupware is its ability to democratize the business, giving people equal access to information and other people as resources. It eliminates the knowledge "haves" and "have-nots."

Currid's Do's and Don'ts for Groupware

Introducing a groupware application into your work environment can introduce quite a few changes, many of them "cultural." We provide a few tips for you so you can make the most of your reengineered processes and the supporting groupware applications:

- ≋ DO change the business process before you apply the new groupware technology. Living with groupware is a way of life, an approach to work.
- ≋ DO consider new ways to evaluate performance once the new group approach is implemented. If you want people to work in teams, you should evaluate their contributions to the team.

Unfortunately, most employee evaluation programs today encourage individual performance, not team performance.

≡ DO invest in your technical infrastructure. A network that supports typical bursty e-mail traffic may not have enough bandwidth to support groupware's exchange of vast amounts of information—especially when you transmit audio, video, images, and other non-text data types.

≡ DO train the users of your groupware application. A new application does little or no good if people don't know how to use it.

≡ DON'T let hierarchies and bureaucracies get in the way of your groupware implementation. The purpose is to effectively share information, not slow it down.

≡ DON'T assume that everyone *wants* to work as part of a team. You may have to conduct team training to get people in the right frame of mind.

≡ DON'T ignore the "people issues" of adapting to groupware and new work habits. Any type of change is unsettling to people, and you may have to counsel them to help them through the process.

≡ DON'T forget to tell everyone what's going on. No one likes to be left in the dark, especially about their jobs and careers. Communicate changes quickly and early on.

Conclusion

Groupware is not just a buzzword, it's a way of life. When used effectively, groupware can transform the way people interact and share information. We've seen how a few companies changed their processes for people working together, using the latest in workgroup technology.

In the next chapter, we talk about electronic commerce, and how companies can do business by exchanging data directly from one computer to another.

CHAPTER 13

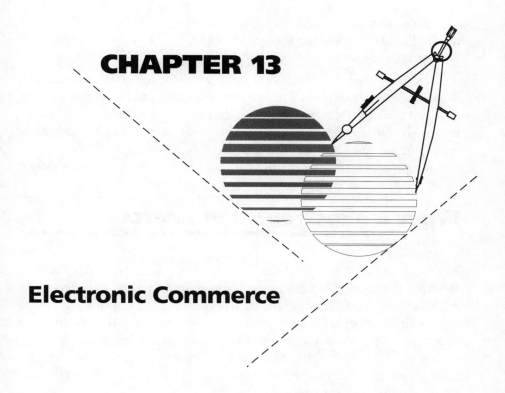

Electronic Commerce

On my way to work this morning, I stopped at my local grocery store and did my day's banking. My bank has an automated teller machine in the store's lobby. I inserted my colorful ATM card, punched in my supersecret code, and was greeted with a friendly and personal message: "Good morning Cheryl C. Currid. Please select your transaction."

First I checked the balance in my checking account. It looked a little low, so I transferred a few dollars from savings into checking. Then, for good measure, I withdrew a few dollars for spending cash and signed off.

Then I went into the grocery store, picked up a few items and headed for the checkout counter. The clerk scanned all my groceries and asked for $12.39. I whipped out my ATM card again and "charged" my groceries directly to my checking account—no check writing was necessary, and no cash changed hands. Within minutes, I was out the door and on my way to work again.

Does this scenario sound far-fetched to you? Probably not. Every day, millions of people use these same techniques to conduct business. Welcome to the world of electronic commerce.

In this chapter, we look at commerce in the age of the computer. We see several examples of how companies and public agencies have changed their business processes—and in some cases, the business they are in—by letting computers do the dirty work of exchanging and processing data. We also discuss the benefits and issues of electronic commerce, and introduce the notion of the information superhighway.

What Is Electronic Commerce?

My trusty old dictionary defines commerce as "trade on a large scale." We use the adjective "electronic" to indicate that computers are enabling trade by facilitating the exchange and use of business data. So, our definition of *electronic commerce* amounts to the electronic exchange of structured business data. Some examples might be the electronic filing of your income tax return, computerized stock trading, on-line shopping via a service such as CompuServe, and direct on-line invoicing for materials received.

The services—both personal and business-oriented—that can and do support electronic commerce are almost limitless. Book your airlines reservations. Pay your bills. Order supplies. Check inventory levels at your company's retail outlets. The list is growing longer every day.

Electronic commerce is a concept that embodies all seven of the guiding principles for reengineering that we discussed in Chapter 2, particularly the rule that says, "Capture data only one time—when it is first created." In many instances, electronic commerce replaces an old process in which people handle and hand off the data many times, often by reentering data from hand-written or printed reports.

Take, for example, the process of filing your federal income tax forms. In just the last few years, the government has agreed to accept returns filed electronically. In 1993, millions of citizens filed their tax forms that way. In the words of the Internal Revenue Service, electronic filing is "safer, faster, and more accurate." Because the information is transmitted directly from computer to computer, there is less chance for errors. As an added benefit, filers can get their returns much faster—in two weeks by mail, or even sooner through direct deposit into a bank account.

Before the IRS adopted electronic filing, the filing process went something like this:

1. You gather together all of your information, such as income and interest statements, proof of charitable contributions, and whatever other documentation necessary.

2. You gather together all of the official government forms, such as the 1040A and the various attachments.

3. You prepare a draft of your taxes on a "scratch" form and use a calculator to add up your income and your expenses, and then calculate your taxable income.

4. You look on a printed IRS schedule to find out how much you owe Uncle Sam. (Why does it seem like he never owes you?)

5. You write the amount you owe onto your scratch worksheet.

6. You verify your deductions and calculations to make sure you didn't overlook anything, then repeat steps 3 through 5.

7. You hand copy the final information onto the official government form 1040, and hope you don't transpose any numbers.

8. You sign the form.

9. You write a check for the amount you owe.

10. You take all the forms and supporting documentation to a copying machine and make a copy for your own records.

11. You package up all the forms, supporting documentation and your check into the official government envelope.

12. You place a stamp on the envelope and drop it in the mailbox.

13. You pray you don't get audited.

Electronic filing has made the process quite a bit easier, although the result is the same—you still have to pay Uncle Sam. The new filing method goes something like this:

1. You enter your household income information into a convenient home software package like MacInTax or TurboTax (by ChipSoft).

2. The program calculates your refund due or amount owed.

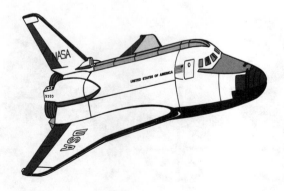

3. You take your final information to an authorized consolidator or tax preparer, who transmits the information to the IRS for a fee. (As of this writing, only authorized personnel may transmit the electronic information. There may soon come a day when ordinary mortals can do it themselves at home.)

4. The IRS computer accepts the information and automatically verifies the information. Your tax preparer receives notice that your file was accepted by the IRS.

5. Assuming there are no glaring omissions or exceptions on your report, the IRS either bills you for taxes due, or sends a refund directly to your bank account.

6. If you owe Uncle Sam a check, you receive notice through the mail.

7. You write the check and drop it in the mail.

Another method for electronic filing is use of the form 1040PC, which is a condensed paper format printed from one of several commercially available PC software packages certified by the IRS. The software computes tax due and prints only those lines from the 1040 and supporting schedules that contain taxpayer data. The IRS said 1040PCs are filed by taxpayers and processed by the IRS faster and with fewer errors than traditional forms. The form also provides for direct deposit of a refund to a taxpayer's bank account.

The IRS has recently implemented another form of "speed filing," called TeleFile. Taxpayers call a toll-free number and enter tax return information through a Touch-Tone telephone during a computerized "interview." The IRS computes the tax and any refund or tax due while the filer is on the phone.

In 1992, taxpayers using TeleFile still had to mail in a special form containing income verification as well as the taxpayer's signature. The IRS experimented with an expanded TeleFile program in 1993, allowing taxpayers to send in a "voice signature" containing the taxpayer's name and social security number via the Touch-Tone phone.

Electronic filing is certainly a popular option with the U.S. public. Table 5 shows the growth in electronic tax filing in recent years.

TABLE 5   IRS On-line: Returns through the First Week in February

Format	1992	1993	% change
1040PC format	80,000	200,000	150.0
Electronic filing	4,205,000	4,814,000	14.5
TeleFile	72,000	75,000	4.2

Source: Internal Revenue Service

The Benefits of Electronic Commerce

There are many benefits to doing business electronically: reduced costs, faster processing of data, better customer service, increased data accuracy of data, expanded services, and more. Astute businesses and government agencies are looking for and finding creative ways to apply computer technology to eliminate time-consuming and wasteful paper-based transactions. Let's look at some innovative solutions to common business problems and the benefits that have been realized as a result of electronic commerce.

Reduced Paperwork and Administrative Costs

We have defined electronic commerce as the electronic exchange of structured business data between computers. It stands to reason that there will be less paperwork, and therefore lower administrative costs, if people don't have to intervene to get information from one place to another. Administrative costs for salaries, facilities, mailings, forms creation and storage, and even waste and abuse can be reduced or eliminated.

The State of Maryland recently implemented a new benefits transfer system that permits all residents eligible for welfare and food stamps to get their benefits electronically. The recipients of these benefits draw their allotments from 1,800 automated teller machines and 3,000 point-of-sale terminals at grocery stores across the state. This system, which nearly eliminates the waste, fraud and abuse involved in mailing checks and food coupons to recipients, is expected to save the state more than $1.2 million per year.

Maryland's traditional paper-based system for processing welfare and food-stamp claims cost the state $5.10 per client each month. The new electronic system cuts that figure to $4.35 per client.

Electronic commerce can also help hold the line on salary expense by letting companies serve more customers without adding new employees. The county of Tulare, California has a chronically high unemployment rate of around 18.5 percent, with about 30 percent of its residents receiving welfare. The county has set up a computerized welfare claims system that is able to handle a growing number of cases without the need for additional service representatives.

At the front end of the claims system are several dozen multimedia PCs that explain the county's welfare services in any of six languages. Citizens use the touch-screen PCs to answer questions to determine if they are eligible for public assistance. The PCs are linked to an IBM mainframe that applies a set of business rules to determine eligibility. The system ultimately produces an eight-page application and a list of the documents needed to verify eligibility.

More Accurate Data

One of our guiding principles of reengineering is to enter data only one time, and at the source. If the data needs to be moved around and used by many people or computers, the data should be transferred electronically and not printed out and reentered manually. Each step of rekeying or rewriting the data is an opportunity to introduce errors and inaccuracies, particularly if handwriting is involved.

In our Tulare County example, the old method would have residents manually filling out complicated and lengthy forms. A clerk would enter the data into a computer system, and a third person would then check to be sure that the data were correct and within bounds. That meant the data were handled (and interpreted) at least three times. The new system captures the data as the residents type them into the computer and immediately applies a set of checks and controls to the data. Information that is outside the bounds of acceptable ranges can be rejected on the spot.

In a test of 200 cases processed the old way and 200 processed by the new system, the error rate for the manual system was 38 percent, while the computerized system made no errors. The system is expected to save the county $20 million a year.

Better Customer Service

Many companies and organizations are reengineering processes to provide better customer service. We can define "better customer service" many ways: getting the product or service into the customer's hands more quickly; allowing the customer to use your service at times that are convenient to him, not to you; reducing the bureaucratic demands on the customer; and so forth.

Electronic commerce supports many examples of improved service. The Pennsylvania Bureau of Motor Vehicles is planning to deploy teller machines throughout the state to simplify the process of vehicle registration. Under the state's current system, all residents have to register their vehicles at a central office in Harrisburg, the state capital, or send the registration via mail or messenger. Last-minute filers must register in person in Harrisburg, where they face long lines.

The regional ATM machines hold great appeal for people in out-lying areas who want to shorten the registration process to minutes instead of days or weeks. State residents can conduct their business whenever it is convenient for them—even at 3:00 a.m.! In addition to providing better service to the customer, the Bureau of Motor Vehicles would reduce its workload by eliminating a significant amount of paperwork.

Additional Services and Incremental Business

Conducting business electronically frees up resources that can begin to focus on expanding services and products to a wider range of customers. Such is the case at Boston College, which has implemented the ultimate network of customer services through electronic commerce facilities.

The college's user information system (UIS) is a campus-wide network that enables 15,000 students, 8,500 faculty members and thousands of staff members to use ATM cards to register for courses, pay dining hall tabs, check out library materials, and obtain many other common services. Kiosks around campus provide access to the network. Students can also use terminals and PCs to access all applications via host-based student accounts.

The school's registrar says that UIS has eliminated the long lines of students that would queue up to register for classes. Now they can register through whatever on-line method is most convenient for them.

Bernard Gleason Jr., the school's executive director of information technology, credits the success of UIS to groundwork carefully laid some 15 years ago. Boston College adopted some very basic yet critical computing concepts. Most important was the notion that all of the college's applications should be part of one system and that the system should be accessible through a consistent graphical user interface. The school also strictly adhered to a consistent format for user names and identification codes.

Boston College continues to make additional electronic services available through UIS, such as the production of student catalogs. As these new services come on line, the college enjoys a few side benefits: reduced labor costs, reduced paperwork and reduced bureaucracy.

New technology continues to lead the charge for companies that want to provide expanded electronic services. Dayton, Ohio-based NCR Corporation (now a division of AT&T) is developing new ATM technology that will soon accommodate a wide range of services. The new ATMs are equipped with two-way audio and video capabilities designed to allow customers at remote terminals to videoconference with service providers. A customer may access his bank accounts through the ATM. If he wants to know about his mortgage loan, he can videoconference with a bank employee, who can immediately provide the information the customer wants.

This technology could enable the bank to offer and sell services that previously could only be offered through a branch bank. But as we all know, ATMs are so much more convenient for the customer.

Electronic Data Interchange

There is a highly specialized form of electronic commerce, called Electronic Data Interchange (EDI), that has actually been around for decades. Digital Equipment Corporation provides the following definition for EDI: "the automated, computer-to-computer, application-to-application exchange of structured business data between a company and its suppliers, customers, banks, and other trading partners." The data are structured according to a set of agreed-upon standards and include common business transactions such as purchase orders, invoices, and remittance advice.

EDI is commonly found within specific industries such as health care, petrochemical, retail and grocery, and automobile manufacturing. Each industry develops its own standard forms for exchanging data. That is, the businesses within each industry agree on data formats, naming conventions, product codes, and so on. The familiar universal product code (UPC), for example, is a data interchange standard in the retail and grocery industry. International standards bodies also have helped define the specifications for information exchange for various industries.

As early as 1960, companies began using EDI as a way to gain competitive advantage. Those forward-thinking companies saw the benefits inherent in directly exchanging product orders, invoices, inventory levels, and pricing information electronically. However, EDI did not enjoy widespread use because of the proprietary nature of the early information exchanges. Companies within the same industry could not agree on the structure and content of the data to be exchanged.

Fortunately, the proprietary nature of EDI is going by the wayside today as more and more industries adopt standards designed to facilitate data exchange among the many players. Suppliers, customers, manufacturers, and distributors can all benefit from timely access to each other's information. Earlier, we mentioned Wal-Mart using its suppliers to manage inventory levels. This was done primarily through EDI technology and practices.

EDI's Role in Reengineering

Although many industries enjoy the benefits of EDI, perhaps the health care industry has the potential to save the most time and most money.

This technology is sure to be at the heart of the Clinton Administration's push to revamp the health care system and provide universal care for all U.S. citizens. Take, for example, the old way of processing a health insurance claim, compared to the electronic way. The typical flow of information without EDI might be something like this:

1. You visit your doctor.
2. The doctor performs the service and makes a note on your medical chart about the diagnosis. She also informs her office assistant what procedure code to bill you for. The doctor may have her own coding system, or may adhere to whatever standards exist.
3. The office assistant enters the procedure code into the office computer system and prints a copy of the bill for you.
4. You pay the bill.
5. You take your copy of the doctor's bill, attach it to an insurance form and mail it to your insurance company.
6. The insurance company logs in the receipt of your claim, and enters the diagnosis and treatment information into a database.
7. The insurance company determines your eligibility and calculates the amount of reimbursement for your doctor visit.
8. If the service is to be reimbursed, the insurance company cuts a check.
9. The check is mailed to you. You endorse it and deposit it into your banking account.

This process could be reengineered with EDI as a supporting technology. The new process flow might be like this:

1. You visit your doctor's office.
2. The doctor performs the service, makes the diagnosis and fills out a standard on-line form. Your treatment has an industry standard code associated with it.
3. At the end of the day, the office assistant transmits all patient treatment records for that day to a health management agency.
4. At the management agency, all patient claims are sorted and cataloged, and benefits are determined.

5. If the service is to be compensated, an electronic funds transfer automatically compensates the doctor's account.

The key to making this last example work is that the service provider (doctor) and the insurance company have agreed to use industry standard codes, terms, and formats to directly exchange information. Moreover, they have agreed on a computer system that runs compatible software on each end, so no rekeying and no translation of data is necessary. The end result of automating this claims process is vastly improved health care services and quite literally billions of dollars of savings throughout the industry.

The potential cost savings are so attractive that Blue Cross Blue Shield of Maryland recently entered into a ten-year contract with Electronic Data Systems Corporation (EDS) for EDI services. Under the contract, EDS will assume the management of Maryland Blue's LifeCard division, putting the manual claims processing operation on-line via an EDI system. Maryland Blue's senior vice president, Thomas Higgins, anticipates that the move will allow the insurance carrier to vastly increase its capacity beyond the current 5.8 million annual claims. Moreover, the company expects to save an average of $5 per claim in administrative and processing costs.

While the dollar figures are attractive, Higgins says the most exciting aspect of the deal is that it lays the groundwork for a planned private-sector, "all-player" network, linking health care providers, payers and patients all across the state.

The Information Superhighway

In the future, we will hear even more about the pending implemen-
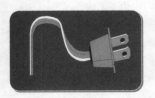
tation of the information superhighway as the means of transport for electronic commerce. The superhighway—portions of which are under construction, under design, or still under consideration—will be a two-way street for data coming into or going out of our homes and offices.

Just who will provide the transport services is a hotly debated issue. Telephone companies, both local and long distance, feel they are the best suited to deliver the services. Cable TV companies argue that they already have "the wire" into the home and should be the service providers. Companies like MCI, Sprint, AT&T, Time Warner Cable, TCI, and others are in the midst of the fray. Since the infrastructure of the information superhighway is projected to cost billions of dollars, it's likely that no one company will ultimately be the sole service provider. More than likely, a consortium of vendors will emerge to deliver us into the age of total electronic commerce.

What can we expect from the information superhighway? If we believe all the claims the potential participants are making, we can expect everything from interactive entertainment to retail shopping through an electronic catalog. We'll have on-line access to every public research library in the country, desktop videoconference capabilities, and a thousand other services, many of which haven't been thought of yet.

The superhighway has a few hurdles to overcome, not the least of which is cost. Just who will provide the services and how much government regulations needed has not yet been decided. Oddly enough, technology is not an issue here, because we already have the technology to deliver the goods and services.

The Issues of Electronic Commerce

So far, we have seen some examples and looked at the benefits of implementing electronic commerce. Now, let's look at the issues that are the potholes in the road.

Standards

There are still many industries that have not adopted or agreed upon a set of standards for identifying data and selecting software. International standards bodies have developed specifications to simplify implementation. The more promising specifications include the Electronic Data Interchange for Administration, Commerce, and Transport (EDIFACT), and ANSI X.12. Even the United Nations is getting behind the standards push. The UN Conference on Trade and Development is promoting the EDIFACT standard across the globe to expedite international trade transactions.

Privacy and Security

Privacy and security are two main concerns for companies that are looking to share business data electronically. Privacy is an especially large concern for the health care industry, where revealing medical records can invite lawsuits and government fines. The current solution is to carefully implement controls and standards that limit who can access the system and what information can be exchanged. One of the key elements of EDI is that it uses standard formats to grant outsiders and business partners restricted access to information that is useful for conducting business, rather than unrestricted access to a company's entire database.

Government Regulations

Many industries, as well as government agencies, operate under strict government regulations and guidelines that make it difficult to abandon paper processes. The Food and Drug Administration wants to accept electronic filings from the drug industry, but it must first rewrite 132 regulations that require handwritten signatures.

In some cases, government regulations may need to be developed or expanded to cover electronic commerce. In the case of EDI where there is no printed invoice, what happens when a dispute occurs between a vendor and a customer? There are no paper records to admit into court, only electronic records. In the early days, U.S. courts didn't trust electronic records, fearing they could be altered too easily. New regulations were required that dictated the preservation of electronic records and the legal status of their contents.

As we begin to look at processes that are ripe for reengineering, we will undoubtedly encounter "sacred cow" processes that appear to be written in stone. We advise our clients to "show us the law" that says the process *has* to be done in a specific way. If there is no law on the books, then you are free to redesign the process to suit your needs. If there actually *is* a law, but it makes no sense for today's business climate, then you have to set about changing or eliminating the law. Government regulations that restrict legitimate commerce have no place in today's economy.

Coordination of Services

In addition to agreeing on standards, companies that want to exchange data electronically with other companies in the industry must coordinate their services and understand who is doing what. In paper-based systems, it's easy to forget or ignore what recipients do with the paperwork we send them—we don't care what goes on in the other guy's shop. With electronic commerce systems, we need to know much more about the full life of the data—where it comes from, where it goes, and how it relates to the services provided.

Conclusion

Electronic commerce is surely the wave of the future. Soon we all may carry ATM cards instead of cash, and the cards will be good at millions of point-of-sale terminals for all types of products and services. The health-care industry may issue each one of us our own personal health card, which can carry information about our past medical histories, our insurance coverage, and critical medical information such as allergies. The information superhighway will have an off-ramp into your living room, and you'll be able to do everything from paying the bills to ordering a pizza from your favorite easy chair. Yes, welcome to the age of electronic commerce.

In this chapter, we looked at a few innovative new ways to conduct business, largely by letting computers be the front end to a complete transaction. We investigated the benefits and issues of electronic commerce, and got a hint of the future with the information superhighway.

In the next chapter, we take a look at mobile and remote computing.

CHAPTER 14

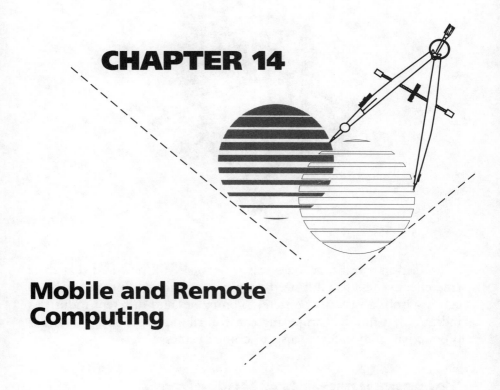

Mobile and Remote Computing

Several communications and computing technologies make up the category of mobile and remote computing. All of them foster a work environment that lets people conduct business away from their desk, whether they are at home or on the road.

The technologies that support mobile computing are quite well developed. The ability to hook up a personal computer to a modem and a standard phone line and dial into a host computer has existed for many years. The technology works very well, and it's very stable.

It turns out that the difficult side of mobile computing has more to do with organizational politics than technology. Many companies still struggle with the issues of policy and procedures that relate to computing away from the organization. In this chapter, we discuss the technologies as well as some of the organizational issues surrounding mobile and remote computing.

Keep in mind that these work styles are still new and that their true effectiveness has not been proven conclusively. But early reports coming from a variety of different companies and different industries indicate that mobile computing can contribute to a boom in worker productivity and in lower costs of doing business.

Telecommuting's Promise

Imagine that most workers in the United States spend between 30 and 90 minutes commuting to and from their offices each day. A trip out of town to a home office or a branch office may take the better part of a

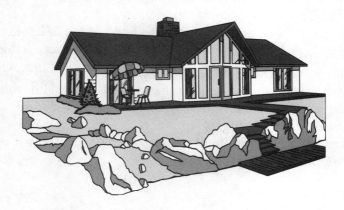

business day just in transportation time. Compare that to the 30 seconds it takes to make a modem connection and log into the company network.

Telecommuters turn out to be, for the most part, salaried or part-time employees who work from their homes or some other site using computers and telecommunications equipment. On average, according to a 1993 survey conducted by the research firm Link Resources, 6.1 percent of the American work force—7.6 million people—already works from home at least one day a week. In all likelihood, that number will double by the end of the 1990's.

According to a government staff director for the National Tele-commuting and Telework Association in Washington, D.C., "Telecommuting is on the correct side of virtually every issue facing society today, whether the issue is concerning family or society, or environment, or business and productivity."

A Florida study indicated that, depending on the job being done, telecommuting improved worker productivity by somewhere between 15 and 25 percent. It also allows companies to reduce rent, utilities, and parking costs. It increases worker morale, frequently increases job satis-faction, contributes to lower turnover rate, reduced absenteeism and tardiness, and alters the equation for disaster recovery. There are other tangible benefits, too, including reduced energy consumption and lower demand on over-taxed transportation systems.

The study also asked telecommuters why working outside the office worked for them. They said they could concentrate better, they were independent and self-starters, and they were motivated by their work.

What Drives Telecommuting?

For some companies, telecommuting is an absolute necessity. In the Northridge earthquake of 1994 roads were damaged so badly that initial estimates said it would take from two to four years to rebuild. The remaining roads in and around Los Angeles were jammed with people trying to commute to work, some of whom took up to four hours each way to get to and from their offices.

One organization estimated it would take less than two weeks to build the information highway so companies could begin implementing telecommuting programs. Compare that with CalTrans' estimate of two to four years to rebuild the concrete highway.

The Clean Air Act of 1990 is also driving the need to look at telecommuting. In 11 states with highly polluted air, companies with more than 100 employees are required to reduce automobile commuting by 25 percent. There is only so much you can do with car pools. Many companies are trying out telecommuting, and have found that the results have allayed managers' fears.

In Orlando, Florida, 160,000 cars a day clog the I-4 corridor, designed to accommodate a little over 100,000. Transportation planners realized that 65 percent of the growth in vehicle traffic would be along the same road. Faced with clean air laws, Orlando employers are looking at telecommuting and telework programs.

Initial reviews are very positive. Employees say their productivity is higher at home than at the office, because they are free from distractions such as telephone calls or casual gossip. In some cases, employees

were so happy with the telecommuting work that they were unwilling to show up at the office every day.

The Downside of Telecommuting

There are, nonetheless, problems with telecommuting. Sometimes employees feel disenfranchised from their coworkers because they don't get to see them very often. Managers feel a loss of control. Workers might not have an effective environment in their own home to act as a workplace. Working mothers often find that they still have to send their toddlers to day care because their children are an unprofessional distraction.

There are other issues as well. How does company insurance affect the teleworker? If someone falls down the stairs at home while getting coffee from the kitchen, who's insurance pays for the fall? What about additional phone lines? A business line usually costs between $40 and $50 a month, while a household line costs about $20 a month. How should the company negotiate these additional lines with the telephone company? (As it happens, we found that many phone companies—among them the phone companies operated by USWest, BellSouth and Nynex—were so delighted to get the revenue from extra lines that they were more than willing to install the lines at the lower non-commercial rates.)

Key Factors for Telecommuting Success

Success comes to those who plan their telecommuting projects well. They get through the issues and management woes and telephone lines and insurance policies and get to the work at hand by assigning people result-based projects that can be done from home. This usually involves the installation of a computer, a modem, fax capability, and an extra telephone line. The worker should have access either through electronic mail or the telephone to any information he or she needs to do the job.

It's important to be sure that the workers take some sense of comradeship with the office-bound staff. Telecommuters should come to the office one or two days a week for meetings or activities with their co-workers.

Technologies for Telecommuting

There are many technologies that allow people to telecommute. Three that we will discuss are remote access, remote nodes, and access through third parties.

Remote access technology lets people dial in from a remote location and take control of a personal computer that could be connected to a LAN or a series of other mini and mainframe computers. Products in this category include Symantec's pcAnywhere, Avalon Technology's Remotely Possible, or Microcom's Carbon Copy. All of them let a user dial in over a modem and take control of a workstation.

Another approach is remote node software, such as DCA's RLN Products. This software turns a dial-in computer into a node on the LAN, giving access to all the information stored on the network. This software is sometimes better than remote access products because it creates a direct link to the LAN. For some applications, however, especially those that pass large numbers of executable files, the users will find this software to be slow.

Access through third-party vehicles allows users to dial in to an e-mail system or a groupware system, or even a public data access tool such as CompuServe. If you only need to exchange a few e-mail messages and a couple of files, these systems might be a little easier to set up. Also, if the remote worker is dialing in from a long distance away, these systems could save money on telephone charges.

Third-party systems are also helpful when the remote worker is not a company employee and there are some security considerations. Because they are somewhat limited in scope and don't allow the user to roam all over the different parts of the system, it is easier to confine the usage to just those applications that you want the user to get to.

Mobile Computing in Action

Mobile computing products now represent a major force in the market. Currid & Company expects that the mobile computing market will experience about a 40 percent compound annual growth rate through the 1990's, accounting for as much as $70 billion in worldwide sales.

Mobile computing is popular because it lets people take their information with them. It's not just for sales people or field service engineers, who are normally away from their offices. Mobile computing has begun to attract a number of traditionally desk-bound professionals, and empowered them to get their work done in many different locations. We need only to look to the banking industry to see how mobile computing devices have changed the way some banks create loans. Some mortgage lenders have found that by going mobile and turning laptop loan origination into a reality, they have achieved a competitive advantage.

Mid-America's Savings Bank of Iowa and Loyola Federal Savings Bank in Baltimore are two mortgage loan organizations who have driven their loan originators out of the office and into the homes of potential customers. It takes about an hour for an originator to walk through the application process with a potential borrower. All of the information—such as credit history, W-2 information, and employment—is taken by the originating officer and transmitted to a centralized organization for processing. The processing has been cut down to as little as three to five days on average.

Central Savings, a Massachusetts-based mortgage lender, has been using laptop computers for loan origination since October 1992. According to officials there, there have been no breakdowns between mortgages originated in the office or on the road because all of the work is done on portables. About 80 agents are equipped with Compaq notebook computers and go about their activities by inputting the loan information into predefined forms and then transmitting it to a central location.

Another interesting use of portable technology comes from the consumer product or grocery field. Companies such as Fastech Information Systems, Inc., Philadelphia, PA, have developed retail reporting applications which let a sales representative go into a grocery store and survey store conditions. They may be checking for out-of-stock items, or the number of shelf facings for both the sponsoring grocery manufacturer or a competitive product. The information is then transmitted from the small computer to a larger server, which combines the information with other reports and produces powerful decision support information for the manufacturer.

These systems are not new; they have been in place for a number of years. What's making them popular today is the recognition that field-based information is vital for making decisions, and field-based information systems can act as a company's eyes on the outside world.

How Does Mobile Computing Support Reengineering?

Mobile computing reorganizes work around results and not tasks. Because they can communicate as freely as necessary with anyone anywhere, it is possible for people in the field to complete their work as though they were down the hall.

Also, mobile computing supports the notion of capturing data only one time, when it is created. Representatives using the Fastech system can collect information about the retail store conditions. The data can be combined with data from other stores and analyzed many different ways—but always from single inputs. Mobile computing also supports the ability to allow decision points where work is performed. If someone in the field is given information, he or she has access to enough information to make decisions on the spot.

Mobile computing also supports the principle of letting people work in parallel instead of sequentially, as each worker can contribute to the central database independently. And because that database is central but the workers are dispersed, mobile computing supports the principle of treating geographical resources as if they were one.

Mobile Computing Technologies

The key words for mobile computing are "small" and "light." Mobile computing products are seen as laptop and notebook computers, personal digital assistants, mobile companions, palmtop computers, and even pen computers and pagers. These devices allow a mobile worker to pull information from various sources, or to push back information when it's needed.

Key Points of Mobile Computing

For all its promise, mobile computing sometimes does not achieve its objective. Usually, that happens when it is deployed incorrectly or when users don't have the ability to move information as needed. Some people ask mobile computing technology to do too much. One company stumbled when it tried to deploy pen-based computers and asked users to write text on the screen. Pen-based computers, good at understanding gestures and marks, still don't do a very good job of handwriting recognition. Users quickly became frustrated with the inability of the computer to interpret handwriting.

Conversely, when they changed the application to let user input only numbers or check marks, the application worked just fine. Because the computer could very easily identify zero through nine or check marks, the applications became very quick to use and the information coming in from it was 100 percent correct.

Conclusion

Mobile and remote computing devices offers many possibilities for changing the way work is done, who does it, and where it is performed. It is also technology that is changing very rapidly, so if your needs aren't met by this technology today, try again in a couple of months. Products are always getting lighter and cheaper and easier to use. There are always opportunities to get work done differently, saving time and effort in the process.

In the next chapter we talk about remote computing's newest relative, wireless computers. As with all the tools we're presenting, wireless computing breaks down barriers in the way work gets done.

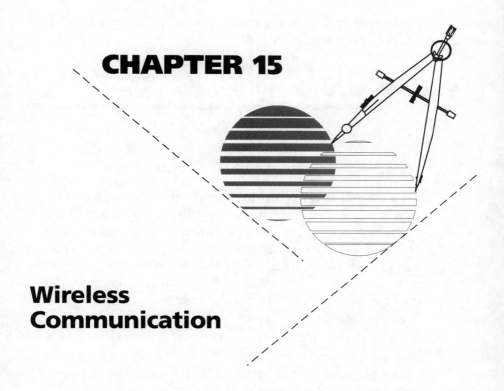

CHAPTER 15

Wireless Communication

Wireless data networks and services are poised to change how people work and where they work. The value of untethered, wireless communications becomes strikingly apparent as work moves toward people instead of people moving toward work.

Just as voice mail did a few years ago, wireless data networks will change the way people communicate on the job. These networks promise to liberate people from telephone tag and, more important, will let them stay in touch inexpensively and easily without needing to be tethered to the phone or computer on the desk. Wireless data will provide a new sense of "location independence" by letting people work from places—like taxicabs, basketball games, or the beach—which are not normally seen as work locations.

This chapter covers both the existing and emerging wireless markets and technologies that make up wireless data communications. It presents the options available for transmitting data in a local or wide-area environment, and provides discussion on the companies leading the way into the wireless future.

New, But Already Productive

Wireless technology is new, but it's already showing great promise for changing the way work is done. Consider a few examples:

≡ Avis, the rental car company, rewrote the rules of customer service a few years ago when it introduced a wireless system. Instead of making customers return cars, then proceed to a cashier inside a building to wait in a long line for a printed receipt, Avis pioneered a system that let representatives greet customers as they pulled up into the rental return line. By the time the customers pull their luggage from the trunk of their car, a receipt has been printed.

≡ A major electric utility in the Northeast is revamping its use of electronic mail so users can take it on the road. They began a pilot program by equipping 12 users with notebook computers and wireless modems. The system only took about 15 minutes to install. It lets users send and receive messages from their cars, taxis, restaurants, and other places uncommon for e-mail. The next step: install 1,000 units on service trucks. All customer data can be updated in real time and at the customers premises.

≡ The Philadelphia office of the United States government's General Services Administration launched a pilot program in 1993 to allow its users to access electronic mail through small wireless computers. With some 500 users who regularly travel for the GSA, they realized the need to get the information to those users on an e-mail system.

≡ A major airline is considering wireless LANs to help ticket agents at busy airports. If ticket lines get too long, the airline would be able to roll up PCs connected to the wireless network and add extra agents right in the middle of the airport lobby. These LAN-on-demand capabilities will surely be welcomed by hurried travelers who don't want to wait in long check-in lines.

≋ Businesses such as British Airways, United Parcel Service, and Otis Elevator use wireless networks to share information with service people in the field. Business people who need to send and receive written messages while on the go are doing just that. Hooked up to a small notebook or palmtop computer, the devices can send and receive mail, make your reservations for dinner, or book a flight to Walla-Walla while you're standing on the 13th tee.

What are these companies attempting to accomplish? Primarily, they are trying to let people access information no matter where they are. As an extension of mobile computing, wireless technologies allow people to take information and conduct business from anywhere they want.

This untethered freedom will be ever more important as the nature of work changes. Companies will consist increasingly of people who interact with customers, usually off the premises, as central-office tasks become the job of fewer workers using better computers. Currid & Company estimates that from 75 to 90 percent of future workers will not be tied to their desk. As the work force becomes more mobile, the ability to move information without wires becomes crucial.

Wireless Emerges

The next big surge in telecommunications will almost certainly involve wireless data. Remember what happened with ordinary phone networks? Data transmission on today's telephone systems is growing dramatically. On certain routes, data—not voice conversations—already constitutes the bulk of the traffic. Between the U.S. and Japan, for instance, fax data make up as much as 90 percent of all telephone signals. You can expect the same evolution in the wireless world.

Data networks will fuel an explosion of new products and services. Already, people can connect laptop and notebook computers to a cellular phone with a special modem and send faxes, messages or retrieve information from a database.

A process called packet switching can be a far cheaper way to send data than waiting for a clear circuit and hogging it for the duration of the call. Messages go as a series of packets, reassembled in their proper order at the receiving end. Pricing is by the packet: about 12 cents each, regardless of the distance the message must travel.

Wireless data systems are still rudimentary. The modems are expensive—up to $700—and, at about eight inches long and weighing more than a pound, they're bigger and heavier than some of the palmtop computers to which they are attached. Not all of the networks are compatible yet with MCI Mail, Microsoft Mail, and AT&T Easylink, the e-mail programs that have become standard in many corporations. You may have to buy new communications software and services, such as the $89-a-month e-mail service from RadioMail of San Mateo, CA.

Today's Wireless Technology

There are several technologies behind wireless computing. The one you'll want to use changes according to distance considerations and what you need to do with it. Analysts divide up wireless computing into three areas: local (or in-building), short-distance (or campus), and remote (or long-distance).

Local Wireless

Local, or in-building, wireless technology lets people put their local area networks together or connect computers within the same building. It lets people roam from room to room, yet still stay connected. There are two types of technology frequently used in in-building: infrared and radio.

Infrared technology requires a clear line of sight between a sender and receiver for the signals to pass back and forth. The signals, however, can be bounced off walls and ceilings. Radio technology generally involves a form of radio transmission that travels along an unlicensed radio band. Radio waves can permeate walls and concrete, but are subject to interference although vendors are quickly finding ways to overcome those issues. For example, in mid-1994 Proxim introduced a high-speed frequency-hopping technology that spreads the signal over several frequencies. This approach resolves the interference problem of signals colliding with other radio-controlled devices.

Short-Distance Wireless

Short-distance, or campus, technology allows people to connect up multiple buildings within a particular area. Most often, people use microwave technology to create the connection. Microwave technology requires a clear line of sight between a sender and receiver. The technology lets companies extend their networks by placing transmitters on top of two buildings. This is far easier than digging up a parking lot or road in order to lay the required cables.

Remote Wireless

Remote, or long-distance, wireless technology spans areas as wide as a continent. These services began to get popular in the early 1990s. Two of them, packet radio and cellular, emerged as stable.

Two suppliers of packet radio networks, Ardis and RAM Mobile Data, have installed nationwide systems which carry mail or data. Having tested both of these systems, Currid & Company finds them very reliable and perfectly acceptable for transmitting short e-mail-type messages. As long as the user is within range, and has the proper equipment, messages are easily received or transmitted. They are ideal for passing text messages or files less than about 10,000 characters (which translates to several pages of single-spaced typed words).

Coverage by packet radio vendors is good, but not yet universal. Ninety percent of the populated area of the United States was within coverage boundaries for packet radio providers (RAM and Ardis) at the end of 1993. Additional coverage areas for small localities is expected throughout 1994 and 1995.

Costs for packet radio services are reasonable for most business applications: $89 to $135 a month.

Cellular services, too, can be used for wireless communication, if necessary. The use of conventional cellular technology, hooking a modem to a cellular phone, can pose difficulties because cellular circuits are not always quiet or clear enough to transmit data. Also, cellular is very expensive, running a minimum of 30 cents per minute for local calls. Long distance transmissions, with roaming charges costing as much as $1 a minute, are prohibitive for most applications.

Emerging Wireless Technologies

A new technology that is based on cellular is called "cellular digital packet data," or CDPD. This technology uses unused space between cellular channels and is designed, as the name implies, to transmit data. Early trials began in 1993, and CDPD networks are beginning to become popular for certain users. CDPD technology offers slightly faster transmission speed than does packet radio.

Low earth orbiting satellites, or LEOS, is another technology under development. LEOS will be small orbiting satellites that will provide very fast ubiquitous global communication services for wireless data. They are expected to be fully deployed by the end of 1997 or later. One such system is Motorola's Iridium project; another is the Teledesic Corp. being formed by Microsoft founder Bill Gates and McCaw Cellular's head Craig McCaw.

The list of would-be network builders is wildly diverse, but all are grabbing for the same gold ring. By the end of the decade, wireless data revenues in the U.S. will hit $10 billion a year, according to BIS Strategic Decisions, a research firm in Norwell, MA. A few of the contenders are well-known forces in communications and computing.

Who Uses Wireless?

The market for mobile wireless offices continues to emerge. The occupations currently using the technology include:

≡ Field service
≡ Transportation
≡ Customer service
≡ Route sales

≋　Wholesale sales

≋　Delivery

≋　Financial services

≋　Health care

≋　Consultants

≋　Accountants

≋　Lawyers

≋　Real estate agents

≋　Investors

Over time, we expect to see wireless technology used by virtually anyone in any occupation. Everyone spends time getting to and from work. Some spend enormous amounts of time in the air as they fly from city to city pursuing business opportunities. Without wireless technology, workers in all professions spend huge blocks of their time unproductively.

Key Players in the Wireless Infrastructure

There are seven notable companies building the wireless future.

Ardis

A wireless-data pioneer, Ardis got its start in the early 1980s as a private network built by Motorola to let IBM keep in touch with service reps. A few years ago, IBM realized the network was grievously under-used, and formed a joint venture with Motorola to open up Ardis to other companies with large field staffs. The workers use custom-made hand-held devices with fill-in-the-blanks electronic displays tailored to particular tasks— transmitting sales orders, or asking a database to find the nearest depot that stocks certain parts.

Ardis has breadth, with service in 400 cities. But like other packet radio providers, it doesn't cover rural areas. Ardis recently added equipment that will let a person send and receive messages while visiting another area (or roaming). The improved system will also allow the use of ordinary laptops.

RAM Mobile Data

This fast-growing joint venture of BellSouth and RAM Broadcasting of New York City has a network that computer-toting executives can use nationwide. Backed with more than $300 million from BellSouth, RAM began building the system in 1991 and now serves over 90 percent of the populated U.S. areas. A subscriber simply hooks his computer to a modem by Ericsson, Sweden's big telecommunications equipment maker, and uses his company's E-mail software to communicate. The system contains built-in roaming, so users need only turn on their radio modems and the system will automatically find them.

CDPD

The brainchild of cellular phone evangelist Craig McCaw, CDPD stands for Cellular Digital Packet Data. McCaw's dream is of cellular phones that will display text as well as handle voice. He aims to convert America's entire cellular infrastructure to a system capable of carrying packet-switched data. For starters, that means adding packet switching equipment to each of his company's 2,225 cell sites.

While McCaw calls CDPD an "extension" of the cellular network, it really looks more like a second system that coexists with the first, with its own transmitters at each site. If it works as planned, CDPD will fix some of the weaknesses that make today's cellular networks an iffy medium for data messages. Contemporary cellular systems are analog and are susceptible to interference. What might be acceptable, if annoying, static during a conversation can ruin a data file. So can the little clicks you sometimes hear when the system hands off your call to another cell. With CDPD, there's no hand-off. If a packet doesn't get through, the system sends it again.

McCaw Cellular has just begun installing CDPD gear and so probably won't be a factor in wireless data until 1995 or 1996. But its commitment to CDPD did help land a big customer: United Parcel Service has equipped its entire fleet of delivery trucks with cellular equipment. Until CDPD arrives, the drivers are making do by sending their data via non-digital cellular calls.

Nextel Communications

A few years ago the Rutherford, NJ-based Nextel was known as Fleet Call and had a handful of taxicab radio-dispatch licenses. It was the telecommunications juggernaut of the month—at least the month of November 1993, when it bought 2,500 radio frequency licenses from Motorola for $1.8 billion in stock. The licenses, combined with those Nextel already owned, put some 70 percent of the U.S. population within receiving range of Nextel's transmitters.

The company plans to replace its antiquated dispatch systems with a voice and data network. That will take at least three years. Until the overhaul is complete, most of Nextel's customers will continue to be companies with vehicle fleets.

Nationwide Wireless Network

NWN is an offspring of Mtel, owner of SkyTel, a major paging company. The new company will sell what is essentially a souped-up paging service, in which messages flow two ways rather than one. You'll be able to use your desktop computer and modem to get in touch with anyone carrying an NWN device, which will transmit an acknowledgment that your message has been received. The device holder, for his part, will be able to send wireless e-mail, either by tapping letters on a touch-sensitive screen or by selecting from a menu of canned replies.

NWN will build its own national network of communication towers and transmitters, separate from SkyTel's. But to jump-start its business, NWN will recruit from among SkyTel's 300,000 customers, perhaps by offering subscribers two-way service for an easy-to-swallow increase in their current beeper bills.

Metricom

Metricom, in Los Gatos, CA, has operated quietly by providing wireless data services to utility companies for remote metering and monitoring. Now Metricom wants to apply its know-how to offer bargain wireless data services on college and corporate campuses and in the surrounding towns. Metricom uses a clever stratagem to keep costs low: it operates in a part of the radio spectrum set aside by the FCC for free use by anyone. There are obvious risks: while access to the airwaves costs Metricom nothing, anyone who wants to transmit on the same frequencies can butt in and interfere. Most uses of the band have little to do with communication—the frequencies are used by garage door openers and anti-shoplifting systems.

Metricom has priced its services very aggressively. Rather than charge by the packet as Ardis and RAM do, it will offer unlimited service for $20 a month or less. Its modems will handle data at a speedy 50,000 to 60,000 bits of information a second, three to six times faster than Ardis or RAM.

Orbcomm

The Orbcomm subsidiary of Orbital Sciences of Dulles, VA, plans to launch budget communications satellites that will fill in the geographical coverage gaps of all the other wireless data systems. It will put up 26 little orbiters for a total cost of $150 million—less than the tab for building and launching a single regular satellite.

Orbcomm's service will be more expensive than that of rival systems—perhaps $1 for a short message. But the satellites will provide data communications anywhere on earth. Though Orbcomm believes personal communications will be its biggest market, it has signed up customers that need to monitor equipment in remote areas.

Other systems are sure to emerge. The FCC will continue to auction off the radio spectrum to encourage new communication services, and some of the winning bidders will certainly enter the wireless data race.

Supporting the Seven Principles

Wireless technology offers strong support for the principles of reengineering. It allows people to organize work around results and not tasks, because it makes them extremely mobile. Consider how Avis reorganized its work and improved customer service by greeting its customers in the rental car return line. Rather then take time away from the customer and require extra people to attend the checkout counters, Avis simply rearranged the work.

Wireless technology also gives people the ability to capture data only one time, as it is created. Rather than writing down the customer information on multiple forms, wireless data terminals let people capture information and put it immediately into their computer systems. Picture a warehouse operation where information is collected by small portable computers and then inventory data are wirelessly transmitted to a server. All the work can be done quickly and inexpensively.

Wireless technology also allows decision points where work is performed. Because new wireless technology can both send and receive information, work can be rearranged to allow decisions to be made as the work is performed.

Also, wireless technology certainly allows people to treat geographic resources as if they were one. People can work just about anywhere yet still maintain two-way communications.

Conclusion

Wireless data technology holds much promise for reengineering because it lets people move from location to location without losing touch. Wireless data technology makes life and work easier, but it does take some getting used to. Companies who successfully deploy wireless technologies quickly learn what works well and what should be left for the next turn in technology evolution.

In the next chapter, we discuss knowledge bases and agents. With the vast storehouses of information available to us, we look at some productive methods that can be used to seek out only what we need to know.

CHAPTER 16

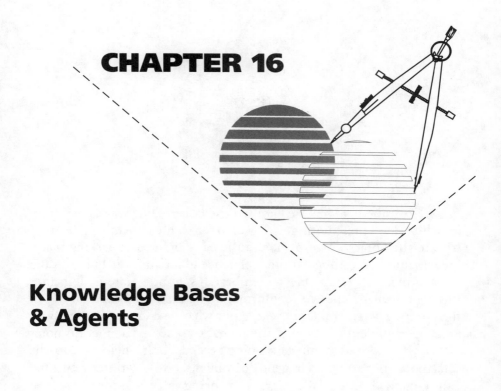

Knowledge Bases
& Agents

At 2:30 one Tuesday afternoon, Craig Gilbert, holding a fresh cup of coffee, returns to his office from the latest of a string of meetings. His mind is churning over a wealth of issues discussed in the last meeting, and he is happy that he is not on the hook for resolving them. He sits behind his desk with a sigh as a familiar bell comes from his computer, signalling the receipt of an important message.

Craig takes a short sip of coffee as he taps a mouse button and gazes expectantly at the computer monitor. "Uh-oh," he says to himself. The message is from his boss, and the subject of the message is "Presentation Required."

The message reads: "Craig: need you to prepare a presentation for the board of directors. They need to hear everything you know about Krumlinger Industries. You'll have 60 minutes to present and take Q's and A's. The board meets Friday at 9. You are on at 10." The impact of the message settles in slowly. "Can he possibly mean *this* Friday?" Craig thinks. Down deep, though, he knows it does.

Remembering what he endured the last time he was called upon for a high-level presentation, Craig shuddered. He remembers the daily trips to the library downtown, and the daily fight for a parking place. He remembers pleading with the reference librarian for help in finding the required materials. He remembers his frantic note-taking after finding out that some of the information could not be checked out of the library. He remembers checking out what he could, packing books and papers under his arm and driving back home to decipher his notes into English. He remembers sending several library helpers into the catacombs, not to be seen again for hours, and sometimes returning empty-handed. He remembers not being able to locate several important documents at all.

He remembers also that it took him well into the fourth week before he was ready to make that presentation. "And now," he muttered under his breath, "I have three days."

Luckily for Craig, he now has access to one of the many powerful on-line information services.

With a click of his mouse he is ready to start. He launches on WinCIM—a special communications program to access the Com-puServe Information Service—and clicks on the green light symbol. He types in "busdb" and hears the familiar whine of the modem and quickly sees an option menu on the monitor. He notices that he is heading into a database with more than 850,000 articles. A few key-strokes and clicks later, Craig locates 439 articles about Krumlinger: its competition, its industry, its products, its strategies, its manufacturing and distribution, its revenues and its management. He narrows the search to deal only with articles from the last two years, and downloads only those that look important to his current search.

Using technology available today, Craig has cut the time to gather information from weeks to minutes. Craig is still going to have to work his way through the material to determine what is usable and what isn't. But there is no more daily scrambling for a parking place at the library. No more shorthand notes. No more frustrated librarians.

Available through a host of commercial services, like Compu-Serve, is a wealth of information. Newspaper and magazine articles, white papers written by experts, even dissertation abstracts. Enter only a few key words and materials are brought to your desk.

This sounds very simple, and it really is. The more familiar you become with these services, the more you'll be amazed at how many sources of information exist. In essence, libraries upon libraries are at your disposal. Vast amounts of knowledge served up—without ever having to leave your office, home, or hotel room.

In this chapter, we discuss services that we call knowledge bases. Most are available on line or through subscriptions on CD-ROM. We also discuss agent technology, which sets up electronic runners that go through storehouses of data and extract desired information, or perform some other service on your behalf.

Today, there exists technology that provides tremendous capabilities for on-line research. It has become so easy and so available that almost everyone can use it.

The Value of Knowledge Bases

It is sometimes difficult for organizations to truly assess the value of knowledge base technology because it is difficult to put a value on making people smarter.

A distributor for a hardware chain recently talked about how his company was gaining a competitive advantage using information that comes directly from an on-line service. The organization had identified a set of key words that would create a clipping file when those key words were mentioned in newspaper articles. Those key words were "Kmart Stores," since Kmart was a very large customer of this particular distributor.

Every time Kmart did anything in the local market, that news story would be clipped from the newspaper and sent to the distributor. He didn't have a very high tech solution; he simply had the story faxed to him by the knowledge base provider.

The distributor told us that Kmart can't put a shovel in the ground without his knowing about it. As a result, every time Kmart does open up a new store or makes a significant change in its distribution mix, he can deploy a salesman to be first on the scene to help Kmart through the changes. It gives him an edge against the competition.

The Major Services

Our goal in this chapter is not to go into great depth analyzing and comparing knowledge bases. Still, we'd be remiss if we didn't at least list the most popular providers.

Business/Professional

- Dow Jones News Service
- First!
- Lexis
- Dialog
- CompuServe

Professional/Personal

- CompuServe
- America Online
- Prodigy
- GEnie

Notice that we intentionally placed CompuServe in both categories because of its wide variety of services.

Depending upon your requirements, one or two of them might be better for you than the others. America Online, Delphi and Prodigy best serve home users, while Dow Jones is geared more for business use. But our purpose in this chapter is less about which service is right for

you and more about discussing how to improve the flow of information and increase productivity.

There are fees—sometimes steep fees—associated with your on-line time. Generally, those services geared more to personal use are less expensive. In any event, you'll want to study the cost structures of the various providers. Don't be too critical of the cost. The value of any information you'll find is often well worth the price. Remember, as you begin to consider using a knowledge base: what do you need to know; what communications functions are offered by a service; is the service easy to use; what does it cost?

The process of getting into a knowledge base service and moving around within it can take some getting used to. Since you are paying by the minute, you want to use the time productively. Many services have free practice areas or introductory offers, so you can learn some of the techniques at no cost. On-line services take a little getting used to, but for what all this information can mean to you, it's well worth stubbing your toe a few times.

What You Use Them For

There is a wealth of information out there, and the ability to access and use it is a powerful weapon in this information age.

You can write to the President or communicate with other government leaders. You can do the same thing with professional athletes. You can move quickly to check out the current status of your stock portfolio. You can book your next flight or do research on on-line databases. You can get help for your PC problem, or discuss medical questions with doctors.

The forums on CompuServe, for example, are excellent resources for getting some quick answers to most any question regarding technology. Technology-related companies too numerous to list here have a presence on CompuServe. Ask your question, or just browse through the forum. Most likely your question has already been asked and answered.

Many services—including small, local bulletin board systems—provide access to the Internet, if only as a way to send and receive e-mail. Once on the Internet, a worldwide network of computers and information is open to you from university campuses, government offices, corporate sites, and research institutions.

The amount of information available on the Internet is staggering. You can find government data on population, agriculture and the economy, as well as full texts of magazines, newspapers, and journals. Keep in mind that the Internet is not as easy to use as other services; in fact, it is not a "service" at all. It is a global mass of uncoordinated computers owned and operated by universities, governments, armed forces, and commercial establishments large and small. Even moving about can be difficult, let alone finding nuggets of information. Software designed to navigate the Internet is becoming better and better, but still

has a long way to go to match the quality of the commercial knowledge bases.

A full discussion of the Internet would take more space than is available here. Most bookstores now carry an array of titles on the subject; we encourage you to browse.

Knowledge Bases for the Professional User

There is a plethora of products available that include knowledge bases. They can be purchased on CD-ROM or accessed through dial-in capabilities. It is possible today to get several years worth of periodicals on CD-ROM from companies such as Newsweek, Ziff Desktop Information, CMP, or International Data Corp.

There is also plenty of business and technology news available on low-cost subscription services to CD-ROM. Generally, these services cost between $300 and $900 a year, and the supplier mails an updated CD-ROM to the customer about once a month or once every two months. CD-ROM solutions are ideal for people needing very focused sets of information. They are less suitable for large research needs where people need to go to multiple sources to get the information.

A broader solution than CD-ROM, albeit a more costly one, is to obtain subscriptions to various business and professional news services. The Dow Jones News/Retrieval offers excellent access to multiple trade and industry periodicals, as well as the Dow Jones, McGraw-Hill, and other news wires.

The amount of information available and the on-line research that can be accomplished is phenomenal. Dow Jones, for example, lets

subscribers put together electronic clipping folders that clip only from selected periodicals on selected topics.

These topics can be refined down to single words such as "reengineering," or phrases such as "reengineering in a manufacturing environment." As information flows out on these topics, they are automatically clipped and placed in a customer's file folder.

The customer can then set up the folders in one of two ways:

🞃 The information is collected in the folder thus allowing the customer to utilize it as required.

🞃 The information is automatically forwarded to the customer by e-mail.

Another such clipping service is made available by Individual Inc., in Cambridge, Massachusetts. The service, called First!, goes one step further. In addition to reading many different sources—both news and industry periodicals—First! uses artificial intelligence techniques that go far beyond what can be accomplished with a simple search for key words. The First! service, like other knowledge bases, will send the appropriately clipped news stories to the customer as requested.

For example, your business is part of the technology industry. You have 20 major suppliers and 10 major customers. You can instruct First! to provide you with all information relating to these 30 companies every day.

First! searches the information that will appear in the day's publications for any and all related information. Once that information is secured, it is downloaded to your system before you get up in the morning. On your way to the shower and while you're drinking your first coffee of the day, you are updated.

First! gets its information from the same sources as the major on-line services.

There are additional services that perform similar type search and retrieval functions. One is Lexis, from MEAD Data Systems. This service is primarily focused towards the legal profession. Another is Dialog, one of the oldest services, which combines a wide variety of databases.

Knowledge Bases for the Personal User

Less-costly consumer-oriented services such as CompuServe, Prodigy, GEnie, America Online, and Delphi provide almost the same capabilities, although the depth of industry news is not quite as great. Each service provides information slightly differently, and CompuServe probably has the widest range of available information.

CompuServe, based in Columbus, Ohio, is perhaps the largest and certainly the oldest of the consumer on-line services. In addition to providing a solid knowledge base and research capabilities, CompuServe also includes very good electronic mail and forums for people with special interests to share information.

CompuServe and America Online provide excellent Windows-based software that makes it easy for people to dial in, get to the information they need, and retrieve it.

Agent Technology

Throughout our discussion of these knowledge bases, we have alluded to the fact that some form of clipping folders can be created that will automatically find information and bring it back. This technology is a primitive use of "agent" technology. It's powerful because it provides automatic access and does automatic work on your behalf.

However, agent technology is maturing to a much more sophisticated level. General Magic, a start-up company based in Mountain View, California, has developed software that creates a "virtual envi-

ronment" in which users can conduct business and multimedia communications. The software, called Telescript, is based on the concept of agents—programs generated by one computer that tell another computer how to perform a task. Telescript, when it's released, will supposedly run on desktop machines and on new portable communications and computing devices. (Other terms for agents that you may come across include "knowbot," "droids," or "gofer technology.")

Agents at Your Command

You are looking to buy desks in volume for the new office building, and you want information on colors available and pricing. In the past, you have poured yourself a fresh cup of coffee, grabbed a legal pad and the Yellow Pages, and began to let your fingers walk.

You make a call and tell the person that you are looking for office desks and that you will be buying a quantity of them. You ask if there is someone there who can help you with color, brands, and pricing. You are put on hold. Maybe you get some music, or maybe you get the happy voice selling you all the virtues of that store. At any rate, no one ever comes back on the line; you hear a click and then the familiar sound of a dial tone.

You try the number one more time. A different voice tells you "Yes, we carry desks." Even though you know it is a mistake, you ask for colors and prices. "One minute please," come the familiar words. Wait. Click. Dial tone again.

Now you have made two calls and you really know nothing. You try store #2, hoping for more success. You continue to call store after store. It can take hours to do a decent job of comparative shopping for one item.

Telescript will send out an agent to retrieve any and all information you require.

And remember the last time you tried to schedule a meeting? Finding the only time that everyone had available in the next two weeks was quite an ordeal. Your secretary needed to involve other secretaries and other calendars to set up a single meeting. Telescript will send out an agent to study the appropriate calendars, find the first available open time slot, schedule the meeting and notify everyone involved.

And how about dinner reservations at your favorite restaurant when your biggest client comes to town? Telescript will send out an agent to set that up as well.

How Telescript Agents Work

General Magic's product consists of two components: a user interface and operating system, Magic Cap, and the communications application and development tools, Telescript.

Magic Cap opens by taking you into familiar territory, a real-world metaphor of streets and buildings. One view shows you a desk, with a phone, postcard, notepad, datebook and Rolodex. Pointing to each activates phone dialing, e-mail, note-taking, calendar, and address-book functions.

Down the hallway are doors for the game room, library, storage room, and so forth. Service providers are reached by going "downtown." Downtown shows several store fronts, from fast food to grocers, florists, and hardware stores. Pointing to one of them activates the interface for that service.

Telescript, the programming scheme, makes the network intelligent. You will wrap graphical objects representing agents in addresses and send them off to do your bidding. The agents will roam freely from your computer to others. They will know what color bicycle tape you like and that your budget only allows you to spend 49 cents per role. And they will also know that if "Ma Shippley's" isn't available for dinner at 8 on Saturday, that your second choice is "Bubba's Big Bone Bar-B-Q."

Telescript's agents also have the intelligence to replicate themselves if they need to. If an agent determines that a task cannot be completed in the time you've allowed, he'll delegate other agents and send them on their way.

You can also instruct the agent on how to deliver its message back to you. Because the desk issue is a priority, you can instruct your agent to deliver the message through your wireless link as soon as possible, but if its unable to do so within an hour, then render the image into a bit map and fax it to you. Or, you could tell the network to route all messages to a wire-line connection, except for messages from certain people—or certain agents—which should be sent over a more costly wireless connection.

Now imagine for a moment that the furniture stores you're dealing with don't want an army of agents roaming in and out of its database. We've all heard the stories of hackers breaking into systems, changing data and deleting information.

General Magic designed Telescript so that no messing around can take place. As soon as the agent arrives, Telescript software will welcome it, and then query the agent to find out what it's come for. Access is not allowed to programs that control the processing and storage of data.

Agents carry electronic permits in their identification satchels, specifying how long they will stay in the computers they visit. Should the host computer realize that the agent is attempting to enter on false pretenses or that the time limit for the visit has been exceeded, the host will be able to amend or rescind the permits and kick out the lingering transients.

This then is your virtual research team. From your desk, you have launched your agents into the world of information to do your bidding. You have given all of them their assignments, specific instructions, and deadlines. And you have told them how to respond to you. Just think of the possibilities!

Creating Your Own Knowledge Base

Many companies have found it helpful to create their own knowledge bases with products such as Lotus Notes or other software that allows the indexing and storage of non-specific textual information. Frequently, companies combine documents and information that they generated internally, such as their own analysis of market reports or certain trend activities, with information that they download from on-line services or obtained from CD-ROM research. They find that their own knowledge base provides them with a more focused view of information based on how the company adds value with their own information.

Lotus Notes users around the world will soon be able to take advantage of a recently announced service from CompuServe. The online service company has added the Lotus Notes Information Service, a customized communications and messaging service for Lotus Notes users.

Supporting the Seven Principles

Knowledge bases and agent technology directly support at least four of the seven reengineering principles. Certainly this technology supports the notion of organizing work around results and not tasks. It provides the ability to send information directly to people, allowing them to achieve results because action can be taken on news immediately.

The technology also supports the principle of allowing decision points where work is performed. Because the information can be sent directly to a sales organization, for instance, sales people can be empowered with enough knowledge to decide who should be called on tomorrow.

It also supports the notion of making people who use the process do the work. In our old paradigms of thinking, we allowed only research people to dig through information. If we had to wait for a librarian to tell management that Kmart was building a new store, chances are that the store would be built and opened by the time the information got the people who could do anything about it.

Finally, the technology also supports the notion of working in parallel instead of sequentially. Because you can get information to the people who need it, knowledge bases support the notion of people working on multiple views of information simultaneously, rather than again handing it off from one person to another.

Conclusion

This is the new information age. There is a wealth of information available to assist in making more informed decisions that will benefit our businesses and our personal lives. It is becoming increasingly important to have the knowledge about the available sources of on-line information and how to access them all.

Combine knowledge bases with agent technology and you'll improve efficiency and productivity in countless ways. Instead of asking one person to become a specialist and slowly filter and transmit information, this technology leverages experts and specialists by simplifying the process of gathering information and providing it to those who need it. It promises to change the way white-collar work is performed in every organization.

In the next chapter we focus on Simulation Tools: CAD, CAM, modeling, and virtual reality.

CHAPTER 17

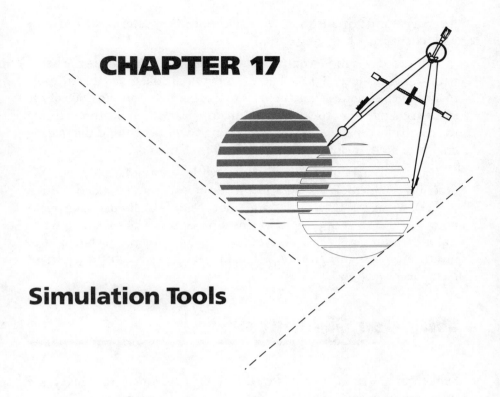

Simulation Tools

A picture, the old saying goes, is worth a thousand words. Sometimes it is. Often, it's worth many more.

Imagine yourself as an attorney in a personal injury case. You are standing before the jury, questioning an expert witness on the physics of braking distance. As your witness is describing the chart that maps braking distance required against time and weight of the automobile, you notice that juror Number Five is nodding off. Undaunted, you charge on. The next witness, a credible eyewitness, describes, in excruciating detail, exactly what she saw. Oops, there goes juror Number Nine. You rest your case, confident that you have presented brilliantly and that any juror who can fog up a mirror will find for your client.

Your opponent stands up and walks over to the TV. As he turns on the set, he explains to the jury that they are about to see a 3-D animation of what actually happened. He further explains that his team has done all the work for the jury because the animation is a certifiably complete and accurate depiction of events leading up to this lawsuit.

Jurors Five and Nine are now wide awake and very interested. You hope your client has a forgiving nature.

Life today is more complex than it used to be, and so are the issues with which we have to deal. There is much more data available to apply to any given situation, whether it is in a courtroom, on the floor of the stock exchange or in the design lab of an airplane manufacturer. Trying to absorb all available detail is like hearing a whisper behind the roaring engine of a 747 or trying to take a sip from a fire hose.

In this chapter, we look at the world of simulation tools. We describe such tools as image processing, computer-aided design (CAD), virtual reality (VR), and modeling. We discuss each technology and how it applies to business processes. Then we investigate some case studies to illustrate the applicability of the technology to business process reengineering. Finally, we show which principles of reengineering apply.

Why Use Simulation?

Spoken and written words are sometimes inadequate to convey the information necessary to complete a thought. It is sometimes easier to draw a picture than to launch into a long dissertation. Computers are very good at dealing with words. Through years of experience, we have

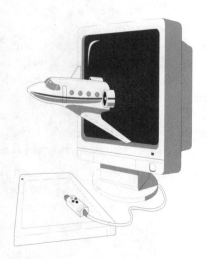

learned to use the computer to create, manipulate, and store words. Only recently, have we learned how to use that same tool to manage other types of data: graphics, video, animation, voice, audio, 3-D, maps, and so on.

Simulation tools merely use the power of the computer to create a reproduction of what we are trying to understand in a form in which we can understand it.

For centuries, architects have drawn pictures to tell people how to build buildings, bridges, and gardens. The pictures would simulate the reality of what the architect intended to create. Only one generation ago, the tools were India ink, straightedges, compasses and triangles. Today, an architect uses CAD—Computer Aided Design. Sitting down at an inexpensive PC, architects can use an inexpensive piece of software (AutoCAD LT for Windows, $495) and draw those pictures. Now, however, those pictures are stored on a hard disk, can be printed, modified, reproduced, transmitted and yes, shown on a TV screen.

Virtual reality (VR) is another form of simulation. You walk up to a VR machine, put on your stereoscopic headset and enter the world of cyberspace. Sounds like a game in your local arcade, right? Well, yes, you could be paying your four bucks an hour to play. But you could also be a member of a tank crew simulating an actual battle of the Persian Gulf War. Or you could be a design engineer working on the F-18 fighter jet. Or you could be a stock broker trying to understand the most recent trend on Wall Street.

Image Processing

In the Good Old Days, pictures didn't lie. Today, digital image processing allows you to create images impossible to see in reality and impossible to duplicate in a darkroom.

Why is this important? Imagine how much easier it would be to visualize a building on a new property if you had a picture of it. Not a problem—overlay a 3-D image of the new building and integrate it into the picture. Now you can see what everything will look like before the building is built. It saves lots of time and money and can help avoid costly mistakes.

Imaging

The ability to alter pictorial reality gives rise to new ways to combine images for advertising. Cleverly created images can be created in a computer rather than spending money and effort to produce special effects and studio time for camera work. Using a computer also speeds the creative process, as the artist can visualize his work while it's in progress rather than waiting for the end of the composition.

There is a growing industry of third-party support for imaging applications, especially with respect to graphic arts, advertising, and publishing. This support provides specialty services that extend the capabilities of image processing application. Some of the products are especially worthy of mention.

Pixar 128 provides 128 different textures that can be applied to objects within an image, to create a more realistic or surrealistic look. It supports imaging applications that support Adobe's plug-in specification, such as PhotoStyler or PhotoShop.

Pixar's Typestry lets you create 3-D type, complete with lighting and textures. The results can be combined with Pixar 128 to extend your imaging software even further. You can create many professional-looking texts, just like those visible on television.

Kai's Power Tools (HSC Software) is a highly rated collection of digital filters and extensions to enhance the special effects functions of imaging programs such as PhotoShop, PhotoStyler, Fractal Design and Paint, Picture Publisher and other programs supporting Adobe's plug-in specification.

Print Processing

Image processing pays off particularly well in the printing process. Photographic images frequently need work on their color and lighting before they can be used. A printer can use the imaging software to correct flaws in the original—such as a reflection on a person's glasses. Done by hand, this is very expensive and labor-intensive. With a computer, it is better, faster, and cheaper.

A perfect example of image processing centers around Micrografx's Picture Publisher and some historical photographs. Mark Tailleur of St. Helens, Oregon, owner of Raven Graphics, took on a project for the Columbia County Historical Society to help preserve some old black-and-white panoramic photographs.

These large photographs depicted life from the early days of St. Helens and are considered to have great historical value. The photographs were badly damaged in spots, with cracks and fading; the images were defocused in sections. Using a Howtek scanner with Picture Publisher, Mr. Tailleur digitized the photographs by sections and proceeded to retouch each section by hand, using the original as a guide. After all sections of a photograph were completed, they were reattached into a single image, which was then reproduced.

Drawing

Another type of image processing is drawing. Drawing programs don't just draw any more. They sketch, draft, paint, and scan. Of all the types of simulation tools mentioned here, drawing programs appeal to the widest audience because they contain features that will be useful in almost any situation.

Charles Schnardthorst of Mobil Oil's Corporate Design and Graphics Department has come to depend heavily upon a drawing package called CorelDRAW to handle much of his team's work. With CorelDRAW, Charles creates logos, technical illustrations and other drawings. He uses it to produce "before and after" drawings of service stations converted to Mobil stations.

Before CorelDRAW came to his department three years ago, all the work was done by outside sources. Within six months, with an investment of $119,000 for computers, printers, plotters, and software, Mobil saved $400,000 in fees for those outside services, and the work was completed faster than before.

CAD/CAM

Remember the example of the architect? CAD/CAM are rather specialized simulation tools that make life easier and better for architects, engineers, and designers.

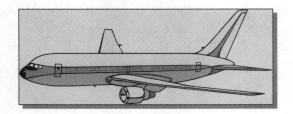

The Boeing 777 airliner, scheduled for delivery in Spring 1995, will be Boeing's first completed design on its new, revamped computer system. The system connects workstations involved in the project to a single, company-wide database. By using CAD, the company expects to save time and money:

≋ Last minute changes can be quickly implemented.

≋ With the use of three-dimensional simulations, there is no requirement for a full-scale mockup.

≋ Because of the accuracy and integrity of the systems used in the design of the airplane, government approval will be easier to get. The entire history and the results of the design effort are available to the government inspectors.

The work of such a project might flow something like this: The engineers come up with an idea for a new part for the plane. Anxious to see a prototype, they fire up their CAD software, create a 3-D shaded image. They save that image on their hard disk and print it on the color printer. They take the printed image to show Manufacturing what they are trying to create.

Manufacturing takes the file. which contains the drawing, and imports it into their CAM system. The CAM system controls the lathes and saws and drill presses that create the prototype, ready for inspection.

Realize that the steps taken here compress what used to be a drawn-out process that would involve at least three departments. Done manually, manufacturing a part, depending on the complexity, could take months. With CAD/CAM software, the process can be reduced to just days, as the computer steps in to streamline much of the labor and math involved in the part's creation. The CAD drawing itself provides a flexible medium for the engineer to fine tune the part before it ever sees the manufacturing floor.

Virtual Reality

Virtual reality (VR) is a technology that makes the communication of large amounts of information more effective. In the logical development of computer technology to communicate information, we have moved from "0's" and "1's", through words, graphs, animation, video, and audio, to VR.

But VR adds another dimension—it involves the user in the data being presented. It could be the elaborate interaction we see in games today, or it could simply be looking at a TV screen and virtually "walking" through a reconstructed crime scene or planned building to get a better feel for the situation—something that a two-dimensional, static drawing could not convey.

VR has moved out of the game room and into the office. Some of the largest stock brokerage companies in the U.S. are experimenting with VR. The idea is to provide highly paid (and highly stressed) securities executives with an understandable look at a large amount of information in a short period of time. Winning or losing in a deal often swings on how quickly a trader can absorb data. He can spend time going over huge columns of numbers or, using VR, can look at an image of a moving Grand Canyon-style graph, with risks of investments corresponding to the height of the rock formations.

One useful application of VR is the flight simulator. Consider letting a complete novice get behind the wheel of a Boeing 747 for flight instruction. By using VR, students—as well as highly experienced pilots—can be presented with any number and combination of situations with which they will be confronted in real life. And there is no risk of loss of life or equipment due to lack of experience.

On the medical front, virtual reality holds out some real promise in training for surgery. With tactile feedback and visual stimulus to create a virtual patient, a surgeon could train for a particular technique without putting anyone at risk. If the surgeon fails, only the virtual patient dies, not the real patient.

A variation on that same theme uses the idea of control via a "power glove." This power glove, when connected to a computer, can be used by a surgeon to direct tiny surgical instruments inside a patient's body to accomplish feats of surgical precision impossible by hand.

Modeling

When we think of modeling, many of us think of the planes and cars we used to make as kids. But here, modeling takes on a much different form. Software modeling generally has two distinct forms, one representing reality and the other used for design verification.

Modeling reality provides us with the means to observe natural events that are difficult or impossible to observe without aid. Scientists use graphical models to observe behavior of atoms, chemical bonds, planetary motion and even the earth's tectonic upheaval. In business, we would use reality models to observe network behavior, transactions within a bank, communication lines, the flow of money through a corporation, and demographic changes in population and product purchasing.

Modeling to verify designs is somewhat different from modeling reality. While modeling reality is based on real data, modeling designs creates data to show potential results.

Let's look at a practical example of design modeling.

A company wants to install a network. They have several different sites where computers will have access to the network. Before installing it, the company wants to distribute networking resources to avoid traffic bottlenecks.

On paper, you can only theorize how well everything could perform based on data sheets, knowledge of the hardware, and practical experience. With modeling software, you can create network configurations, move resources around and pinpoint potential problems before you ever pull cable through your buildings.

For another example of modeling, we need look no farther than our local grocery store. Chapter 7 mentioned the amount of data that a grocery store can generate through the use of its bar code scanners.

The merchandising manager can use those data to help with the layout of goods on store shelves, too.

Data generated by UPC codes and cash registers (or POS terminals) can be fed into a program that produces a picture of a shelf full of goods sold that day. While the UPC codes determine the specific brands (which can be computer-generated to appear on the shelf), the POS terminals give data about the amount of goods sold. Using other criteria—such as whether a given product is to be given a special promotion soon—a manager can create a model of what the shelf would look like, and where other brands might be placed to situate the promotional item better.

If the "look" does not meet the necessary criteria, the computer model can suggest other arrangements to her, and she can tweak the model to get just the right appearance. The same modeling software can suggest how to balance the inventory and when to buy more goods.

Supporting the Seven Principles

Because simulation tools are devices that leverage human resources to capture and understand information, they nicely support many of the principles of reengineering.

- ≋ They allow us to organize work around results, not tasks. Designing the airplane is the result and all the tasks that support the result have access to the tools.

- ≋ Because the tools are computer-based, data is collected only when it is created and then used by anyone who needs it throughout the process.

- ≋ Decisions can be made at the point where the work is performed. When the stock broker has the information at his desk, he can make the decision to buy or sell.

- ≋ Clearly, all the examples support the principle that work can be done in parallel instead of sequentially.

- ≋ Networked simulation tools let users be where they need to be and still have access. All geographic resources are treated as one.

Conclusion

We took you to the courtroom, the design shop of architects and aircraft designers, and even stepped into virtual reality. Put this new technology to use while you reengineer business processes. Don't leave it up to your competition to force you to move in the right direction.

The next chapter is about the promise of expert systems, which emulate the ways humans come to decisions.

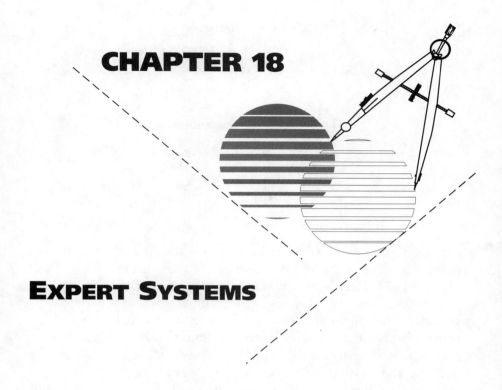

CHAPTER 18

EXPERT SYSTEMS

The term expert system (ES) projects an image of a whiz-bang bleeding-edge technology. It is not. Many businesses have implemented ESs over the last 25 years quite profitably.

One of the most famous business ES applications is XCON (for eXpert CONfigurer), developed by Digital Equipment Corporation. In the early 1970s, Digital had a wide range of continually changing computer components that could be configured in a vast number of ways. Human experts—known as technical editors—ensured that each computer system on order had all the necessary components and no extras, and made diagrams showing how to assemble the system.

The initial configurations sometimes had omissions or errors, which had to be fixed before the manufacturing department could schedule production. After the systems were built, 90 percent of them were checked again at Digital's final assembly and test facility in Westminster, Massachusetts, where the pieces of the computer were

physically plugged together and run. Once they passed this test, the computers were disassembled and shipped to the customers.

In 1973, faced with the prospect of adding tens of millions of dollars worth of assembly and test facilities to accommodate sales growth, DEC sought an alternative. The result was XCON, an expert system that could check sales orders and design the layout of each computer order it analyzed. The system, along with the creation of a database and an improvement in component quality, allowed DEC to ship most components directly to the customer for final assembly, eliminating the need to build additional final assembly facilities.

Digital's managers credit XCON with about $25 million of the savings realized from minimizing the final assembly and test process. They also cite XCON as an important contributor to their strategy of offering customers many options.

In this chapter, we discuss the pros and cons of expert systems. We explain what they are and what they can accomplish, and provide examples of business problems that were defeated at the hands of ESs. We even include some do's and don'ts.

What Is an Expert System?

Very simply, an ES is software that seeks to emulate the decision-making process of a human expert.

In XCON, for example, the knowledge of the human integration experts was loaded into software. Decisions about what options could be used in a specific system's design were made electronically, saving millions of dollars in time and facilities, and improving the employee productivity. Customer satisfaction was also improved, because product shipments were expedited.

In very general terms, here are the five pieces that combine to make a typical rule-based ES:

- ≋ **Knowledge base.** The knowledge base is a collection of data that contains the domain-specific knowledge about the problem being solved.
- ≋ **Inference engine.** The inference engine performs the reasoning function.
- ≋ **Blackboard.** The blackboard is a communications facility that serves as a clearinghouse for all information in the system.
- ≋ **User interface.** The user interface lets the user input information, control the reasoning process, and display results.
- ≋ **Explanation facility.** The explanation facility interprets the results by describing the conclusions that were drawn, explaining the reasoning process used, and suggesting corrective action.

Some have said that expert systems take too much time to develop, largely because ESs are critically dependent on identifying a qualified expert, and then digging deeply into that expert's behavior and knowledge. Others believe that ES development is not a lengthy process, and have developed programs in a matter of weeks.

The Requirement for an Enterprise Model

Over the last 20 to 25 years, many companies automated only pieces of their businesses, scattering networks and incompatible computer platforms throughout their organizations. The resulting disarray has created information islands throughout companies.

Because there was never an "enterprise" plan to enable the flow of information from one area to another, significant decision making has taken place without knowing critically important data. With the passing of time, the information islands have drifted further and further apart, often representing conflicting and competitive departments within the same company.

The decentralized islands of information need a unified view of the larger organization. Coherent behavior requires more than blockbuster applications and network connections; it must be governed by an enterprise model that codifies the corporation's intent and procedures.

More important, a coherent model should include how to *change* procedures. The institutional ability to change in a dynamic environment has become a survival imperative for most companies. It is an ability that may very well differentiate the companies that survive from the companies that don't.

Let's face it: most companies don't have an enterprise plan. Even in the companies that do, it is very likely that the plan is not consistent with the always-changing needs of the business it supports. ESs can help in both cases; either the ES would be improvement on an outdated or

outgrown system, or it would help in the search for accurate and realistic information.

A company that created an enterprise plan early in its existence may have less need for an ES than a company that grew in a fragmented and unorganized manner. In their effort to achieve constantly extending goals and objectives, many companies implemented patchwork systems where they were needed at the time. As companies look for areas to reengineer, those are prime targets.

The goal of reengineering at any company is to have each of its departments produce the best possible flow of reliable information. With that in mind, whether or not there is a "plan" in place, ESs are a very helpful tool.

The ES: Where to Begin

It's one thing to study the successes of other companies and quite another to produce a success of one's own. So how does a manager court the new technology?

First, you have to identify a likely subject for an expert system. Look for design, diagnosis, or monitoring procedures that are not being performed as well as they could be. Ask: "Is there a task in my organization that would be improved if:

≋   ...we had more time?" Organizations are replete with tasks for which doing things faster means doing them better. Basic transaction systems for credit, purchasing, and so on are promising areas to explore.

≡ ...the best expert always did the job?" Digital couldn't afford to have its design engineers configuring computer systems, even though they understood the process best. XCON lets the company apply expert knowledge to a task that is routine but important.

≡ ...we had consistent decisions?" The use of human beings to make decisions brings variation into the equation. Every one of us will read and react to guidelines in different ways. The utilization of technology incorporating artificial intelligence enables consistency.

The notion of the thinking machine is seductive. ES builders are often drawn to build flashy applications. But observation of dozens of systems indicates that the more mundane tasks are among the most fruitful areas for new applications. Business and government have many jobs that are important but routine or even boring. Tasks such as contracting, negotiating, and auditing pervade business and are promising opportunities.

Likely candidates are jobs that currently use complex questionnaires. Meeting the requirements of government agencies like the Environmental Protection Agency or the Occupational Safety and Health Administration could be simplified by encoding the regulations in an expert system and making the system available to companies who need to comply.

The improvements in quality, timeliness, or consistency may seem small, but they can have a great impact on overall business. Texas Instruments uses its Capital Investment Expert System to help employees who make capital budgeting requests. The ES provides a complete and consistent set of questions covering all aspects of any proposal. The system guides users through the questions relevant to a particular project. Higher executives at TI are assured of comparable analyses, so they can make more informed capital allocation decisions. The system also helps individual managers analyze their situations more completely.

People sometimes talk of a "standard" ES application, but that is often an oxymoron. If a company needs experts to solve a particular problem, it usually needs a customized approach. Consequently, implementation of an ES is often as much a process of transferring a point of view or set of beliefs as it is providing a solution to a problem.

Consider how many "experts" you have in your business—people who know the processes and procedures better than you do. They can help you make some improvement in those areas.

Most likely, you already have everything you need to make the improvements necessary and move forward with an ES. You have a company full of experts, the latest information technology equipment, and an able IS department.

The next step is to form the team that will perform the analysis, write the code, and implement the system.

At the Disney retail stores, it was determined that the people creating the ES would be those who actually lived and breathed situations on a day-to-day basis. Rather than bringing technologists into the equation and having them try to answer questions that haven't been asked or needn't be asked, they brought in people from the store organization, or people in the accounting or merchandising arenas, and made them part of the systems team.

One of the Disney's goals was to take the most tedious administrative tasks involved in running a store—such as ordering supplies—and make them as paperless and automatic as possible. The objective was to get the management people on the store floor as much as possible and out of the back room, in order to deliver and maintain the highest level of guest service.

The Company IQ

We have talked throughout this book about the islands of information that exist within your business, scattered activity that most likely has been ongoing and growing for years. Managers of companies with hundreds of millions of dollars in revenue and tens of thousands of employees can't track everything that happens, much less coordinate millions of elements into a timely, coherent response. That's why functional hierarchies were originally created.

The old chain of command was designed for a relatively stable—and now increasingly rare—make-and-sell kind of business. But many fast-growing sense-and-respond companies never adopted functional hierarchies in the first place. In the process of expanding, they have

used IT-enabled networks as the tendons that hold the skeleton and muscles of the company together.

In an attempt to compete with agile niche players, executives in many large companies are loosening the reins. Rather than explicitly specifying "do it this way," they are empowering employees to "do it the best way you know how." However, without coordination, accountability, and shared objectives, this approach can often lead to paralysis rather than coherent company-wide behavior.

A company's complexity is a function of how many information sources it needs, how many business elements it must coordinate, and the number and type of relationships that exist among those elements. We think of a company's corporate IQ as its institutional ability to deal with complexity—its ability to capture, share, and extract meaning from marketplace signals. Corporate IQ directly translates into three IT infrastructure imperatives for connecting, sharing, and structuring information.

In most large companies, a low IQ results from change occurring so rapidly that it's neither feasible nor affordable to keep computer applications up to date. Low IQs are particularly prevalent when processes have been automated over decades without any framework to integrate disparate applications and databases.

Clearly, corporate managers, not IT professionals, should design a business. And business design extends beyond procedural design; it includes making strategic decisions about what market signals should be sensed, what data or analytical models should be used to interpret those signals, and how an appropriate response should be executed.

To faithfully represent management's design, a model must consistently characterize any process at any scale, exhaustively account for the possible outcomes of every process, and unambiguously specify the roles and accountabilities of the employees involved in carrying them out.

In a test at a large manufacturing company, an enterprise modeling tool was used to map an engineering change process for electronic circuitry. Senior executives considered this process among the best in the organization. However, the new modeling tool not only revealed opportunities for procedural improvements, such as removing manufacturing bottlenecks, it also uncovered a startling fact: during the entire operation, not one person in the organization made a single commitment on volumes, cost, or delivery dates. Only forecasts, estimates, and targets were set. No one was accountable for making the goals stick.

If accountability isn't specified, business processes lack discipline and predictability, making them difficult to manage. A model that defines both procedures and accountability for outcomes can help managers do the job of managing.

Decision Making: Where Is the Information?

Making the "right" decision is not always possible, but making the "best possible" decision is. If a manager believes that he has all the information required to make the best possible decision, he will usually make that decision with all confidence. However, given the state of

information technology in today's businesses—those "islands" out there—all the information required to make the best possible decision does not usually make it into the hands of the decision maker.

In the middle of this required process of information flow is the ES. An ES can serve a dramatic purpose. By combining logic and employee expertise into software code, a practice or procedure that used to require days can now be reduced to minutes or seconds. Thus, information becomes available quicker.

Executives have been intrigued for years by the idea of computer programs that can replace the human element, so that the repetitive intelligence required to make decisions can be incorporated into a "never-failing" computer program. ("Never-failing" in this context is used with the understanding that the program is updated systematically to reflect changes in business climate.)

Once expertise is revealed, it can be reviewed, discussed, and communicated in whole new ways. Studies have shown that experts are seldom able to retrace the analytic steps taken to arrive at a particular decision. They may be able to highlight important factors that went into a decision, but usually cannot describe the whole process. They are not being intentionally evasive. In the process of becoming expert, individuals distill many observations into intuition and deep understanding but may not be able to articulate them.

That can make it difficult to mine the expert's knowledge. But once the information has been drawn from the expert and the software created, the rules, examples, and data provide a mental mirror with which the expert can explore, explain, and elucidate the nature of his or her expertise. The understanding revealed is therefore of value both to the expert and to the members of the organization dependent on the expertise.

Once expertise is outside someone's head, more people can work at refining it; as the expertise is fine-tuned, problem solving moves from art to science. It can then be more easily captured in other computer languages. Thus, today's ground-breaking ES may be tomorrow's traditional solution.

It will be tempting to look back at an ES and say that the task should have been solved with a more traditional programming approach. But to take that position is usually to misunderstand (and underestimate) the process by which expertise is captured. Once a complex problem is solved, the solution seems obvious.

Another benefit of ES is that once the knowledge has been captured in code, it can be protected and shared. If a human expert is hired away or is too busy to teach younger colleagues, an ES can help by serving as a training tool. Many people can, in effect, become apprentices to a few experts. People who are afraid to ask questions because they are expected to know the answers can consult with an ES in private. And the experienced person can benefit by seeing how another expert approaches the task.

And finally, building an ES is a foot in the door to artificial intelligence. Most systems are custom built, and even the few available turnkey systems often need customization. Knowledge engineers are scarce, and it takes time to develop people with the skills needed to make ESs and AI work. Of course, these facts can be used competitively. By getting in early, an organization can gain experience and develop technical staff, thereby creating a barrier competitors will have a hard time overcoming.

Who's Using Expert Systems?

Westinghouse Electric Corporation designed an expert system to monitor the steam turbines it sells. When a turbine fails, it sometimes throws pieces of steel, whirling at thousands of revolutions per minute, into protective castings, causing tens of thousands of dollars worth of damage and weeks of downtime. Detection of potential failures is extremely useful. Westinghouse's process diagnostic system (PDS) continuously tracks data from monitors on the turbine and makes recommendations for maintenance. PDS is sold as part of Westinghouse's service contract.

American Express Company uses an ES to help its credit authorization staff sort through data from as many as 13 databases. The American Express credit card has no set spending limit, an important feature for competitive reasons. Determining the appropriate credit level for each customer, however, poses a stiff administrative challenge.

Each time the customer makes a large purchase, the merchant telephones AMEX to authorize the charge. The AMEX employee then has to make a quick judgment call. Authorization requests outside the normal buying pattern require a search of the data bases for more information. Now the Authorizer's Assistant ES performs that search and makes recommendations to the person who makes the authorization decision. The entire process takes only seconds.

Coopers & Lybrand has an ES called ExperTAX that helps accountants in reviewing the way their clients accrue taxes and in offering tax planning advice. ExperTAX improves the quality of the tax service because it never forgets a question and it checks each policy against the client's financial statistics. Furthermore, it allows relatively inexperienced junior staff to perform more complete and accurate tax planning.

XCON, Authorizer's Assistant, and ExperTAX didn't disappoint the companies that funded them. The improvements they delivered were real and measurable. We've already discussed how XCON saves Digital money and furthers its corporate goals. AMEX expects its Authorizer's Assistant not only to raise an authorizer's productivity by as much as 20 percent but also to reduce losses from over-extension of credit. (The exact financial benefit is kept secret.) Authorizer's Assistant supports the company's strategy to differentiate itself by offering individualized credit limits. ExperTAX makes better use of junior people's time.

As these examples show, expert systems can support various competitive strategies by differentiating a product or by lowering costs. Sometimes projects begun with one objective in mind have led to another. In some instances, new businesses have sprung up. Both Texas Instruments and Digital first developed expert systems for internal use but have since spun off organizations based on the technology that offer new products, such as expert systems "shells," and consulting and training. (An ES shell is a software tool that provides an integrated set of building blocks that can be used to create an ES program.)

Learning from an ES

Often more interesting—and ultimately more valuable—than the hoped-for gains in productivity and effectiveness are the many unexpected benefits that flow from ESs. One such benefit is the way an ES can help people in the organization understand a problem better.

For years, IBM had a set of standard prices for installing, relocating, or removing computers. These prices were the starting point for negotiations among the customer, the field service representative, and service management. Because each customer had different ducting, wiring, and flooring and because experience of the estimators varied widely, consistent bidding was a problem. IBM field service employees needed a better shared understanding of how to price complex jobs.

Now IBM uses an ES called CONSULTANT to help price bids. The representative simply specifies the machine types and the location-specific factors, and the system generates a bid. Bids are negotiated only if the field person's price differs from CONSULTANT's by more than 20 percent. This procedure has eliminated many administrative problems.

Neural Networks: An ES Variation

A variation to the ES, called neural networks, is beginning to be seen, and its adaptability may eventually overshadow efforts at further developing expert systems. Neural networks (NNs) seek to mimic the ability of the human brain to learn from experience. They analyze past decisions and find patterns, concentrating not so much on *what* the expert decided, but *how* he decided.

The most common use for NN programs involves finding previously unnoticed relationships in collections of data.

In retailing, for example, the advantages of such a program are apparent. Through their POS systems, retail collects very accurate, detailed data on sales. This is extremely valuable information because it can help retailers determine how consumers will make future purchases.

In practice, however, attempts to combine POS, pricing, promotion, demographic, consumer preference, market trends and other seemingly disparate data to forecast sales have been fraught with difficulties. Standard forecast techniques are based on linear regression, using prior sales as the only variable. But that really isn't how buyers buy. So while forecasting based on last year's sales data alone is better than not forecasting at all, it isn't the entire answer.

Neural networks might be the answer.

Neural networks work by modeling the relationship between things we know—which are called independent variables or predictors—and things we don't know, which are dependent variables or predictions. But rather than relying on a human's estimate of the correct formula, a neural network builds its own model by guessing, testing, and modifying.

The NN then will analyze multiple variables to develop a forecast. Variables might include promotional activity planned for the product, promotions of similar products, price changes, competition within a five-mile radius and weather conditions. As the model is being developed, its accuracy can be tested with and without each variable to determine the variable's effect on the forecast's accuracy.

Whichever approach you utilize—the ES or the NN—with proper planning and your best available sources of information, you will experience a dramatic result. In the process, you will most likely learn more about outdated business processes within your company.

As exciting and promising as ESs are, over-enthusiasm can sometimes lead to unfounded assumptions and unrealistic expectations. A typical claim is that expert systems help companies "clone their experts." That claim is overblown. Problem-solving is only a small part of what an expert does in a company.

The best ESs to date capture only a portion of the expert's knowledge. Moreover, even the most advanced expert systems, such as XCON, do not replace experts; they augment their capabilities or allow less-experienced individuals to perform better. Generally speaking, humans are supported by—not replaced by—expert systems. Moreover, expert systems are regularly, if not continually, monitored and updated by humans.

Though most ESs are written internally, an example of Expert System suppliers to the insurance industry are Aion Corporation (Palo Alto, CA), and AICorp, Inc. (Waltham, MA). These companies have recently merged to form Trinzic Corporation.

Supporting the Seven Principles

Expert Systems support the following reengineering principles:

≋   They organize work around results, not tasks. An ES achieves the task by including tasks within

≋   They use data that is captured one time. The expert does not have to review each and every occurrence

≋   People who use the process do the work—the perfect example of expertise and IS working together

≋   They treat geographic resources as one. The ES can be centrally located.

Conclusion

Expert systems are not new. No matter how much technology evolves, changes, and brings about wonderful things, ESs continue to be a part of building new sophisticated information systems.

The packaging of ESs continues to change. More and more of the human methodology and thinking processes are becoming computerized. As long as productivity increases are possible, the knowledge stored within the mind will evolve into even more productive information systems.

Multimedia will likely provide the next breakthroughs in intelligent behavior. The perception of ease-of-use will increasingly become based on ideas from the entertainment arena. Multimedia—all the glory and excitement of sights and sounds—is reviewed in the next chapter.

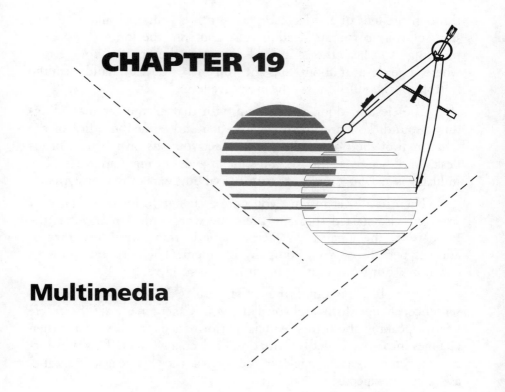

CHAPTER 19

Multimedia

You walk into the large auditorium for your division's annual meeting. It's been a tough year but your department has done well. In the front of the room is a large 10-foot screen. As the lights dim, you hurry to find a good seat.

In the background you hear the faint sound of a helicopter. As the sound gets louder, a distant view of the skyline of a city that seems somehow familiar appears on the screen. As if you were a passenger in the craft, the buildings become closer and more distinct. Suddenly you realize this is the city where your corporate headquarters is located, and there's the company's building.

The scene switches. You are on the ground looking up. The helicopter is descending toward you with your firm's name painted across the bottom.

The scene changes again. The helicopter has landed as the sounds of the motor and whirling blades start to diminish. As if looking through the lens of a video camera, you find yourself walking up the steps of your corporate headquarters and into the lobby. It's a busy morning. You hear the sounds of people as they move about everywhere. The elevator door opens and you enter. You see a hand push the button for the 50th floor—the executive level.

The elevator door opens again with that all too familiar "ding-ding" sound. You proceed down the hall and enter the office of the Chairman of the Board. He rises to greet you, sits on the edge of his desk, and begins to speak. His message is strong and clear. The industry is growing, and your firm is a vibrant part of that growth.

Then in a brief instant, you note a change in his voice. It's as if someone else started speaking the same words mid-sentence. At the same time, the Chairman's face and body transforms into that of another person. It's your company President. The corporate message continues, but from another executive's perspective.

After a brief period of time, it happens again. The President, mid-sentence, changes form and voice into your Chief Financial Officer. He begins speaking about the financial performance for last year. He then changes into your Chief Information Officer, a woman. This transformation generates a few giggles in the room as the change is so dramatic, as well as unexpected.

As the presentation continues you find yourself spell-bound wondering who the presenter will change into next. What will they say? The underlying message is clear yet ever so subtle—the members of your firm's senior management are a real team. They all share a common message.

Your division Vice President is next and a cheer erupts in the auditorium. As he begins to speak, he moves from his sitting position on the corner of the desk to one of standing. His figure is life-size on the screen. He casually begins walking to the left. Just as he is about to walk off-camera, he appears in real life from behind the screen, still talking. The effect is as if he magically came out of the screen. A cheer goes up again. You, and the rest of the audience are captivated. He quickly moves to the illuminated podium, and continues.

His presentation is powerful and informative. He talks about the people in your division and the real contributions each has made. Video clips of live interviews with key employees are interwoven with colorful graphs and bullet slides that support his statements. He commands the flow of the presentation from what seems to be a touch-screen device.

A hand goes up with a question. It pertains to something covered five minutes earlier. With a simple touch of the screen, a previous portion of his presentation instantly appears. The question is answered completely with supporting detail. Once again, a touch of his screen brings him, without delay, back to where he left off.

The presenter makes his closing remarks regarding the challenges that lie ahead for the company. The lights dim once more. The screen displays a distant view of the corporate headquarters building again. Triumphant music fills the room.

The company building starts to melt into a sphere of silver liquid, and then reforms into the shape of the starship Enterprise. It slowly rises from among the other office buildings, circles around the city, and then jumps into hyperspace with a boom. In its wake is a trail of glittering particles that gather together to spell out the company theme for the new year: "CHARTING THE COURSE FOR THE FUTURE."

What type of presentation would you choose to attend? The one above, or one where the presenter subjected you to black and white transparencies that have you nodding off after the first five minutes?

This dynamic presentation could have been taken on the road and shown at each of the company's division locations, and it would not have required senior management to travel to each location.

What if this were a sales presentation being given to your company? Would you rather sit through black and white slides, or something like the annual meeting? Which presentation method would motivate you to buy? How about a sales presentation given by your company representing your products and services? Which presentation method would you prefer your company use? What method does your competitor use?

In the world of presentation support tools, black and white transparencies were the predominant medium used in the 1960's. Color was added in the late 1970s, which helped a great deal. At least, it seemed to keep audiences awake a bit longer.

In the mid 80s the industry moved to 35mm slides. We put our audience in the dark and back to sleep. Most slides were too busy, upside down, or backwards, or all three. And have you ever dropped a tray of slides just before a major presentation and have to explain away the delay?

Starting in the late 1980's, PC-based presentation software such as PowerPoint (Microsoft), Freelance Graphics (Lotus), and Harvard Graphics (Software Publishing Corporation) became the predominant choices for presentation support. You can still bore your audience to tears, but you can no longer blame the presentation medium.

But let's get back to that hypothetical "annual meeting" described earlier. It actually took place. The company was a major natural gas conglomerate in Houston, Texas, and this creative and power-packed presentation was for its annual report to management.

The technology used to create such attention-grabbing effects is collectively referred to as multimedia. It is becoming the choice for presentation support, corporate training programs, and a host of other business applications. In this chapter, we explore this technology, its growth, and various examples of how and where it can be applied to business processes.

Multimedia: Our Definition

Pull together a group of six or seven corporate PC managers and support people. Ask them what they think the word "multimedia" means. After at least two hours of lively discussion, you will easily document more than 100 definitions.

In the context of our discussion, "multimedia" is simply a set of capabilities—including digital sound, video, and animation—that can be integrated with text and graphics to create computer applications that are more enriched and have more impact.

You've almost certainly seen multimedia presentations at trade shows. Lots of razzle-dazzle, sure. But you probably don't think it has much to do with your business problems. For many people, multimedia is still Rodney Dangerfield technology—it doesn't get much respect. It looks good, sounds great, and is exciting to watch. Often, however, it is judged to be too complicated, too expensive, and too much trouble for too little purpose.

What you need to keep in mind is that multimedia, or "new media" as some are starting to call it, is the use of multiple types of media—text, graphics, sound, animation, and video—to convey information. Multimedia applications do not have to be the grandiose and often unreal applications we see at trade shows. They do not have to be as extensive as our utility's annual company meeting described earlier. For that matter, it doesn't even have to be labeled as a "multimedia" application.

The PC in your research department may be configured with a CD-ROM drive to provide access to the huge amounts of data now available in that medium. Even if the CDs contain video and sound clips, you may not think of this application as being multimedia. Rather, you merely view the CD-ROM as just another form of storage device.

Or how about the executive who has video installed in his computer to permit him to watch TV on a real-time basis. He may also have a fax send/receive modem and telephone answering software, which permits the computer to double as a voice mail system. He may not consider his application to be multimedia; he merely sees his PC as a more productive business tool.

Why Use Multimedia?

One of the most widely accepted principles of teaching is that people retain in short-term memory about 20 percent of what they see, 40 percent of what they see and hear, and 70 percent of what they see, hear, and do. It stands to reason that the more we involve all the human senses, the better job we will do at communicating our message.

For a long time, the PC has been relegated to number crunching and word processing. Numbers and text are the easy stuff, but use only a small part of our senses. For the PC to become a full extension of ourselves, it must be made to capture, store, process, and communicate in multiple types of media. Improvements in each of these areas can also increase our effectiveness.

Take audio, for instance. How long have we suffered with the limitations of that silly speaker in the PC, capable of little more than a beep? We've moved from 78 rpm phonographs to CD-ROM players to enhance our enjoyment of music. Why should we accept less progress in the technology we use to run our businesses?

The Elements of Multimedia

Let's digress for a moment and briefly discuss the basic elements of multimedia.

Text and Graphics

These two traditional elements of computing we are all familiar with.

Text consists of words. Graphics consists of any visual method of displaying text information, such as charts, graphs, or pictures. Both text and graphics are the basis of what multimedia technology will manipulate.

Audio

Audio is the use of pieces of sound to convey information using a

person's auditory senses rather than their visual senses. In order to incorporate sound into an application, you first must use a sound digitizer to record and convert the sound into a digital format your PC can understand. From there, you can edit or manipulate the sound, adding special effects like reverb, or changing its pitch.

The PC records sound through a microphone in much the same way you record onto a cassette tape. The PC translates the sound into a binary code using a chip on the audio capture or sound card you have installed, and then stores the sound in a regular computer file. Instead of a text or graphics file, you have a sound sample, or audio "clip," as it is called.

Many Windows-based software programs comply with Microsoft's OLE standard. OLE stands for Object Linking & Embedding. The standard allows you to embed an audio clip anywhere in a text or graphics file, and have that audio clip become a physical part of the file. This "voice annotation" capability is like Post-It notes for files shared on a network, and is something many users use almost immediately.

A voice annotation capability may not make sense if you're just doing a spreadsheet for yourself, unless you merely want to store some kind of reminder to yourself. Consider, however, the idea of work-group computing. Both first-round and successive voice tags become extremely important to the spreadsheet on a network, where others see and work with it.

Video

Pieces of video used in multimedia applications can take two forms: live video being received as input through a camera, as in videoconferencing; or a previously recorded piece of video, or video "clip."

Video capture boards, also known as digitizers or frame grabbers, convert analog video signals from a source like a VCR or video camera into digital images. These digital images can be stored in a file on your hard drive.

Animation

We're not talking cartoons here, but the process of creating a computer generated animation is not really all that different than the process a cartoonist uses. It involves producing multiple frames of an image, in which part of the image changes over time to simulate motion.

The process of producing each frame of an animation is called "rendering." Even on the most powerful 486-based PCs, rendering a single frame may take anywhere from three minutes to as much as an hour, depending on the complexity of the drawing. Full-motion animation runs at thirty frames per second. Therefore, if you were producing an animation that had a run-time of five seconds, your potential rendering time to produce the animation could be 150 hours! (5 seconds × 30 frames/second × 1 hour per frame.)

Isn't This Pretty Expensive?

Until just recently, the answer was yes. To get started in multimedia, you had to have a super-fast processor in your PC, a sound board, speakers, lots of RAM, a big hard drive, a CD-ROM drive, and a high resolution monitor. Integrating all these capabilities into your PC and making them work correctly was no easy task either. You'd be ready to go only after you spent $7,000 to $8,000. The question was: go where? There were not a lot of multimedia products on the market.

 In today's market we find two types of multimedia users: those who are *authoring* or creating multimedia applications or "titles," and those who *play back* existing applications.

The *playback* user still needs all the hardware pieces noted above, but prices have plummeted. CD-ROM drives are getting faster and cheaper. PCs from Apple, Compaq, IBM, and almost every major computer manufacturer now support sound, voice input, video playback, and other multimedia features. Most all of these multimedia-ready PCs can be found at very affordable prices, often less than $2,000.

Multimedia upgrade kits containing everything necessary to upgrade your current 386 or 486 machine are also available. Companies like Creative Labs, CompuAdd, Media Vision, Tandy, and others are shipping kits with prices ranging from $800 to $1,200. Prices, however, continue to drop almost daily. Some predict that multimedia capabilities added to a PC will soon come free of charge, much like preloaded software is today.

Speaking of software, manufacturers continue to stamp out tons of new silver platters. CD-ROM-based software, databases, reference

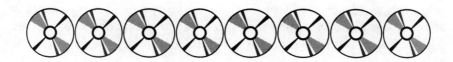

guides, talking encyclopedias, and scores of other information and training titles are being issued daily. Even the latest business presentation software such as PowerPoint, Freelance Graphics, and Harvard Graphics all bring presentations to life with new sound, animation, and graphics. There is even a CD-ROM-based interactive training course available today that teaches you how to reengineer business processes.

If you are *authoring* or creating multimedia titles, your PC hardware and software requirements are much more extensive, and will keep you at or even above the $5,000 mark. Unlike a *playback* user, you will need a video capture versus playback board, a much higher-quality microphone, authoring and animation software, and a hard drive that might approach 1GB or more.

What About Standards?

Does the multimedia industry have standards? Does it ever! There are more standards in the industry than languages spoken at the World Trade Center. There are standards for every "media" we have mentioned. Are there conflicts between all the standards? Yes. But fear not; there is a safe haven from the storm.

In May of 1991, Microsoft joined with 11 other leading industry PC suppliers and established what is now called the Multimedia PC Marketing Council. Members of the council agreed on what it refers to as "a widely accepted industry standard for multimedia computing." It further referred to the standard as one which "allows millions of existing PCs to be easily upgraded with the CD-ROM drive, sound board, and software required for multimedia use." The council uses an "MPC" trademark as a symbol of multimedia plug-and-play functionality, in the same way that "VHS" signifies compatibility between video cassette recorders and video tapes.

Users can now purchase products that display the MPC-trademark, and feel confident that compatibility among components is assured. For more information about these products or to request an MPC catalog, you can contact the Multimedia PC Marketing Council at:

Multimedia PC Marketing Council, Inc.
1703 M Street
Suite 700
Washington, DC 20036
(202) 331-0494

Gotchas, Do's, and Don'ts

Everyone can't upgrade. If you have older, less powerful PCs or operating environment, odds are you will never gain full access to the powers of multimedia. You really need to be using the latest version of Apple Computer Inc.'s Macintosh operating system, or Microsoft Corp.'s Windows along with a VGA or better board and monitor.

Networked multimedia isn't quite here yet. Today's popular networks are optimized for "bursty" data traffic created by productivity and business software. The compressed digital video or other high bandwidth audiovisual data found in multimedia applications produce continuously flowing "streams" of data. This streaming nature conflicts with PC networks, which are based upon contention schemes to ensure resource equality. When the network becomes busy, everything slows

down. This slowdown creates bottlenecks for audio, video, animation, and other real-time data.

There is, however, hope for networking multimedia too. Higher-bandwidth networks such as ISDN and ATM will help provide net-worked multimedia applications in the future. There are also many companies that have unused or underutilized cable and bandwidth that can carry their multimedia applications. For these companies, there isn't even an incremental cost to use the network for these type applications. Check it out. Your firm's network may be one of them.

You may not have the talent. There is an old saying in the com-puter industry, and it certainly applies to multimedia: You can teach an artist to use a computer; you cannot necessarily teach a computer person to be an artist. If you are going to "author" a multimedia application, we strongly suggest that you either take a lot of art classes before you begin, or find the creative types in your organization and give the job to them. The ease with which you assemble this type of talent will dictate how easy it is to make a transition from the old way to the new way.

Reengineering with Multimedia Magic

Two areas within corporate America top the list of multimedia implementation today: presentations and training. Let's focus on training for now.

We all know that to remain competitive in today's markets, busi-nesses need highly skilled employees. Corporate training programs cost a lot of time and money. Customer studies show that between 30 to 50 percent of total training costs can be saved when computer-based mul-timedia training is used along with traditional classroom programs. The same studies note productivity increases of 15 percent or more.

Take the experience of a large, well-known consulting firm. Part of the required training for all new consultants was to complete an intense business practice course. This course was made up of approximately 60 hours of self-study in local offices, coupled with 40 hours of instructor-led sessions at their corporate training facility.

A headquarters team took the assignment of designing a sophisticated multimedia version of the course. This course allows the new consultant to "wander" on-screen through a simulated company, making good and bad decisions, and solve various problems in every area of a make-believe business.

As a result of their investment of time, effort, and dollars, new consultants now complete the course in 35 hours instead of the previous 100 hours, and with better course results. In addition, the firm estimates they will save $2 million a year in payroll and $8.5 million a year in delivery costs. Their ROI, in real money, is less than six months.

By applying some of the principles of reengineering, the firm was able to reach their goal of reduced training time and expense without sacrificing quality.

- The desired result is to have better, most cost-effective training.
- Make people who use a process do the work. The firm provides an environment were the students basically teach themselves.
- Incorporate controls into information processing. The training is now consistent for all students rather than variable and based upon the expertise levels between course instructors.

Hospital Use of Multimedia

 A good example of where multimedia was applied as part of reengineering a process can be found at a major not-for-profit hospital in Houston, Texas. In this case, multimedia technology was a "must have."

As part of their charter, the hospital is required to accept low-income patients who are entitled to Medicaid benefits. A major concern is the growing numbers of pregnant teenagers. Each year, more than 4,000 girls ranging in age from 12 to 22 show up at the hospital's door in various stages of pregnancy. Some are only three months pregnant; others deliver their babies within 24 hours of arrival.

Most of these young women share many characteristics. They are single, poor, and illiterate, and come either from broken homes, half-way houses, or right from the street. Most know nothing about caring for an infant.

Part of the task of caring for these young women includes training on the various stages of pregnancy, to insure a healthy result for both mother and baby. Training is provided in three phases:

≋   **Prenatal** includes do's and don'ts in the early stages of pregnancy to reduce the likelihood of birth defects. This one step alone could save having to care for another 4,000 patients: the newborns themselves.

≋   **Labor and Delivery** details what is going to happen to the mother's body, and what the patient should expect during delivery.

≋   **Post Partum** outlines how to keep the baby healthy. What the hospital doesn't want is to have the new mother return to the hospital three months later because her baby has diaper rash up to its throat. Even worse, the mother could show up three months later, pregnant again.

Efforts to provide training to the girls is complicated by several issues. Pamphlets covering some of the more important things are available, but most of the girls can't read. Video tapes are limited, dated, and ineffective. Most of the training is conducted by Registered Nurses, and the last thing a troubled girl wants to hear is advice from an adult. Training is inconsistent due to changes in personnel and variance in teaching skills of the nurses.

Applying the principles of reengineering, the hospital first looked at *the desired result, not tasks*—communicate the information to the young women in such a way that learning could actually take place. The obvious question was "What communication media do women of this age like?" Simple: the telephone, a stereo, the TV. There was one other thing the young women liked as well—video games! Could a video game, which somehow included a telephone, stereo, and TV, be designed in such a way that the necessary information is communicated?

Responding to the next reengineering principle generated the need for multimedia. *Make people who use a process do the work.* Make the girls themselves do the work. But most of the girls can't read, but they can hear and see. Obviously, the requirement for audio and lots of visual graphics was mandatory. No text could be used.

Using the resources of an outside multimedia integrator, the hospital designed a PC-based video game in which each patient was presented with a house to explore using a mouse. Each room of the house was filled with familiar objects such as a TV, a phone, a stereo, furniture, a cat, pictures on the wall, and so forth. Many of the objects were designed with motion—the cat wags its tail, smoke rises from a burning cigarette in the ash tray on the table, etc.

When they click the mouse on almost any object in the room, the girls learn something about pregnancy and child care. If the burning cigarette is selected, a graphic appears showing the difference in fetus development between a mother who smokes and one who doesn't. If the cat is selected, the girls learn that the cat is OK to play with during their pregnancy, but don't change the cat's litter box. Have someone else do it. There is a germ in cat litter that can cause birth defects in unborn infants.

Several clever steps are designed into the game to address some of the other issues noted earlier. All the audio information is conveyed using young girls' voices, rather than adult voices. It's like the girls are talking with one of their friends their own age. To avoid any possible ethnic origin issues, all the "people" figures in the game are ethnically non-specific. They are not white, or African-American, or Asian. They are green, blue, and purple with triangular and square heads. The information is what is important, not the source of the information.

While the girls are having fun learning, another principle of reengineering is silently at work. *Incorporate controls into information processing.* The program tracks the progress each girl makes and writes the results onto a diskette for later analysis by the hospital staff.

The program is currently in beta test, so there is still no measurement as to the overall impact this new process will have. Both staff and patients that have been involved with the project, however, are ecstatic. Nursing staff members are being freed from training responsibilities and can return to normal duties. The young female patients love to "play the game." The hospital plans to share the program with others in Houston. One of the county hospitals in the area is providing services to more than 10,000 teenage pregnant girls annually. The excitement and promise of cutting those numbers is overwhelming.

Conclusion

Undoubtedly, the most important message we can convey to you through this book is simply this—Use IT or lose it. Use IT (Information Technology) in reengineering your business processes, or lose it—"it" being your competitive edge or profits. Explore the part of IT called multimedia. We know unfamiliar technologies can be somewhat intimidating at first. Many people feel the same hesitation about multimedia as they did when they first moved from DOS to Windows. Today, they are glad they invested the time and energy. Find a way to wade through what may seem like a jungle of multimedia terms, products, and standards. Discover this real technology treasure. Multimedia will empower you and your company. You won't be the first to use it—don't be the last.

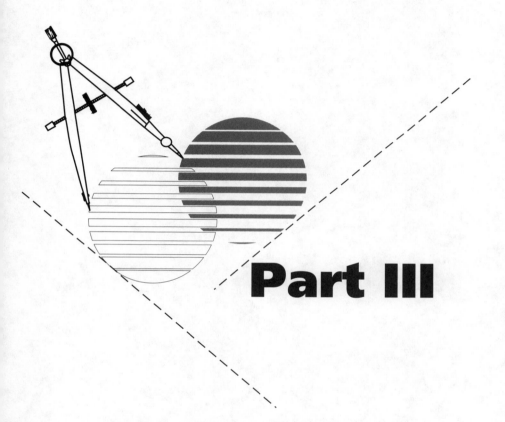

Part III

Getting It Together

It is time to create your plan. You know what the information technologies are that will enable your plan. Perhaps you are well aware of several areas within your business that need to be reworked. Perhaps—as you read of these technologies here—you have become aware of others.

Hold on tight. There are some potential stumbling blocks in front of you. We have learned of some of these do's and don'ts from those who have been down this path before. Understanding where the demons are before you begin the creation of your plan and its implementation will undoubtedly save you time and ensure that others continue to focus on them.

CHAPTER 20

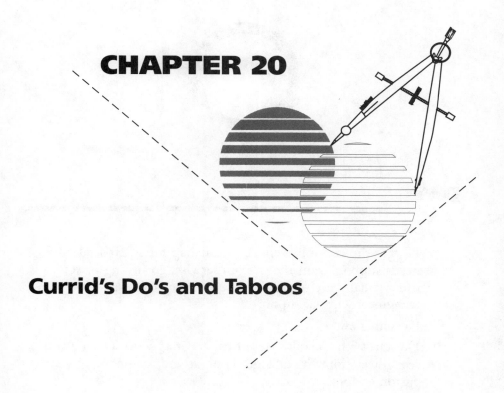

Currid's Do's and Taboos

Throughout this book, we have provided you with a wealth of useful information about bringing together teams, techniques, and technologies. But it's only a start. As John Locke said more than 300 years ago, "No man's knowledge here can go beyond his experience." With the knowledge you have gained in the preceding pages, you can now dive in and make something happen.

Remember, however, that reengineering is the fundamental rethinking and redesign of an entire business system. It is not a trivial undertaking. We are not dealing with changing the font on a personnel requisition form. BPR involves processes, jobs, organizations, management systems, values and beliefs. It strikes to the heart of your company.

We've gathered two lists: one, a list of activities that will enhance the process, the other a list of taboos. Consider them as you progress into your own project.

Do's

- ≡ Do get the commitment of top management. Radical BPR needs support from the top. Otherwise, go fishing or something equally useful. You will be wasting your time trying to reengineer without support.
- ≡ Do start now.
- ≡ Do start with a blank sheet of paper (or a "clean screen") and reengineer from the outside. Look at your company as your customer does.
- ≡ Do develop a clear vision early in the process.
- ≡ Do establish a common language. Get everyone to agree on the terminology you will use. It's important for the steering committee to set up the company mission and project objectives. It should be short and easily understood.
- ≡ Do document everything. Consider using a groupware product, like Lotus Notes, to collect all project materials. That way, you can easily organize and share your working activities.
- ≡ Do get teams established with the right people. Create a cross-functional team of people who are capable of doing the job. Use the best and the brightest on these teams—not just people who have time to participate.
- ≡ Do train them. Take the team to reengineering seminars.
- ≡ Do empower the team to act.
- ≡ Do establish in the organization a sense of urgency.

- Do set realistic, achievable schedules.

- Do pick the right process to reengineer. If the boss's daughter designed the order entry system, and the boss thinks his daughter hung the moon, don't start with the order entry process. Pick another one to begin.

- Do make sure that the benefits of reengineering are visible and understandable by the "customers," both internal and external.

- Do pick a quick winner first—a process that can be reengineered fairly quickly so the team can see some results.

- Do change the way the organization, and its people, work.

- Do pay attention to politics. We are dealing here with people and organizations. There will be turf wars. Be sensitive to the needs and desires of all team members and all ultimate users of the new process.

- Do consider bringing in an outsider. If you can't see beyond "the way we've always done it," then find someone who can. An outsider offers a fresh perspective untainted by organizational turf concerns.

- Do question everything. The presumption is that the process, and all its elements, are wrong. Only when they are proven right are they retained.

- Do apply the right technology. Make sure you use the right tool for the job. For example, virtual reality probably has little to do with accounts payable today. Likewise, don't put the customer list in a spreadsheet—use a database.

- Do include a technology expert on every reengineering project. If you don't have people with knowledge of advanced technologies, rent someone who does. You'll never find the best way if you never stumble over it.

- Do pick solid technology vendors for both hardware and software. Make sure the companies will be there tomorrow to support you and your systems.

- Do communicate broadly. Everyone needs to know what is happening. Use whatever it takes to get the message across—broadcast e-mail, voice mail, or newsletters. And don't forget to work the grapevine and rumor mill.

≋ Do set and reset your priorities. Prepare the roadmap properly and then continuously question it to see if it is still valid.

≋ Do use common sense but unconventional wisdom. If an idea doesn't withstand the test of reasonableness, discard it. But think outside the box without traditional constraints.

≋ Do bring lots of money. Reengineering isn't cheap. While most successful projects end up saving money, you'll end up spending a lot to get projects off the ground.

≋ Do take reasonable risks and surround yourself with people who are also willing and able to do so.

Taboos

≋ Don't do it if you don't have to. Don't fix a process that turns out to be the best in the industry. Choose obviously broken processes.

≋ Don't fix it if it doesn't matter. Go for the big processes and don't spend any time reengineering the color of paper on the third copy of the purchase order form.

≋ Don't be shy. You have to make changes.

≋ Don't wait around for someone to come ask you to change the way they work.

≋ Don't let the sponsors, the top managers from whom you have gained commitment, off the hook. Keep them committed.

≋ Don't fight a losing battle. If the team, the customer, or the management doesn't support the particular idea you're working on, move on to something else.

≋ Proceed carefully if you must use an untried, unproven technology. That does not mean to avoid leading-edge technology. It is often a competitive advantage to be first. But, as the wise man once said, don't test the depth of the water with both feet.

≋ Don't abandon total quality management (TQM). Reengineering complements TQM but does not replace it. For badly functioning processes, reengineer first, then follow with TQM methods to continuously improve the process.

≋ Don't expect to complete the job. Reengineering is not a one-time effort. When you finish one process, it is likely you'll find others.

≋ Don't give up. You will be frustrated. You will get angry. You will meet resistance. Be prepared for it. Keep moving forward.

Conclusion

So there you have it. We've covered the reasons for reengineering, the teams and techniques, and the information technologies that can become the basis for your company's transformation. Not only do you know *who* to get involved in the project and *how* to gain support from key players and employees, but we have given you the benefit of many years of experience in helping companies transform and transcend into a heightened state of competitiveness through the effective use of technology. We know, as you now do, that properly deployed technology allows people to share and make the most of pertinent business information. Your people can make faster, more accurate, and more informed business decisions as a result.

The business decision that you now face is an important one: do you want your company to be among "The Quick" or among "The

Dead"? It's time to position your organization for the 21st Century—by rethinking, reinventing, and reengineering anything that slows you down.

APPENDIX A

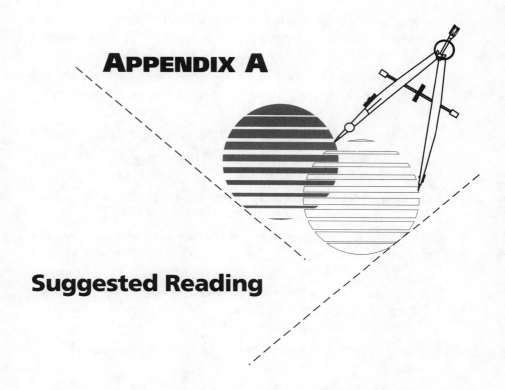

Suggested Reading

Books

Bancroft, Nancy H. *New Partnerships for Managing Technological Change*. New York: John Wiley & Sons, Inc., 1992.

Belasco, James. *Teaching the Elephant to Dance*. New York: Crown Publishers, 1990.

Conner, Daryl. *Managing at the Speed of Change*. New York: Random House, 1992.

Currid, Cheryl. *Computing Strategies for Reengineering Your Organization*. Roseville, CA: Prima Publishing, 1993.

Currid, Cheryl. *The Electronic Invasion*. New York: Brady Books, 1993.

Davis, Stan, and Bill Davidson. *20-20 Vision: Transform Your Business Today to Succeed in Tomorrow's Economy.* New York: Simon and Schuster, 1991.

Davenport, Thomas H. *Process Innovation Reengineering Work through Information Technology.* Boston: Harvard Business School Press, 1993.

Drucker, Peter. *Post Capitalist Society.* Harper Business, 1993.

Hammer, Michael, and James Champy. *Reengineering the Corporation: A Manifesto for Business Revolution.* Harper Business, 1993.

Hyatt, Carol, and Linda Gottlieb. *When Smart People Fail Rebuilding Yourself for Success.* New York: Penguin Books, 1993.

National Institute of Business Management. *Mastering Meeting. The Essential Guide for Successful and Productive Meetings.* Berkley Publishing, 1990.

Opper, Susanna, and Henry Fersko-Weiss. *Technology for Teams. Enhancing Productivity in Networked Organizations.* New York: Van Norstrand Reinhold, 1992.

Peters, Tom. *Liberation Management.* New York: Random House, November 1992.

Popcorn, Faith. *The Popcorn Report.* New York: Doubleday, 1991.

Senge, Peter. *The Fifth Discipline.* New York: Doubleday, August 1990.

Sideline. *Creative Wack Pack.* ISBN 0-880-79-3589.

Sproull, Lee, and Sara Keisler. *Connections: The New Ways of Working in the Networked Organization.* Cambridge: MIT Press, 1991.

Stuckey, M. M. *Demassification: A Cost Comparison of Micro vs. Mini.* New York: Fourth Shift, 1989.

Stuckey, M. M. *Demass: Transforming the Dinosaur Corporation.* New York: Productivity Press, 1993.

Tapscott, Don, and Art Caston. *Paradigm Shift.* New York: McGraw Hill, Inc., 1993.

Toffler, Alvin. *Powershift: Knowledge, Wealth, and Violence at the Edge of the 21st Century.* New York: Bantam Books, 1990.

Wycoff, Joyce. *Mindmapping: Your Personal Guide to Exploring Creativity and Problem-Solving.* Berkley Publishing, 1991.

Zuboff, Shoshana. *In the Age of the Smart Machine*. New York: Basic Books, 1988.

Articles

"Advertising: Roman Wins WPP Battle." *The Wall Street Journal*, November 11, 1992, p. B6.

Ayre, Rick. "Mail-enabled Applications Help Groups Work Together." *PC Magazine*, October 27, 1992, pp. 268–269.

Bannon, Lisa. "Italy Privatization to Start with Sale of Credito Italiano." *The Wall Street Journal*, November 10, 1992, p. A20.

Berezhnaya, Olga. "All Together to Bankruptcy?" *Moscow News*, November 8, 1992, p. 11.

"BfG Bank: Gothic Takeovers." *The Economist*, October 24, 1992, p. 88–89.

Bray, Nicholas. "Makes $1.5 Billion Bid for RHM, Topping Hanson Offer." *The Wall Street Journal*, October 30, 1992, sec. A7.

"British Airways Said to Consider a Bid for Qantas." *New York Times*, October 28, 1992, p. D3.

Brousell, David, Elaine Appleton, and Jeff Mood. "Levi Strauss's CIO On: The Technology of Empowerment." *Datamation*, June 1, 1992.

Bruousell, David R. "Multimedia's Giant Conceptual Leap." *Datamation*, January 15, 1993, p. 114.

Buzzard, James. "The Client/Server Paradigm: Making Sense Out of the Claims." *Data Based Advisor*, August 1990, p. 72(8).

Carr, Grace M. "Share and Share Alike." *Lan Technology*, November 1992, pp. 74–81.

Choi, Audrey. "Conflict Besets Eastern German Steel Industry." *The Wall Street Journal*, November 4, 1992, p. A10.

Choi, Audrey. "France to Sell Rhone-Poulenc Shares to Public." *The Wall Street Journal*, October 30, 1992, p. A9C.

"Computerland's Seven Suggestions for Successful Client/Server Computing." *Computerland Magazine*, January/February 1992.

Drucker, Peter. "The New Society of Organizations." *Harvard Business Review,* September 1992.

"Dunhill Is Said to Seek Gucci." *The New York Times,* November 2, 1992, p. D7.

Dunn, Peter. "GenRad Plans 2750 Model to Run Software for 1970." *Electronic News,* February 17, 1992, p. 18.

"East German Companies: Private, Perhaps." *The Economist,* November 7, 1992, p. 87.

Edwards, Billy, and Adrienne Moch, "From Water to Public Works: One City's Privatization Success Story." *American City & County,* November 1992, pp. 38–39.

Edwards, Morris. "Some Notes On Groupware for LANs." *Communications News,* July 1992, p. 42.

Ehrenman, Gayle C. "Meetings Go Electronic, for a Price." *PC Magazine,* May 12, 1992, p. 31.

Eng, Paul M. "Bits & Bytes." *Business Week,* January 25 1993, p. 88D.

Fischer, Bryan J. "Privatization in Poland, Hungary, and Czechoslovakia." RFE/RL Research Report, November 6, 1992, pp. 34–39.

Garneau, George. "Zuckerman and the 'Bleeding Dinosaur.' " *Editor & Publisher,* October 31, 1992, pp. 12, 35.

"Gillette Plan to Buy Parker Pen Receives Scrutiny on Antitrust." *The Wall Street Journal,* October 7, 1992, p. All.

Goff, Leslie. "High School Goes Prime Time." *LAN Magazine,* April 1993, pp. 151–156.

Hammer, Michael. "What is Reengineering." *Information Week,* May 5, 1992, p. 10.

"Hanson: Hunter's Return." *The Economist,* October 10, 1992, pp. 84–85.

Herman, James, Christopher Serjak, and Perter Sevcik. "Switched Internets: The Coming Gigabit Revolution in Enterprise Networking." *Distributed Computing Monitor,* February 1993, 3-28.

Hudson, Richard L. "Hanson Offers $1.35 Billion for Bread Baker." *The Wall Street Journal,* October 6, 1992, p. A15.

Job, Mark. "What is Groupware Anyway?" *Data Based Advisor,* August 1992, pp. 60–62.

Kantrowitz, Barbara, and Joshua Cooper Ramo. "An Interactive Life." *Newsweek*, May 31, 1993, pp. 42–44.

Kaplan, Alan, Robert Lauriston, and Steve Fox. "Groupware (Buyers Guide)." *PC World*, March 1992, pp. 208–15.

Koehler, Scott. "The Scoop on OOP." *Computerworld*, February 8, 1993, p. 52.

Kramer, Matt. "E-mail May Hold Key to Groupware's Future." *PC Week*, October 26, 1992, p. S20.

"Kroger Co." *The Wall Street Journal*, August 19,1992, p. B4.

Leonard, Jonathan S. "Unions and Employment Growth." *Industry Relations*, Winter 1992, pp. 80–94.

"Managing by Wire." Harvard Business Review, September/October 1993.

Marshak, Ronni T. "Focusing our Workgroup Coverage: Concentrating on the 3Cs: Communications, Collaboration, and Coordination." Patricia Seybold's Office Computing Report, May 1992, pp. 2–3.

Nunamaker Jr., Jay F. "Automating the Flow: Groupware Goes to Work." *Corporate Computing*, October 1992, pp. 187–91.

Powell, Bill, Anne Underwood, Seema Nayyar, and Charles Fleming. "Eyes on the Future." *Newsweek*, May 31, 1993, pp. 39–41.

Quinnel, Richard A. "Llama Alert!" *EDN*, June 28, 1990.

Quint, Michael. "Takeover Set for a Bank in Colorado." *The New York Times*, November 10, 1992, p. D3.

Rao, Anand. "Team Spirit." *LAN Magazine*, March 1993, pp. 109–114.

Raskin, Robin. "For the Good of the Group?" *PC Magazine*, January 12, 1993, p. 30.

"Russia: Reform in One City." *The Economist*, November 7, 1992, p. 60.

Senese, Gene. "Get Ready to 'Morph' Yourself." *Computerworld*, June 7, 1993, p. 33.

Sheridan, John H. "JIT Spells Good Chemistry at Exxon." *Industry Week*, July 1, 1991, pp. 26–28.

Skorstad, Egil. "Mass Production, Flexible Specialization and Just-in-Time: Future Development Trends of Industrial Production and Consequences on Conditions of Work." *Futures*, December 1991, pp. 1075–1084.

Slofstra, Martin. "Is E-mail About to Explode?" *Computing Canada*, February 15, 1993, pp. 1–2.

Spiegel, Leo S. "Expanding Brain Bandwidth." *Lan Technology*, November 1992, pp. 39–43.

Stark, David. "Path Dependence and Privatization Strategies in East Central Europe." *East European Politics & Societies*, Winter 1992, pp. 17–54.

Stone, M. David, Steven Chen, and Steve Rigney. "Have Your Computer Call My Computer." *PC Magazine*, Februrary 9, 1993, pp. 271–288.

Weimer, George, Bernie Knill, et al. "Integrated Manufacturing: Compressing Time-to-Market Today's Competitive Edge." *Industry Week*, May 4, 1992, pp. IM2–IM16.

"World Wire: Argentine Nuclear Privatization." *The Wall Street Journal*, October 28, 1992, p. A14.

"World Wire: Philippines to Speed Sell-Offs." *Wall Street Journal*, November 4, 1992, p. A10.

"World Wire: Portugal to Privatize Radio." *The Wall Street Journal*, October 30, 1992, p. A7.

Valdes, Ray. "Sizing Up Application Frameworks and Class Libraries." *Dr. Dobb's Journal*, October 1992, pp. 18–35.

APPENDIX B

Software and Hardware Manufacturers

Adobe Systems, Inc.
1585 Charleston Road
Mountain View, CA 94039-7900
415-961-4400

America Online
8619 Westwood Center Drive
Vienna, VA 22182-2285
703-448-8700

Apple Computers, Inc.
20525 Mariani Avenue
Cupertino, CA 95014
408-996-1010

Arabesque Software, Inc.
2340 130th Avenue NE
Bellevue, WA 98005-1754
206-869-9600

AT&T Global Computing
1700 S. Patterson Blvd.
Dayton, OH 45479
513-445-5000

Automap, Inc.
1309 114th Ave SE, Suite 110
Bellevue, WA 98004-6999
206-455-3552

Avalan Technology
116 Hopping Brook Park
Holliston, MA 01746
508-429-6482

Borland International
1800 Green Hills Road
Scotts Valley, CA 95066
408-438-8400

Compaq Computer Corporation
20555 SH 249
Houston, TX 77269-2000
713-370-0670

CompuADD Corp.
12303 Technology Blvd.
Austin, TX 78727
512-250-1486

CompuServe, Inc.
P.O. Box 20212
Columbus, OH 43220
800-848-8199

Corel Corporation
1600 Carling Avenue
Ottawa, Ontario, Canada K1Z 8R7
613-728-8200

Creative Labs
1901 McCarthy Blvd.
Milpitas, CA 95035-7442
408-428-6600

Delrina Corporation
6830 Via Del Oro, Suite 240
San Jose, CA 95119
800-268-6082

Digital Equipment Corporation
146 Main Street
Maynard, MA 01754-2571
508-493-5111

Dragon Systems, Inc.
320 Nevada Street
Newton, MA 02160
617-965-5200

FileNet Corporation
3656 Harbor Blvd.
Costa Mesa, CA 92626-9916
714-966-3400

Fractal Design Corporation
335 Spreckels Drive, Suite F
Aptos, CA 95003
408-688-5300

Fujitsu Computer Products of
America, Inc.
2904 Orchard Parkway
San Jose, CA 95134-2022
800-626-4686

General Electric Company
GE Information Services
3135 Easton Turnpike
Fairfield, CT 06431
203-373-2211

General Magic
2465 Latham Street, Suite 100
Mountain View, CA 94040
415-965-0400

HSC Software
1661 Lincoln Boulevard, Suite 101
Santa Monica, CA 90404
310-392-8441

IBM Corporation
Route 100
Sommers, NY 10589
914-766-3700

Individual, Inc.
84 Sherman Street
Cambridge, MA 02140
617-354-2230

Intel Corporation
3065 Bowers Avenue
Santa Clara, CA 95052
408-765-8080

Intersolv, Inc.
3200 Tower Oaks Blvd.
Rockville, MD 20852
301-230-3200

Lotus Development Corporation
55 Cambridge Parkway
Cambridge, MA 02142
617-577-8500

Madge Networks
2310 North First Street
San Jose, CA 95131-1011
408-955-7000

McCaw Cellular Communications
P.O. Box 97060
Kirkland, WA 98083-9760
206-827-4500

MCI Communications Corp.
1801 Pennsylvania Avenue NW
Washington, DC 20006
202-872-1600

Media Vision
3185 Laurelview Court
Fremont, CA 94538
510-770-8600

Metricom, Inc.
980 University Avenue
Los Gatos, CA 95030
408-339-8200

Microcom, Inc.
500 River Ridge Drive
Norwood, MA 02062-5028
617-551-1000

Micrografx
1303 Arapaho Drive
Richardson, TX 75081
214-234-1769

Microsoft Corporation
One Microsoft Way
Redmond, WA 98052
206-882-8080

Motorola, Inc.
1303 E. Algonquin Road
Schaumburg, IL 60196
708-576-5000

Novell Corporation
122 E. 1700 South
Provo, UT 84606-6194
801-429-7000

Omron Advanced Systems Inc.
10201 Torre Avenue, Suite 330
Cupertino, CA 95014
408-996-3088

Oracle Corporation
500 Oracle Parkway
Redwood Shores, CA 94065
415-506-4651

PC DOCS, Inc.
124 Marriott Drive, Suite #203
Tallahassee, FL 32301
904-942-3627

Pixar
1001 W. Cutting Blvd.
Richmond, CA 94804
510-236-4000

Polaris Software
17150 Via Del Campo, #307
San Diego, CA 92127
619-674-6500

Powersoft Corporation
70 Blanchard Road
Burlington, MA 01803
617-229-2200

Prisma Software Corporation
401 Main Street
Cedar Falls, IA 50613
319-266-7141

Prodigy Services Co.
445 Hamilton Avenue
White Plains, NY 10601
914-993-8000

Proxim
295 N. Bernardo Avenue
Mountain View, CA 94043
415-960-1630

RadioMail
2600 Campus Drive
San Mateo, CA 94403
415-286-7800

Reach Software Corporation
872 Hermosa Drive
Sunnyvale, CA 94086
408-733-8685

Road Scholar, Inc.
2603 Augusta, Suite 1000
Houston, TX 77057
713-266-7623

SkyTel Corp.
200 S. Lamar Street
Jackson, MI 39201
601-944-1300

SoftSolutions Technology
Corporation
625 S. State Street
Orem, UT 84058-9989
801-226-6000

Software Publishing Corporation
3165 Kifer Road
Santa Clara, CA 94056-0983
408-986-8000

SWFTE International Ltd.
724 Yorklyn Road
Hockessin, DE 19707
302-234-1740

Sybase, Inc.
6475 Christie Avenue
Emeryville, CA 94608
510-596-3500

Symantec
10201 Torre Avenue
Cupertino, CA 95014-2132
408-253-9600

Tandy Corporation
1800 One Tandy Center
Fort Worth, TX 76102
817-390-3700

Trinzic Corporation
404 Wyman Street, Suite 320
Waltham, MA 02254-9156
617-891-6500

TRW Inc.
1900 Richmond Road
Cleveland, OH 44124-3760
216-291-7000

Ventana East Corporation
Oakdale 700 Building
700 Harry L. Drive
Johnson City, NY 13790
800-295-8640

Verbex Voice Systems, Inc.
1090 King Georges Post Road,
Bldg. 107
Edison, NJ 08837-3701
908-225-5225

WordPerfect Corporation
1555 North Technology Way
Orem, UT 84057
800-451-5151

XIRCOM
26025 Mureau Road
Calabasas, CA 91302
818-878-7600

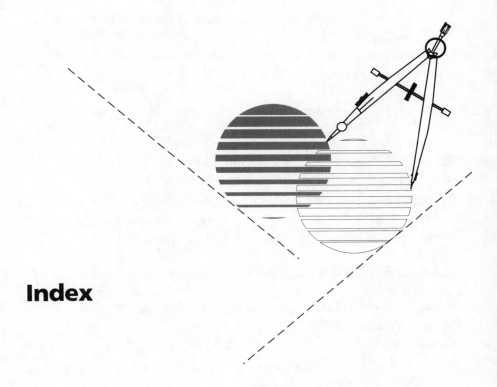

Index

A

ABC Flow-Charter (Micrografx), 32

A.C. Nielsen, 91, 104

Agent technology, 213–16

AICorp, Inc., 242

Aion Corporation, 242

All Clear (Clear Software), 32

All-Hazards Situation Prototype-LAN (ASAP-LAN), 110

America Online, 208

American Airlines reengineering project, 32

American Express Company expert system, 239–40

Animation for multimedia, 251–52

ANSI X.12 standard for electronic commerce, 180

Application development
choosing the right tool for, 73–74
productivity as measure in, 72
revisiting technologies for, 68–71
tools for, rapid, 63–75

Application portability, 71

ArcView for Windows, 103–4

Ardis as key player in wireless communication, 199–200

Articles about reengineering, 273–76

Artificial intelligence, expert system as preliminary to, 239

Atlas GIS, 104

Atlas GIS for Windows, 103

Audio for multimedia, 250–51

Authorizer's Assistant (American Express), 240

AutoCAD LT for Windows, 221

Automated input, 87–97
  case study of, 95–96

Automated teller machines (ATMs), 167, 174–75, 181

Avis car rental, customer service by, 194, 202–3

B

Bar code reader, 91

Bar coding devices, 27, 87, 93–94

Barker, Joel, 33

Blackboard used in expert systems, 231

Blue Cross Blue Shield of Maryland, 178

Boeing 777 airliner, 224

Books about reengineering, 271–73

Borland Office, 59

Boston College user information system, 174–75

Brainstorming, 33–34, 163

British Airways
  customer service at, 6
  wireless communications at, 195

Bulletin boards systems (BBSs), electronic, 135, 140–41, 144–45

Bush, George, 87

Business audio, 83–84

Business process reengineering (BPR), 9, 266

C

C++, users of, 70

CAD/CAM, 223–25

Calendars, electronic, 145–46
  groupware, 156, 164

Caller ID, 81

Capital Investment Expert System (Texas Instruments), 234

Carbon Copy (Microcom), 188

CASE Associates Inc., 68

Cash register, 89–91

Catastrophe Management Information Network (CatMan), 109

CD-ROM
  for multimedia, 249
  publications available on, 211
  types of products on, 252–53

Cellular digital packet data (CDPD), 198, 200

Cellular service for wireless communication, 197–98

Central Savings, 189

Centralized resources, 29–30

Champy, James, 9–10

"Cheap" computers, problems with, 61

Chevron Corporation, 24–25

City Streets for Windows (Road Scholar Software), 109

Clarke, David, 160

Clean Air Act of 1990, 186

Client/server databases, 57–58

Clinton, Bill, 133, 148–49

Company IQ, 235–37

Compaq Computer Corporation, 143–44, 159–60

CompuServe, 55, 57
  electronic town meeting hosted by, 141
  gateways to, 148
  as knowledge base, 206–8, 210
  as largest and oldest consumer on-line service, 213

Computer-aided design (CAD), 221, 223–25

Computer-aided software engineering (CASE), 67–68, 73–74

CONSULTANT expert system (IBM), 241

Continental Insurance of New York insurance claim predicting tool, 109–10

Controls
  incorporated into information processing, 28, 74
  user, 28

CorelDRAW, 223

Corporate chain of command changed by e-mail systems, 139–40, 143

Corporate culture, changing, 139–43

Corporate IQ, 235–37

CDPD as key player in wireless communication, 200

Crain, William, 24–25

Credit card reader, 91–92

Currid & Company, 143–46, 157, 188

Customer service, improving, 174

D

Data
  accuracy of, 173–74
  captured only once, 26–27, 74, 173
  demographic business, 104

Data sharing of tools, 60

Data networks, 195–96

Database partitions, 126

Databases, 27, 54, 57–59
  checklist for, 58–59

shared freeform, 161–62

technology for, 57–58

Decision making, desire for expert system involved in, 237–39

Decision points where work is performed, 27, 74

Delivery Information Acquisition Device (DIAD), 96

Delivery Information Automated Lookup System (DIALS), 96

Delivery routes, GIS for, 106

Desktop tools, 54
  consistent, 59–60

Desktop videoconferencing, 157

Dialog knowledge base, 208, 212

Digital signal processors (DSPs), 84

Disaster management, GIS for, 106

Disney retail stores, expert systems at, 235

Distributed user directories, synchronizing, 151–52

Docucon, Inc., 128

Document management, 121–31
  defined, 122–23
  example in banking of, 128–30
  need for standards in, 128
  scanning for, 125–27
  support of the seven principles of reengineering by, 130
  vendors for, 128

Dow Jones News Service, 208

Dow Jones News/Retrieval, 211

Drawing as image processing, 223

Dun & Bradstreet, 104

E

Earthquake of 1994, Northridge (L.A.), 186

Electronic calendars, 145–46

Electronic commerce, 167–82
  benefits of, 172–75
  coordination of services for, 181
  defined, 168–69
  delivery of, 178–79
  government regulations for,
    180–81
  issues of, 179–81
  privacy and security of, 180
Electronic conferencing, 155–57
Electronic data interchange (EDI),
    27, 175–78
  defined, 176
  role in reengineering of, 176–78
Electronic Data Interchange for
    Administration, Commerce,
    and Transport (EDIFACT),
    180
Electronic Data Systems Corpo-
    ration (EDS), 178
Electronic etiquette, 150–51
Electronic mail (e-mail), 133–52
  attaching files to, 135–36, 141,
    145
  correspondent scope increased
    by, 141
  defined, 134–36
  differences between traditional
    communications and, 137–39
  expectations for communication
    changed by, 140–41
  fax services merged with, 149
  features and capabilities of,
    144–49
  filtering agents for, 148–49
  gateways, 148
  geographically dispersed people
    united using, 141–43
  as great equalizer, 139–40

  interoperability of different
    products for, 151
  issues for implementing and
    using, 149–52
  mobility widened by, 142, 188
  role and promise of, 136–37,
    143–44
Electronic meetings, 159
  using meetingware, 162–63
  using videoconferencing, 163–64
Enabling technologies for reengi-
    neering, 49–259
  fundamental, 53–61
Enterprise model for expert system,
    232–33
Equifax, 104
Etak, Inc., 104–5, 107
Evaluation apprehension, 34
Expense report system
  example of document man-
    agement, 124
  example of workflow man-
    agement, 115–17
Expert systems (ESs), 229–43
  components of, 231
  for decision making, 237–39
  defined, 230–31
  as lead-in to artificial intelligence,
    239
  learning from, 240–41
  neural networks as variation of,
    241–42
  preparing for, 233–35
  support of the seven principles of
    reengineering by, 243
  users of, 239–40
ExperTAX (Coopers & Lybrand), 240
Explanation facility in expert
    system, 231

F

Fastech Information Systems, Inc., 189

Fax (facsimile) services merged with e-mail, 149

Fax-back, 82–83

Federal Emergency Management Agency (FEMA), 110

Fidelity Investments, 29

File server databases, 57–58

Filtering agents for e-mail, 148–49

First! knowledge base, 208, 212

Flashback (Norris Communications Corporation), 80

Flight simulator, use of virtual reality in, 225

Ford Motor Company
accounts payable department and processes of, 7, 23–24
financial problems of, 6

Four-phase reengineering approach
activate phase of, 30–31
analyze phase of, 31–33
annihilate phase of, 33–34
assimilate phase of, 34–35

Fourth Generation Languages (4GLs), 69, 73

Frederick, Doyle, 104

Freelance (Lotus), 248

Functions versus processes, 10–15

G

Gates, Bill, 198

Gateways
e-mail, 148
to the Internet, 57

General Magic, 213–16

General Services Administration, e-mail at, 194

GEnie, 208

Geocoding, 105

Geographic information system (GIS), 100–107, 109–11
case studies for, 109–11
costs of, 103–5
data for, 100–101
problems with, 101–3
uses for, 105–7

Geographically dispersed resources, treatment of, 29–30, 74

Gilbreth, Frank, 16

Gilbreth, Lillian, 16

Gleason, Bernard Jr., 175

Global positioning system (GPS), 99, 107–11
case studies for, 109–11
mapping and GIS applications with, 109
operation of, 108
receiver for, 108–9

Goals for reengineering, 9, 32–33

Goodyear Tire and Rubber, 4GL for application development at, 73–74

Gore, Al, 7, 133, 141, 149

Government Printing Office Electronic Access Bill, 140–41

GPS MapKit SV, 103

Groceries, flow of, 87–90

Group of Seven (G–7) nations, paper produced by workers in, 123

Groupware, 155–66
criteria for, 157
defined, 135, 156
do's and don'ts for, 165–66

effects of using, 164–65

remote access to, 188

support of the seven principles of reengineering by, 164

technologies included in, 156–57

types of, 160–64

uses of, 158–64

GTE, customer service at, 6, 8

Gulf War, 107

Gupta Corporation, 68

H

Hammer, Michael, 9–10, 26

Hardware, 60–61

manufacturers' list for reengineering, 277–80

Harvard Graphics (Software Publishing Corp.), 248

Health care industry

EDI's uses in, 176–78

privacy issues in, 180

survey, 7

Hendricks, Keith, 107

Hewlett-Packard (HP), centralization at, 30

Hierarchical management structures, processes fostering, 27

Higgins, Thomas, 178

Hipparchus 2.2 for Windows NT, 103

Hospital use of multimedia, 256–59

Host-terminal databases, 57–58

Howard, Thomas, 143

Hurricane Andrew, 110

I

IBM, losses of, 5–6

IBM Credit, processing new customers at, 7

Idea blocking, 34

IDEF/0, 32

Illinois Criminal Justice Information Authority, 111

Image processing, 221–23

Imaging, 222

Income tax returns, filing federal, 169–72

before electronic filing, 169–70

using electronic filing for, 170–71

Individual Inc., 212

Inference engine of expert system, 231

Information processing, controls incorporated into, 28

Information Resources, 91

Information sharing

via e-mail, 141

via groupware, 157

Information superhighway, 178–79

networking as first stop to, 54–57

planning for, 55–56

Information Systems group, 63–64

deadline pressure for, 66

transition time in reengineering, 69–70

Information technology (IT)

parallel work activity using, 29

using or losing, 259

Insurance claims, paperwork for, 27

Integrating as level of reengineering, 23–24

Intel Corporation, personal conferencing capabilities developed by, 164

Intelligent hubs, 56

Interactive voice response (IVR) systems, 80–82

Internet, 55, 57, 105
   public addresses on, 141
   navigating, 210–11
   receiving messages on, 148
   U.S. president and vice pres-
      ident's addresses on, 133
   uses of, 142
Interoffice correspondence, 137–41
Iridium project (Motorola), 198

J

Johnson-Lenz, Peter, 156
Johnson-Lenz, Trudy, 156

K

Kai's Power Tools (HSC Software),
   222
Knowledge bases and agents, 205–
   18
   creating custom, 216–17
   in expert systems, 231
   major services for, 208–9
   for professional users, 211–12
   support of the seven principles of
      reengineering by, 217–18
   uses of, 209–11
   value of, 207–13

L

Laptop computers, 190
Lee, Charles, 8
Legal knowledge base, Lexis as, 212
Lexis knowledge base (MEAD Data
   Systems), 208, 212
Life insurance company new cus-
   tomer application process, 8
Link Resources, 185

Loan workflow management, case
   study of, 118–20
Lotus Notes, 156, 159–62, 266
Low earth orbiting satellites
   (LEOS), 198
Loyola Federal Savings Bank, 189

M

McCaw, Craig, 198, 200
MacInTax, 170
McKesson Water Company, 40
Magic Cap operating system, 215
Magnetic-ink character recognition
   systems, 88, 94–95
Magnetic-strip readers, 88, 92–93
MapInfo for Windows, 104
Marketing research, GIS for, 106
MCI Mail, 148
Meetingware, 162–63
Message Handling Services (MHS)
   gateway, 148
Message routing, 147
Metricom as key player in wireless
   communication, 201–2
MICR printer, 91, 94–95
Microsoft Office, 59
Microsoft Windows, 59–60
MicroTracker (Rockwell), 109
Mobile companions, 190
Mobile computing. *See* Remote
   computing
Mobile GPS Sensor (Trimble-Socket
   Communications), 109
Modeling, software, 226–27
Modem
   for remote access to e-mail, 147
   time savings of using, 185
   for wireless data system, 196

MPC-trademark, 253–54

Multimedia, 245–59

    authoring applications using, 252–53, 255

    costs of, 252–53

    defined, 248–49

    elements of, 250–52

    examples of business consultants and hospitals using, 255–59

    industry standards for, 253–54

    minimum requirements for, 254

    on networks, 254–55

    playing back applications using, 252–53

    reasons to use, 249

    reengineering using, 255–56

Multimedia PC Marketing Council, Inc., 253–54

Multimedia upgrade kits, vendors for, 252

Multitasking tools, 60

N

National Center for the Analysis of Violent Crime (NCAVC), 110–11

National Productivity Review, 7

National Telecommuting and Telework Association, 185

Nationwide Wireless Network as key player in wireless communication, 201

NCR Corporation, ATM technology of, 175

NetWare Global Messaging (NGM) (Novell), 148

Network operating system (NOS), stable, 56

Network

    enhanced to handle groupware information, 166

    grocery store example of, 90

    technology checklist for, 56–57

    traffic on, 152

Network vision, 54

Networking, 54–57

    beginning, 55

    multimedia, 254–55

    technology checklist for, 56–57

Neural networks (NNs) as variation of expert systems, 241–42

Mew media. *See* Multimedia

News services, 211

Nextel Communications as key player in wireless communication, 201

Notebook computers, 190

O

Object Linking & Embedding (OLE), 250–51

Object-oriented programming (OOP) techniques, 70

On-line databases, 135

Open Database Connectivity (ODBC) standard, 128–29

Operation Desert Storm, 107

Optical-character readers, 87

Optical-character recognition (OCR), 94

Optical storage devices, 126–27

Orbcomm as key player in wireless communication, 202

Organizational structures, 10–15

    function-based, 10–12

    process-based, 12–15

P

Pacific Power and Light, 42–44

Packet radio networks, 197

Packet switching, 196

Palmtop computers, 190

Paperwork, electronic commerce to reduce, 172–73

Parallel activities, integrating, 26, 29, 74

pcAnywhere (Symantec), 188

Pennsylvania Bureau of Motor Vehicles, 174

Personal Computer Memory Card International Association (PCMCIA) type II slot standard, 108

Personal conferencing, 164

Personal Dictation System (IBM), 84

Personal digital assistants, 190

Personal navigators, 108

Phone card, 92–93

Picture Publisher (Micrografx), 222–23

Pilot or prototype of the reengineered system, 34–35

Pixar 128 imaging software, 222

Point-of-sale (POS) terminal, 90–91, 227, 241

Power glove, 226

PowerPoint (Microsoft), 248

Pregnancy and child care training using multimedia, 256–59

Presentation support tools, 245–48. *See also* Multimedia

Principles of reengineered work (Hammer), 26–30

  supported by expert systems, 243

  supported by groupware, 164–65

  supported by knowledge bases and agents, 217–18

  supported by RAD tools, 74

  supported by simulation tools, 227–28

  supported by UPS and automated input, 97

  supported by voice systems, 85

  supported by wireless communication, 202–3

  supported by workflow management, 120

Print processing for photographic images, 222–23

Private Branch Exchange (PBX), 78

Process diagnostic system (PDS) (Westinghouse Electric Corp.), 239

Process improvement efforts, survey of companies for, 7

Processes

  changed before applying groupware, 165

  functions versus, 10–15

  history of, 15–16

  overspecialized, 28

  picking reengineering, 267–68

  workers put in control of, 26, 74

Prodigy knowledge base, 208

ProGen 4GL (Business Computer Design), 73

Public forums, 135

Q

Quality management versus reengineering, 17–18

R

RadioMail, 144

RAM Mobile Data as key player in wireless communication, 200

Rapid Application Development (RAD) tools, 64–75
application development process with, 70
benefits of, 65–66
deadline pressure for, 66
four points for achieving success with, 64–65
support of the seven principles of reengineering by, 74
tips for success with, 67
Redundancy, reducing, 165
Reengineering. *See also* business process engineering (BPR)
approaches toward, 22–25
defined, 9–10
do's and taboos for, 265–70
EDI's role in, 176–78
e-mail's role in, 143–44
four phases of, 30–35
goal of, 9, 32–33
guidance for, 39
levels of, 23
mobile computing's support of, 190
multimedia for, 255–56
other theories versus, 17–18
from outside, 266, 267
plan for, 263–70
principles of, 25–30, 74
quick winner for, selecting, 267
reasons for, 8–9
resources to read about, 271–76
schedules for, 267
scope of, 5–19
to simplify expense reporting system, 117
teams for, 32, 37–47, 266

techniques for, 21–35
terminology for, 266
turf wars and politics in, 267
updating priorities for, 268
vendor names, addresses, and telephone numbers for, 277–80
vision for, 266
Reengineering ToolKit, infrastructure technologies for, 61
Regulatory monitoring, GIS for, 106
Reinvention, entering age of, 6–8
Remote access, 147–48
products for, 188
technology for, 188
Remote computing, 183–91
key points of, 191
products for, 188
support of reengineering of, 190
technologies for, 190–91
uses of, 189
Remote node software, 188
Remotely Possible (Avalon Technology), 188
Repositories of reusable application objects, 70–71
Resources for reengineering, 271–76
RLN Products (DCA), 188
Routers for LANs, 56

S

Sales forecasting, neural networks for, 241–42
Sales support, GIS for, 106
Savings Bank of Iowa, 189
Scalability of application development technologies, 71

Scanners, document and image, 87, 91, 93–94, 125–27

Schnardthorst, Charles, 223

Scientific Management, 16

Senior management involvement in reengineering, 31

Service fleets, GIS for, 106

Seven principles. *See* Principles of reengineered work (Hammer)

Simulation tools, 219–28

    reasons to use, 220–21

    support of the seven principles of reengineering by, 227–28

Site selection, GIS tools for, 105

SmartSuite (Lotus), 59

Smith, Adam, 15–16

SoftSolutions Document Desktop, 129–30

Soft-Switch Corporation, gateway products of, 151

Software manufacturers' list for reengineering, 277–80

SPANS GIS 5.0 for OS/2, 104

Spatial analysis, 105

Spatial and Temporal Analysis of Crime (STAC), 111

SQL Base (Gupta Corporation), 68

SQL Windows (Gupta Corporation), 68

State of Maryland benefits transfer program, 172–73

Steering committee, 38–41

    champion on, 40, 46

    czar on, 41

    roles for, 39–41

    selection of, 37–38

Streamlining, 22–23

Structured query language (SQL), 58

Suggested reading materials for reengineering, 271–76

Sure!MAPS (Horizon Technology), 109

Sylvania customer buying habits system, 110

T

Tactician 2.3 for Windows, 104

Tailleur, Mark, 222–23

Task tracking, 146

Task-switching, multitasking for, 60

Taylor, Frederick, 16

Teams

    evaluating contributions to, 165–66

    training people to work in, 166

Teams for reengineering, 32, 37–47

    insider for, 47

    outsider on, 46–47, 267

    process owner, 45–46

    process reinvention by, 33

    reengineering, 41–47

    selecting, 37–38, 266

    steering, 38–41

    team captain for, 44–46

    team members for, 46, 267

Techniques for reengineering, 21–35

Technology-enabled teamwork, 165

Techpaq (Compaq), 159–61

Telecommuting, 183–91

    disadvantages of, 187

    equipment required for, 187

    impetus for using, 186–87

    key factors for successful, 187

    products for, 188

    promise of, 184–88

    technologies for, 188

Teledesic Corp., 198

TeleFile, 171–72

Telephone Access Service (TAS) (WordPerfect Corp.), 81, 147–48

Telescript (General Magic), 214–16

1040PC condensed paper format, 171–72

TerraView 4.0, 103

Text and graphics for multimedia, 250

Thematic mapping, 105

Top management support of reengineering, 266, 269

Topographically Integrated Geographic Encoding and Referencing (TIGER) data files, 104, 107

Total quality management (TQM), 269

TotalTrack, 96

Touch-activated screens, 88, 92

Touch-Tone phone, 82–83

Transformation level of reengineering, 24

Travel expenses, reducing, 156

Travelers Insurance, RAD at, 66

Trinsic Corporation, 242

Tulare, California computerized welfare claims system, 173–74

TurboTax (ChipSoft), 170

Typestry imaging software, 222

U

Uniform Product Code (UPC)
  data generated by, 227
  standard for, 90

United Parcel Service
  case study of automated input, 95–96

cellular equipment for, 200

Universal product code (UPC), 176

University of Texas Health Services group, 32

University of Virginia, 110–11

U.S. Department of Defense, 107

U.S. News Online, 141

User interface in expert system, 231

User-independent continuous-speech recognition products, 84

V

Vendors for reengineering software and hardware, 277–80

Vennet groupware communications network, 158–59

Video capture boards, 251, 253

Video for multimedia, 251

Videoconferencing, 158, 163–64

Viking Express (Ericsson/GE), 142

Virginia Department of Taxation, RAD tax accounting system at, 66

Virtual environment, 213–14

Virtual meetings, 159

Virtual reality
  business uses of, 225–26
  as simulation, 221, 225

Visual Basic (Microsoft), 70

Voice mail, 79–80

Voice recognition, 84

Voice response unit (VRU), 78

Voice systems, 77–86
  functions of, 79–83
  justifying, 78–83
  support of the seven principles of reengineering by, 85

Voice-activated systems, 88, 95

W

Wal-Mart, inventory system at, 29

Wells, Mike, 160

Wessex Corporation, 104

Westinghouse Electric Corporation expert system, 239

White House, electronic mail at, 133–34

WinCIM communications program, 206

Windows Sound System, 83

Wireless communication, 144, 193–203

    examples of productivity enhancements by, 194–95

    key players in, 199–202

    local, 196–97

    remote, 197–98

    short-distance, 197

    support of the seven principles of reengineering by, 202–3

    technology for, 196–99

    users of, 198–99

Wiring architecture for networks, 56

WordPerfect Office 4.0, 147, 164

WordPerfect Office TeleMail, 144

Work, organizing, 26, 74

Workflow, 113–20

    case study of loans improving, 118–20

    defined, 114

    document management tied to, 122

    software for, 22

Workflow management, 114

    support of the seven principles of reengineering by, 120

WP Office, 81

X

X.400 communication standard, 151

XCON (Digital Equipment Corp.), 229–31, 240, 242

Computing Strategies for Reengineering Your Organization

Cheryl Currid & Company

Effective use of computers in business today is an evolving art, not a science. Formulas that worked well for businesses yesterday may not be effective today—and may be dead wrong tomorrow! To remain a competitive player in the fast-paced world of commerce and computers, you need to find the right path through the confusing maze of options that have come with the corporate technology explosion. Drawing on the expertise of industry mavens and computer gurus alike, Currid & Company explains how you can smoothly integrate today's new systems and technologies with your corporate goals.

Cheryl Currid is a columnist for *WINDOWS Magazine*. Her Houston-based organization, Currid & Company, helps clients assess, prepare for, and apply new information technology.

304 pages, hardcover
$24.95
1-55958-481-5

Wave Three: The New Era in Network Marketing

Richard Poe

Become a Part of the New Entrepreneurial Revolution!

Fueled by new technology and innovative marketing ideas, cutting-edge network marketing companies have set out to change the way North Americans live and work. To the corporate world, these companies offer a secret formula for lightning growth and global dominance. To consumers, they offer the chance to start a business at minimal cost and to work comfortably from home. And—for the fortunate few—to achieve rapid wealth beyond your wildest dreams. This is the Wave-Three Revolution.

In today's Wave-Three network marketing organizations, distributors rely on a twenty-first century network of systems, procedures, media, and technology that simplifies, standardizes, and even automates the most difficult aspects of the business. Richard Poe tells you what you need to know about network marketing and how to get started right away on this exciting path toward financial independence.

Richard Poe is former Senior Editor of *Success* magazine.

$14.95, paperback
320 pages
1-55958-501-3